West Africans in Britain 1900–1960
Nationalism, Pan-Africanism and Communism

West Africans in Britain 1900–1960

Nationalism, Pan-Africanism and Communism

Hakim Adi

Lawrence & Wishart
LONDON

Lawrence & Wishart Limited
99a Wallis Road
London E9 5LN

First published 1998

© Hakim Adi 1998

The author has asserted his right under the Copyright, Designs and Patents Act, 1988, to be identified as author of this work.

All rights reserved. Apart from fair dealing for the purpose of private study, research, criticism or review, no part of this publication may be reproduced, stored in a retrieval system, or transmitted, mechanical, optical, photocopying, recording or otherwise, without the prior permission of the copyright owner.

British Library Cataloguing in Publication data.
A catalogue record for this book is available from the British Library.

ISBN 0 85315 848 7

Photoset in North Wales by
Derek Doyle & Associates, Mold, Flintshire.
Printed and bound in Great Britain by
Redwood Books, Trowbridge.

Contents

Acknowledgements	1
Introduction	2
Pioneers of Student Politics	6
West African Student Organisations 1923–30	23
The Search for a Black United Front 1930–39	52
The War Years 1939–45	89
Africanisation and Radicalisation: Cold War Responses 1945–49	120
The 1950s: Communism and Nationalism	151
Conclusion	186
Appendix	188
Abbreviations	214
Index	216

Acknowledgements

This book started life as a doctoral thesis at the University of London and I wish to thank all those who have helped me conduct my research and assisted in its writing over a period of many years, especially the staff of many libraries and archives. I am grateful to the Central Research Fund Committee at the University of London for a grant from the Irwin Fund, which allowed me to conduct research in Nigeria, and to the Thornley Bequest Committee for a grant towards the cost of publication.

This study of West Africans in Britain has been possible only because many people were kind enough to devote their time and share both information and ideas with the writer. I would particularly like to thanks Mrs Olu Ogunbiyi, who has over 60 years of memories since she first came to Britain in 1932 to help open and run the first WASU hostel. I would also like to thank all those who shared their lives and experiences with me, particularly the late Kay Beauchamp; Biddy Bryan, who spent many hours showing me the sites of West African student hostels in London; Nii Odoi Annan, Cathy Coker, Aliyi Ekineh, the Earl of Listowel, and Billy Strachan.

I would also like to thank Professors Gabriel Olusanya and John Saville, who both encouraged me and provided me with significant leads when my research was still in its early stages. I extend a special thanks to Professor George Shepperson for his support, encouragement, information and advice. His interest in my research has been very greatly appreciated. I also wish to thank Professor Richard Rathbone at the School of Oriental and African Studies, London, who encouraged me to embark on this study and who supervised my thesis. For his constant friendship, support, encouragement, advice and criticism, I am deeply grateful. I would like to give special thanks to my friend and colleague Marika Sherwood who has put her time, energy and considerable knowledge at my disposal over many years.

Finally my thanks go to my family and friends for their constant encouragement and support.

Introduction

The history of Africans in Britain can be traced back to the Roman period, but currently documentary evidence suggests that it is only from the sixteenth century onwards that Africans from the western part of the continent regularly visited or resided in Britain. West Africa became closely linked with Britain from the time of the trans-Atlantic slave trade, and large parts of this region were eventually conquered and placed under British colonial rule. Over the centuries the West African population in Britain has included slaves and abolitionists, servants and seamen, merchants, stowaways and students whose histories await further research. This book is intended as a contribution to the study of one of the most significant groups of West Africans who resided in Britain throughout the twentieth century - West African students.[1]

Since the 1950s a number of books and articles have been written on the subject of West African students in Britain. Some have focused on individual student organisations or students from one particular part of West Africa. Others have highlighted the political significance of the students' activities in wider studies of nationalism in West Africa and the development of Pan-Africanism.[2] The memoirs and other writing of former students, some of whom became leading political figures, such as Kwame Nkrumah, Joe Appiah and H.O. Davies, have added personal details and insight to this literature.[3] This book is an attempt to trace the development of West African student politics in Britain, from the early years of this century, when student and other Pan-African organisations first appeared, until the latter part of the 1950s, when the struggle for self-government in West Africa seemed to have been won, as Britain granted independence to Nkrumah's Ghana, the former Gold Coast. A large part of this book is concerned with the West African Students' Union (WASU), the most prominent and enduring of West African student organisations, which was formed in

INTRODUCTION

the 1920s, and was still active in the early 1960s. Every attempt has been made to place the activities and politics of WASU in historical context, and also to document the political activities of other West African organisations and some individuals, as far as sources of information have allowed.

A central theme of this book is the influence of British social and political life on West African students, and more particularly on their politics and political organisations. The focus is on students who came to Britain for higher education from the four British colonies in West Africa - Nigeria, the Gold Coast, Sierra Leone and Gambia. The vast majority of such students were, until the mid-1940s, male and from wealthy, even royal, families. It is clear that such families maintained a tradition of educating their children in Britain over several generations. Such students might have been expected to have some interest in the political destiny of their homelands even before they reached Britain. However, in many cases they became much more aware of their colonial status during their sojourn in Britain, as well as the hypocrisy of colonial rule. The difficulties which life in Britain presented often led to a greater concern with anti-colonial politics in the colonies. It also meant that the students found it necessary to organise themselves in order to overcome the colour bar and racism, to find accommodation or to secure the jobs for which they were qualified. The colour bar and the discrimination they faced in Britain often altered their political outlook, while their presence at the political heart of the empire seemed to favour them with the opportunity to agitate for a change in their colonial status, as well as the opportunity to challenge colonial rule itself.

The position of the students as probable future leaders in the colonies meant that while in Britain they became the concern of various interests who hoped to exert some influence over them. The Colonial Office, those who economically exploited the colonies, religious and humanitarian organisations, even though sometimes in rivalry, all attempted to preserve and strengthen Empire and Commonwealth by courting the students. In particular, there was concern that the racism faced by the students in Britain might strengthen individual and general anti-colonial sentiments, therefore efforts were made to protect the students from what were seen as the worst aspects of British life by the provision of suitable accommodation and introductions to 'respectable' acquaintances. At the same time, it was feared that the students' conditions might throw them into the arms of 'subversive elements', whose aims were openly anti-colonial and anti-imperialist.

Colonial rule and racism did indeed lead many West African students to seek radical solutions to the problem of colonialism, and they did come into contact with anti-colonial forces in Britain such as the League Against Imperialism (LAI) and the Communist Party of Great Britain (CPGB), as well as those whose aim was to reform the Empire such as the Fabian Colonial Bureau (FCB). As a result the student organisations often found themselves in the midst of a struggle for their hearts and minds, but in a strong position to act as a pressure group, negotiating with many temporary allies, so as to further what they saw as West Africa's and therefore their own political and economic future.

The attempts by the Colonial Office to influence the students might be seen as some of the first steps along the neo-colonial road. The more radical and communist affiliations of some students, although sometimes of a passing, youthful nature, added another political dimension to nationalism in West Africa and to Pan-Africanism. At the same time the concerns and activities of the students contributed to anti-imperialist and anti-colonial politics in Britain.

West African students, especially prior to the 1940s, comprised one of the most important sections of Britain's black population. As the century progressed they increasingly came into contact with the other often more permanent sections of this population. This book attempts to document some of the most important of these contacts, especially those with such organisations as the African Progress Union, League of Coloured Peoples (LCP) and the Pan-African Federation (PAF). There is no doubt that a particular Pan-African political milieu developed in Britain throughout the twentieth century, to which the West African students made their contribution. This has been internationally significant, but it is also an important part of the evolving politics of black people in Britain.

Clearly not all West African students in Britain took part in political activities or were members of the various student and other organisations. This book is not a general social history of students' lives, although it has attempted, where possible to provide sufficient background detail of some aspects of student life in Britain. This fascinating social life requires further research and documentation, but lies beyond the scope of this book.

INTRODUCTION

Notes

1. For a general introduction to the history of Africans in Britain see D. Killingray (ed), *Africans in Britain*, Frank Cass, Ilford 1994.
2. G.O. Olusanya, *The West African Students' Union and the Politics of Decolonisation, 1925-1958*, Daystar, Ibadan 1982; A.T. Carey, *Colonial Students – A Study of the Social Adaptation of Colonial Students in London*, Secker and Warburg, London 1956; Political and Economic Planning, *Colonial Students in Britain – A Report by PEP*, PEP, London 1955; G. K. Animashawun, 'African Students in Britain', *Race*, 5, 1963, pp38-48; P. Garigue, 'The West African Students' Union: A Study in Culture Contact', *Africa*, 23/1, January 1953, pp55-69; P.O. Esedebe, 'WASU's Pan-African Role Reconsidered', *Journal of the Historical Society of Sierra Leone*, 2/2, July 1978, pp1-10; P. Rich, 'The Black Diaspora in Britain: Afro-Caribbean Students and the Struggle for a Political Identity, 1900-1950', *Immigrants and Minorities*, 6/2, July 1987, pp151-173; P.O. Esedebe, *Pan-Africanism: the idea and movement, 1776-1963*, Howard University Press, Washington D.C. 1982; J. A. Langley, *Pan-Africanism and Nationalism in West Africa 1900-45: A Study in Ideology and Social Classes*, Oxford University Press, Oxford 1973; UNESCO, *The Role of African Student Movements in the Political and Social Evolution of Africa from 1900 to 1975*, UNESCO Publishing, Paris 1994; R. Jenkins, 'Gold Coasters Overseas, 1880-1919: with Specific Reference to their Activities in Britain', *Immigrants and Minorities*, 4/3, November 1985, pp5-52.
3. J. Appiah, *Joe Appiah: The Autobiography of an African Patriot*, Praegar, New York, 1990; H.O. Davies, *Memoirs*, Evans, Ibadan 1989; K. Nkrumah, *Ghana: The Autobiography of Kwame Nkrumah*, Thomas Nelson & Sons, Edinburgh 1957.

Pioneers of Student Politics

West African students have been coming to Britain since the days of the trans-Atlantic slave trade. In the eighteenth century British and African traders found it mutually advantageous to educate African children, especially males, in Britain, and each party strove to maximise advantage from the arrangement. One of the most famous of these early West African students was William Ansah the son of the Fante King of Annamboe, in what is today Ghana, who was kidnapped and enslaved in Barbados before being freed and in 1736 taken to Britain, where he received some education. Philip Quaque, another Fante student of royal birth, was sent to Britain as a thirteen-year-old in 1754. In 1765 he became the first African to be ordained as a priest in the Church of England. As early as the mid-eighteenth century, West African boys and girls were being educated in Liverpool, and by 1788 there were said to be as many as fifty West African students in the city, in addition to others being educated elsewhere in Britain.[1]

African rulers and merchants found it useful to send their sons, and sometimes daughters, to Britain to learn what they called 'white man's book', which assisted them in their trading activities, including the trade in slaves. The British philanthropists and abolitionists also took an interest in such students. In particular they tried to give them a 'good Christian education' whilst they were in Britain, so that they might, 'carry back to their own country minds considerably enlightened', and even exert some beneficial influence on surrounding countries. After the establishment of the Sierra Leone colony in 1808, British abolitionists established a school in Clapham, south London, to educate Africans who could then be placed in situations, 'as would afford the best means of promoting the great ends of the settlement', which included the spreading of Christianity throughout West Africa, as well as the suppression of the slave trade and the development of alternative 'legitimate' trade.[2] Both humanitarians and the British government hoped that Africans so educated would be a useful influence amongst their compatriots. They were particularly eager to educate the sons of hereditary rulers, who might one day themselves succeed to power. In this way they hoped that, 'there would be a fair prospect of their carrying into effect in the countries which they would ... govern, plans more or less similar to those inculcated in them in England.'[3]

Thus began the tradition of educating teachers, priests, and prospective West African rulers in Britain; a tradition developed and encouraged by all those in Britain and West Africa who thought that they might profit by such an arrangement. Perhaps not surprisingly, African students were as much influenced by the social conditions which they experienced in Britain, as they were by the formal education they received. In particular, many were shocked by the many forms of racial discrimination and prejudice they found, which served to create an unfavourable impression of the 'Mother country'. In 1791 John Naimbana, the eldest son of the Temne paramount ruler in what was to become Sierra Leone, was sent to Britain to be educated and entrusted to the care of the abolitionist Granville Sharp. But it was impossible to shield the prince from the racist attitudes prevalent in English society at the time. Despite attempts to encourage his spirit of Christian forgiveness, the prince, evidently speaking from experience, declared: 'If a man takes away the character of the people of my country, I can never forgive him.'[4]

The contradictory nature of Britain's relationship with West Africa, which combined slave trading with abolition, education with exploitation and the pursuit of profit with philanthropy, had a profound effect upon those West African students who came to Britain in the nineteenth century. Sierra Leonean James Africanus Horton, who graduated from Edinburgh University in 1859, exhibited both pro-British and pro-West African sympathies. Horton welcomed British civilisation and Christianity, especially for what were considered to be their modernising influences, whilst at the same time he spoke out against the notions of African inferiority and championed the cause of 'the Self-government of Western Africa'.[5] Horton was one of the first in a long line of West African nationalists educated in Britain who, consciously or unconsciously, reflected in their political views and activities the contradictions of both their education and privileged background. The social and economic conditions and various political influences which they found in Britain, played an extremely important part in their political development. The rise of imperialism, and the accompanying national chauvinism and racism which developed at the end of the nineteenth century, had a profound effect not only on African students, but also on the relationship between them and those who sought to influence them and West African affairs in general. The impact that British society had on students, who might well become future political leaders, was therefore a matter of major concern to all those, both in Britain and Africa, who hoped to benefit from and maintain the Empire.

British missionary societies were also in contact with West African students. The Church Missionary Society sponsored a number of students to come to Britain for education during the latter part of the nineteenth century. In 1888 the ex-Baptist missionary William Hughes founded the Colwyn Bay Training Institute in Wales, specifically to train young Africans as missionaries. Ex-student Mojola Agbebi and another early Nigerian nationalist James 'Holy' Johnson even organised a support committee for the Institute in Lagos. Another graduate of the Institute was Oladipo Lahanmi, who later became the secretary of the British-based West African Christian Union.[6]

West African students from those areas which were ultimately to become the colonies of Nigeria, Gold Coast, Sierra Leone and Gambia, were mainly, but not always from wealthy families. They were sent for schooling and higher education in Britain which could not be found in West Africa, so their ages ranged from those who were quite young children to mature adults coming to further their careers in such popular professions as medicine and law. By the mid-nineteenth century Queen's College in Taunton had established itself as one of the most popular destinations for school age students, while the Oxbridge colleges and the universities of Edinburgh, Durham and London, as well as the Inns of Court in London, were often favoured by the older students.[7] Several women students studied at Portway College in Reading, but although there were some female students, males clearly outnumbered them in higher education. 'In an hour's walk through the Strand, Regent-street or Piccadilly', William Wells Brown, the fugitive American slave wrote in 1852, 'one may meet half a dozen coloured men, who are inmates of the various colleges in the metropolis. These are all signs of progress in the cause of the sons of Africa'.[8]

Some of those who came to Britain as students followed in Horton's footsteps and published their views on the political issues of the day.

Racism was clearly a problem for many of them, including the Sierra Leonean doctor David Taylor, father of the composer Samuel Coleridge Taylor.⁹ A.B.C. Merriman Labor wrote of the abuse and insults he had received in the streets of London and the discrimination practised by some English landladies. He also accused newspaper editors of stirring up racism by allowing sensational and inaccurate reports in the press. At least one student at Oxford University had a different experience. Joseph Renner Maxwell, who graduated from Merton College in 1879, reported that 'I was not once subjected to the slightest ridicule or insult, on account of my colour or race, from any one of my fellow students'. On the basis of his experience Maxwell argued that the solution to the problem of discrimination was increasing intermarriage between African men and European women. But he later found that racism was still the preferred policy of the Colonial Office who barred his employment in government service. Others, such as Bandele Omoniyi, Kobina Sekyi, and J.E. Casely Hayford, recorded their experiences in Britain, or drew on them in their published writings in order to educate their compatriots, and add fuel to the fire of nationalism in West Africa. Such literary efforts also alerted the humanitarians, and other interested parties, to the imperial implications of what was known as the 'colour problem'.¹⁰

Pan-Africanism, Ethiopianism and student politics

By the end of the nineteenth century, students from Africa and the Caribbean had begun to organise themselves, both to promote the interests of their colonies of origin, and to forge unity and combat the effects of discrimination in Britain. After a number of unsuccessful attempts to form African political organisations, in 1897 the African Association, under the leadership of the Trinidadian student Sylvester Williams, was formed in London.¹¹ A Sierra Leonean law student, T.J.Thompson became its vice-chairman, and a Nigerian, Moses Da Rocha, a medical student at Edinburgh University, was assistant-secretary. The Association was formed:

> To encourage a feeling of unity: to facilitate friendly intercourse among Africans in general; to promote and protect the interest of all subjects claiming African descent, wholly or in part, in British Colonies and other places, especially in Africa, by circulating accurate information on

all subjects affecting their rights and privileges as subjects of the British Empire and by direct appeals to the Imperial and local governments.[12]

Owing to its presence in the capital of the Empire, the Association acted as a kind of African lobbying group. The following year it convened the first Pan-African Conference in London, which was attended by delegates from the US and the Caribbean, as well as West African representatives including Dr Richard Akiwande Savage, the delegate and president of Edinburgh University's Afro-West Indian Literary Society, and a future editor of the *Gold Coast Leader*. The Afro-West Indian Society was one of the forerunners of African student organisations in Britain. It was situated in one of the leading medical schools, which had been a destination for prospective West African doctors since the days of Horton.[13]

Edinburgh University was clearly an early hotbed of West African student activity. In 1902 West African medical students from Edinburgh persuaded the Dean of the Medical Faculty to write in complaint to the Colonial Office against the openly discriminatory policies of the West African Medical Service, which barred from appointment those of 'non-European parentage'. A letter was also sent to the Colonial Office on behalf of all the West African students at Edinburgh. It made clear their opposition to a policy, which not only threatened their careers, but was also a complete reversal of former government policy in West Africa.[14]

Another example of student politics at Edinburgh is connected with the appearance in 1906 of Keir Hardie's 'Zulu Letter'. The 'Zulu' in question was actually the Sierra Leonean medical student H.R. Bankole-Bright, who was to become one of the founders of the National Congress of British West Africa and the West African Students' Union. Bankole Bright had written to Hardie, approving of his criticisms of British misrule in Africa and giving the impression that he was a Zulu student. In his reply Hardie included a fiery denunciation of British imperialism, and expressed the hope that 'the day will speedily come when your race will be able to defend itself against the barbarities being perpetuated against it by hypocritical whites'.[15] Following the publication of the letter, questions were raised in Parliament, while at the university Moses Da Rocha wrote a scathing criticism of Bankole-Bright in a letter to the Nigerian paper the *Lagos Standard*. Da Rocha's response suggests that there were some important political differences between West African students at Edinburgh, a situation which Da Rocha appeared to acknowledge when he wrote of 'jealous Black Traitors and conspirators' in his correspondence with the African-American journalist John Edward Bruce.[16] What is also clear is the high level of political activity amongst West Africans in Edinburgh at this time, who lobbied politicians and wrote to the press both in Britain and in West Africa. It was this kind of activity that was to occupy Prince Bandele Omoniyi, another Nigerian student in Edinburgh in the early years of the twentieth century.

Omoniyi is best known for his book *A Defence of the Ethiopian Movement*, which was published in Edinburgh in 1908. Unlike many West African students, and despite his royal title, Omoniyi lived in poverty and conducted nearly all his political activities independently. He wrote in the Scottish and West African press and in the *Labour Leader*, the paper of the Independent Labour Party (ILP); and he corresponded with Ramsey Macdonald and members of the Government, including the Prime Minister Campbell-Bannerman. Known at the university as 'a genuine enthusiast in the cause of the Negroes', most of Omoniyi's student life in Britain was spent attempting to defend the interests of Africans throughout the British empire. As a result, like many who would follow him, he fell foul of the Colonial Office, and official indifference probably contributed to his early death in Brazil at the age of twenty-eight.[17]

Ethiopianism, another name for early Pan-Africanism, was popular amongst African and Caribbean students in Britain during the first years of the twentieth century. By 1904 there was an Ethiopian Association in Edinburgh, and in Liverpool in the same year the Ethiopian Progressive Association (EPA) was founded 'by West African and West Indian natives, students at the various colleges'. The Association seems to have had a short life, but it attempted to contact both Booker T. Washington and W.E.B. Du Bois in the US and published at least one edition of a journal, *The Ethiopian Review*. The EPA aimed:

> To create a bond of union between a) all other members of the Ethiopian race at home and abroad, b) to further the interest and raise the social status of the Ethiopian race at home and abroad; and to try to strengthen the friendly relations of the said race and the other races of mankind.[18]

Such sentiments were precisely those expressed at the Pan-African Conference in 1900 and show how racism and the general effects of imperialism remained the main concerns of the students.

Both individual West Africans and those organisations they formed were Pan-African in orientation. West Africans and those from the Caribbean often joined together to further their interests, and established links with prominent African-Americans and their organisations. As the EPA expressed it, they were concerned with 'matters of vital importance concerning Africa in particular and the Negro race in general'. These concerns ranged from the 1906 Natal Uprising in South Africa, to discrimination in the West African Medical Service and the 'pacification' campaigns in Nigeria. The students were also concerned to raise the status of African people in general. They stressed the achievements of Africanus Horton and Edward Blyden and extolled the virtues of a glorious African past.

J.E. Casely Hayford's autobiographical novel *Ethiopia Unbound* was published in London in 1911 and gives us some evidence regarding the political concerns of the students at that time. Casely Hayford had himself been a law student at Cambridge and in London. The book's hero, Kwamankra, is a supporter of the views of Edward Blyden but the writing of the book was also clearly influenced by international events, such as the military defeat of 'European' Russia by Japan in 1905. The book is able to look to the future and hope for 'mighty changes' in Africa, like those evident in Japan's economic development. But Casely Hayford also extols the glories of Africa's great past as the 'cradle of civilisation', and looks forward to the development of an 'African nationality', 'race emancipation', and the modernisation and regeneration of African societies.[19]

The students were also concerned about racism and the 'colour bar' in Britain. Omoniyi wrote that: 'The treatment accorded to Africans in the Nativeland and abroad by the ignorant classes of white men and those who ought to know better generally "makes one's blood boil"'. So establishing good 'race relations' was often high on their agenda. In their appeals to the Government regarding colonial issues, the students exhibited a remarkable faith in the former's good offices, generally viewing government policies as simply mistaken or misapplied by 'the man on the spot', and it was seldom that colonial rule was challenged directly. Nevertheless their stay in Britain usually served to heighten the students' awareness of political issues, often as a result of the racism they found there, and familiarised them with a range of political opinions and organisations.

The African students' hostel

In 1911, as part of the developing international peace movement, the Universal Races Congress was held in London to encourage 'friendly feeling and co-operation among all races and nations'. Following the Congress many interested parties in Britain urged the development and fostering of 'inter-racial unity' of one sort or another. Commercial and humanitarian interests, represented by such organisations as the African Society and the Anti-Slavery and Aborigines' Rights Protection Society (ASAPS), were alarmed at the development of Ethiopianism and Pan-Africanism, especially after the 1906 Natal Rebellion against the colonial authorities in South Africa. They were concerned that the existence of racism and a colour bar in Britain might provoke anti-British feelings amongst African students, which they would then transmit to their compatriots in Africa. They were also concerned that African students might follow in the footsteps of Indian students, who in 1905 had formed the Indian Home Rule Society. In 1909, despite police surveillance, one member of this society, Madan Lal Dhingra, assassinated Sir William Curzon Wyllie, an assistant to the Secretary of State for India. Sir Harry Johnston and other imperialists therefore saw the need to 'foster a more sympathetic spirit', and 'to remove certain social disabilities', as they expressed it, in order that anti-colonial sentiments might be extinguished, and the British Empire preserved.[20]

Various schemes were suggested: a 'Universal Races Club' for example, or some other way of bringing African students into contact with 'the better side of British life'. The aim of these 'well-wishers', such as ASAPS, to shield African students from untoward or subversive influences, remained as a major goal for government, religious and humanitarian organisations throughout the colonial period. However, they pursued this goal in the face of the British state's racism and the colonial system itself and from these it was impossible to shield the students. Those Africans resident in Britain, both students and others, also began to organise themselves, stirred by such indignities as the announcement by London University Graduates' Club in 1914 that it would operate a colour bar and therefore Africans would be ineligible for membership. A new publication appeared, the *African Times and Orient Review* (*ATOR*), founded after the Universal Races' Congress by Dusé Mohammed Ali.[21] *ATOR* became extremely influential not only in Britain but also throughout West Africa and the Pan-African world. Its contributors included Marcus Garvey and W.E.G. Sekyi from the Gold Coast, who as a young law student in London in 1917 wrote one of his first articles for the journal entitled 'The Future of Subject Peoples'.[22]

In 1912, after consultation with the Colonial Office, ASAPS, under the guidance of its energetic secretary Reverend John Harris, and the African Society began to plan for a conference of all Africans in the country, even though African students had already begun independently to organise themselves. Harris' aim was to organise a meeting place and accommodation for the students in London, so as to keep them away from what were viewed as 'the worst influences of our modern civilisation'. He had the support of missionaries, educationalists and government officials, as well as prominent African merchants and professionals resident in London, many of whom attended the 'Conference for Africans' in April 1913.

In total about forty Africans attended the conference, including Merriman Labor, and Dusé Mohammed Ali, although most were businessmen rather than students. The declared aims of the conference – tackling the problems of discrimination and the colour bar, encouraging loyalty to the Empire, and spreading Christian civilisation – were acknowledged by all the participants, while students such as the Nigerian Adeyemo Alakija cited examples of the racism they faced, which included discriminatory treatment as passengers travelling on ships to and from West Africa.[23] One of the main issues discussed at the conference was how African students might be shielded from the racism and chauvinism in Britain, which accompanied colonial occupation and conquest. Concern was expressed about the prospect of disgruntled Africans shifting their allegiance to Britain's imperial rivals, France and Germany; the dangers of sexual relationships between African men and British women; and the possibility of Africans studying in the US and thus becoming aware 'of the inferior conditions of the negro as a citizen under the British flag'.[24] If educated Africans had bad experiences in Britain this would damage Britain's colonial interests, since they might become anti-British and as strongly nationalistic as many Indian students. The well-wishers wanted to prevent this in the hope of nurturing what they hoped would be a pro-British leadership in the African colonies.

Initially Harris had the support of the students for a proposed hostel or residential club, but they gradually turned against the idea as it became clear that this would lead to increasing government control of their lives. In *ATOR* the proposed club was unflatteringly described as: 'a sort of rounding up place for West Africans with a sprinkling of ex-West African and ex-Colonial officials thrown in as patrons'. In West Africa too, the project was criticised. In June 1914 an article entitled 'Sir Frederick Lugard and the Education of West African Natives', appeared in the *Lagos Standard*. The article bluntly pointed out:

> It is important that West African students in British Universities should not be under the leading strings of Government with local West African Governors having educational and political policies like those of Sir Frederick Lugard. A freer atmosphere than that of hostels under West African Government auspices is necessary for a healthy and vigorous development of African students. It is necessary for our advancement as a race that our young men studying for the professions in the United Kingdom should be proficient not only in the professions but imbibe also some of that spirit of independence, freedom, liberty, fair play and justice so characteristic of the Britisher in his own home. Our professional men fall very naturally into the rank of our leaders and it will be a bad day for our progress when our doctors and lawyers and engineers through the cramping influence of Government hostels in the UK come back to us with all manly spirit knocked out of them and become mere weaklings with no backbone and courage to stand for the rights of their people.[25]

On the eve of the Great War the stage was set for the confrontations which would continue until the 1950s. The idea of a student hostel was at the heart of the matter, for who would assume control: the students, the Colonial Office or the 'well-wishers'? African attitudes would undergo a radical change as a result of the war years, the international demands for self determination, and as a result of the racist violence which broke out in many British cities after the war. Increasingly, after 1918, African students realised that in order to attempt to change conditions in Britain and West Africa they had to become more organised. They would need allies, but at the same time they would seek to preserve their independence and self-reliance.

The African Students' Union

Even during the war the students began to form new organisations. The first of these was the African Students' Union, founded in

December 1916, possibly as a direct response to the activities of ASAPS and the African Society. The aims of the Union were said to be primarily social, and designed to cater for Africans resident in Britain. The Union was a non-political organisation, founded for the purpose of discussing African history and sociology, and for exercising the minds of the African students in London. The founding president was E.S. Beoku-Betts of the Middle Temple, who was the son of a leading Sierra Leonean merchant. Born in 1895, Beoku-Betts had come to London in 1914 to study law. A Fellow of the Royal Anthropology Society, he was credited with being the main organiser of the Union; the other elected officials were mainly from the Gold Coast.[26]

In August 1917, *ATOR* published Beoku-Betts's presidential address to what was now referred to as the African Students' Union of Great Britain and Ireland. Entitled 'The Negro - Pre-historic and Historic', the address was an historical outline of the 'evolution of the Negro', and the 'affinity of Egypt, Ethiopia and Ashanti due to race origin'. In short, it was an attempt, however inaccurate, to reclaim and re-establish Africa's past and to counter the racist doctrine that Africa and Africans had no history. The Union does not seem to have lasted for long, and probably ceased its activities when its president returned to Africa later that year.[27]

The West African Christian Union was formed in 1916 by the Nigerian Oladipo Lahanmi. It soon collapsed, but was re-launched under the auspices of the Student Christian Movement (SCM) 'as a joint union of West African and West Indian students'. The SCM was also concerned about the effects of the colour bar and racism, which gave rise to what it referred to as the 'seditious tendencies alleged among foreign students' and 'natural nationalist dissatisfaction with their position as subject races'. According to the SCM, the new Union devoted 'a good deal of time to the consideration of race and colour questions', and its members exhibited 'some rather undefined bitterness on the score of exploitation and bad government at home'.[28]

The African Progress Union (APU) and the Society of Peoples of African Origin (SPAO)

A more enduring, and more influential, organisation was APU, formed in December 1918 for 'voicing African sentiments', and 'furthering African interests', following a series of consultative meetings by

Africans and 'descendants of African blood'. APU was 'an Association of Africans from various parts of Africa, the West Indies, British Guiana, Honduras and America, representing advanced African ideas in liberal education.' It declared that it was not in rivalry with other organisations, but, 'actuated by love of country and race'; and it emphasised that, 'only Africans and those of African blood can truly interpret the aspirations of kin'. APU's first chairman was J.R. Archer, Labour councillor and Britain's first black mayor, but businessmen rather than students were the dominant force amongst its early members. Amongst its aims was the intention to 'establish in London "a home from home", for social recreational and intellectual improvement, where movements may be promoted for the common welfare, and friends entertained'.[29] Perhaps under the influence of Archer, the APU did claim to be in touch with 'the masses'. However, at the inaugural dinner, members were also quick to express loyalty to King and Empire. So as to leave no ambiguity about their aims they stressed the need for 'racial consciousness before inter-racial communism'.[30]

It is clear that the war had raised the expectations of many black people in Britain and throughout the colonies. Colonial troops and auxiliaries had played an important part in the war, and the British war effort had been directly financed by the colonies. However, many soon realised that the principle of self-determination was not to apply to the colonies. 'We shall be told - Africa is not ready', declared Archer at the APU's inaugural meeting, as he raised the demand not only for self-determination but also for reparations for 'the Black race'.[31]

Another new organisation was the Society of Peoples of African Origin (SPAO), formed at the end of the First World War by Sierra Leonean businessman John Eldred Taylor, the owner of *The African Telegraph*. The Trinidadian F.E.M. Hercules became general secretary of the Society, and editor of the paper from the end of 1918. Hercules had an influential role in both the SPAO and APU, and he appears to have been instrumental in establishing a temporary merger between the two organisations in July 1919. The SPAO called for an end to the colour bar and discrimination, for racial pride and unity, and political and social reforms in the colonies. It even called for a federation of Caribbean and West African colonies, accompanied by limited self-government within the British Empire. But it made clear that these aims should be 'pursued constitutionally'. The SPAO 'would have no truck with irresponsible agitators'. It declared, 'let us be moderate', and added that 'talk of sedition and revolution' would only alienate what were referred to as 'these our best friends'. It openly contrasted its own aims and methods with those of the Indian intelligentsia, who were agitating for Home Rule.[32]

It was however the problem of racism in Britain which became the main concern of these organisations, as attacks on African, Arab and Caribbean seamen, and other residents intensified after the war. Cardiff, Liverpool, Manchester, South Shields, Glasgow, Hull, London, and other towns and cities were all affected by 'race riots' in 1919, a consequence of a concerted campaign by government departments, the press, Labour Party, and certain trades unions such as the Seaman's Union, during a period of great political tension which included both labour unrest within Britain and anti-colonial rebellions throughout the Empire.[33] The First World War had led to a significant increase in Britain's African and Caribbean populations, who defended themselves against attack and strenuously demanded that as British subjects and contributors to the war effort their rights should be respected and safeguarded. The post-war climate was of concern to the newly formed Committee for the Welfare of Africans in Europe (CWAE), led by Reverend Harris, which in 1919 together with the SCM, the United Missionary Board and APU once again began to focus on the alleged problems of African students, who, according to Harris 'pick up all the worst side of our political and social life and return to the Colonies and Dependencies in anything but a helpful spirit'. Having correctly gauged post-war African sentiments, he also declared that it was an opportune time to establish a hostel which could be viewed as 'a memorial to the African race for its part in the Great War'.[34]

But APU refused to have anything to do with the scheme. They and the SPAO were pursuing their own independent hostel plans, which included providing a hostel for seamen, and were opposed to 'a place run entirely by Englishmen for Africans'. It was evident that a new spirit of self-reliance and anti-colonial feeling had developed amongst many of those represented by these two organisations, who were constantly comparing their wartime loyalty to their peacetime ill treatment. Africans and those of African descent had only recently been prevented from taking part in the post-war victory parades. However, Harris continued with his mission to save Africans from 'pernicious doctrines and habits' and began his lifetime role as a guardian to young African students in Britain, while APU continued with its own schemes to exercise 'benevolent guardianship' over the 'hundreds of African students who go to England each year', but in rivalry with

Harris and the CWAE. The hostel came to symbolise a wider struggle in the colonial world between those asserting the need for some form of self-government and those supporting colonial rule. The CWAE, made up of what Harris called 'the principal energies of African progress – administrators, missionaries and merchants', clearly recognised that the students 'would be leaders of public opinion tomorrow' and stressed the importance of keeping them on the right lines. It was even suggested that the Government should officially receive and train the students 'so that they could go back with ideas that should be helpful to the community out there and a safeguard for the future administration of these colonies'.[35]

Those involved with the CWAE expressed a number of concerns. Many wished to limit the number of African students who arrived in Britain, and argued for the provision of a West African university, fearing the consequences of racism and 'subversive influences' on African loyalty to the empire. Some were concerned about the possibility of increased intermarriage or sexual relationships between African men and British women. All were concerned to take the measures necessary to maintain the Empire. Many Africans, on the other hand, were concerned that under CWAE control the hostel scheme would be a form of segregation and political control. They were mindful of the fact that attempts had already been made to restrict the political activities of Indian students, and were therefore adamant that any such scheme should be under independent African control.

In February 1922 a further joint conference was held attended by a third of the three hundred Africans, who, according to APU, were resident in London at the time. The conference showed that disagreement over the hostel question existed even within APU, which some students claimed did not represent their interests. To some extent the conference signalled the end of West African student reliance on the leadership of APU, and the realisation that they would be better served by organising themselves both at a social and a political level. Such aspirations were probably influenced by the emergence of the National Congress of British West Africa (NCBWA) and a new West African nationalism and self-reliance.

Notes

1. P. Fryer, *Staying Power*, Pluto, London 1984, pp423-4, 426-7, and K.

Little, *Negroes in Britain*, Kegan Paul, London 1947, pp186-90.
2. F.O. Shyllon, *Black People in Britain*, 1555-1833, Oxford University Press, Oxford 1977 pp48, 51-4.
3. *Ibid*. p53. See also D.A. Lorimer, *Colour, Class and the Victorians*, Leicester University Press, Leicester 1978, pp217-19.
4. Fryer, *op.cit.*, p428.
5. J.A. Langley, *Pan-Africanism and Nationalism in West Africa 1900-1945*, Oxford University Press, Oxford 1973, p111.
6. See Hazel King, 'Mojola Agbebi: Nigerian Church Leader', in R. Lotz and I. Pegg (eds.) *Under the Imperial Carpet – Essays in Black History 1788-1950*, Rabbit Press, Crawley 1986, pp84-109.
7. For some details of the early history of students from the Gold Coast in Britain see R. Jenkins, 'Gold Coasters Overseas, 1888-1919: With Specific Reference to Their Activities in Britain', *Immigrants and Minorities*, 4/3, 1985, pp5-52.
8. P. Jefferson (ed.) *The Travels of William Wells Brown*, Edinburgh University Press, Edinburgh 1991, pp175-6.
9. Lorimer, *op.cit*. p66.
10. Kobina Sekyi (1892-1956) studied law in Britain and subsequently became one of the leading journalists and politicians in the Gold Coast. He was a founder member of the National Congress of British West Africa (NCBWA). J.E. Casely Hayford, (1866-1930) who studied law in Britain became one of the most influential of the early West African nationalists and led the founding of the NCBWA. See also A.B.C. Merriman, *Britons Through Negro Spectacles*, The Imperial and Foreign Co., London 1909. J.R. Maxwell, *The Negro Question, or Hints for the Physical Improvement of the Negro Race*, T.F. Unwin, London 1892; B. Omoniyi, *A Defence of the Ethiopian Movement*, J&J Gray, Edinburgh 1908; J.E. Casely Hayford, *Ethiopia Unbound*, Phillips, London 1911; K. Sekyi, 'Extracts from "the Anglo-Fanti"', in N. Cunard, *Negro: An Anthology*, Ungar, London 1979. See also Lorimer, *op.cit.*, pp 64-68.
11. I. Geiss, *The Pan-African Movement*, African Pub. Co., New York 1974, pp166-69 and *West Africa*, 14 March 1922, p168. As early as the eighteenth century Olaudah Equiano and other Africans had united to form the Sons of Africa, to give an organised voice to the political concerns of Africans in London, and probably elsewhere in Britain.
12. Fryer, *op.cit.*, p280.
13. On Savage and the Afro-West Indian Literacy Society see *The Student*, 20 October 1898 p8, and Langley, *op.cit.*, p189.
14. H. Adi, 'West African Students in Britain, 1900-60: The Politics of Exile', in

D. Killingray (ed.) *Africans in Britain*, Frank Cass, London 1994, pp107-29.
15. *The Scotsman*, 5 July 1906, p7.
16. G. Shepperson, 'An Early African Graduate', in G. Donaldson (ed.), *Four Centuries, Edinburgh University Life 1583-1983*, Edinburgh University Press, Edinburgh 1983, pp96-7, ref. 3.
17. H. Adi, 'Bandele Omoniyi – A Neglected Nigerian Nationalist' *African Affairs*, 90/361, 1991, pp581-605. For an example of Omoniyi's writing see Appendix.
18. H. Adi, *op.cit.*, p583, note 9.
19. R. Jenkins, *op.cit.*, pp24-5. Edward Wilmot Blyden (1832-1912) was born in the Caribbean but migrated to Liberia where he subsequently became a professor of Greek and Latin, a government minister and ambassador to Britain. He was one of the most influential black thinkers and writers of the nineteenth century, who challenged the ideas of African inferiority in his writing and called for African unity to create the conditions for African greatness in the future.
20. See 'Conference with Africans', *Journal of the African Society (JAS)*, Vol. XII (1913), p425.
21. Duse Mohammed Ali, 'Foreword', *African Times and Orient Review (ATOR)*, July 1912. See also I. Duffield, 'Duse Mohammed Ali, Afro-Asian solidarity and Pan-Africanism in early twentieth-century London', in I. Duffield and J.S. Gundara (eds) *Essays on the History of Blacks in Britain*, Avebury, Aldershot 1992, pp124-50.
22. *ATOR*, October-December 1917.
23. Sir Adeyemo Alakija (1884-1952) became one of Nigeria's most prominent lawyers and politicians and the founder of one of the country's most important newspapers the *Nigerian Daily Times*. He became a member of the Nigerian Executive Council in 1942 and was knighted in 1945. See also *JAS*, XII, 1913, p425.
24. *Anti-Slavery Reporter and Aborigines' Friend*, April 1913, pp50-61.
25. *ATOR*, April 1914, p98 and the *Lagos Standard*, 7 June 1914.
26. *ATOR*, February 1917, p36 and December 1917, p113. Sir E.S. Beoku-Betts (1895-1957) became a judge in the Sierra Leone Court of Appeal and a member of the Legislative Council in 1924. He was knighted in 1957.
27. *ATOR*, August 1917, p46 and September 1917, p61.
28. SCM Archive, 'Memo on present condition of work among foreign students', 1918.
29. *The African Telegraph*, December 1918, pp89-90.
30. *West Africa*, 8 February 1919, pp38-40.
31. *West Africa*, 4 January 1919, pp840-42.

32. *The African Telegraph*, January-February 1919, p117 and March 1919, p139. Both the APU and the SPAO attended the Pan-African Congress organised by W.E.B. Du Bois in Paris in 1919.
33. On the riots see J. Jenkinson, 'The 1919 Race Riots in Britain: A Survey' in R. Lotz and I. Pegg, *op.cit.*
34. Anti-Slavery Society Papers, MSS. Brit. Emp. S23 H2/56. Harris to Sir Owen Phillips, 24 February 1919.
35. *African World*, Supplement, 30 November 1921, pviii.

West African Student Organisations 1923-30

The Union of Students of African Descent (USAD)

By the early 1920s West African students had formed new organisations to further their interests. The African Races Association had been formed at Glasgow University in 1917, with the aim of promoting 'closer union of Africans and African descendants in the British Isles' and the 'discussion of subjects pertaining to, or affecting the general welfare of the African race'.[1] In the same year an African Union, with mainly West African officers, was formed at Edinburgh University.[2] In London, APU continued to play a prominent role, especially in the Pan-African congresses of 1921 and 1923, but it also began to lose much of its influence. Most of its members were wealthy and elderly merchants, or politically conservative and they were increasingly out of touch with the aspirations of the younger African students.

It was the Union of Students of African Descent (USAD) which became the most prominent organisation of the African students during the early 1920s. The Union grew out of the activities of the London-based West African and West Indian Christian Union, which after attracting a number of non-Christian student members, changed its name to USAD, and grew in size from 25 members in 1921, to around 120 by 1924, including Indian and English associate members.[3] The first president of USAD was the Trinidadian Percy Acham Chen, and in its early years the Union was dominated by West Indian rather than West African students, although a Nigerian woman A.M. Fanimokun, was one of its most active members. In 1923 C.F. Hayfron-Benjamin from the Gold Coast became the Union's president, and more African students were encouraged to join, including those at Cambridge and Edinburgh universities. According to Hayfron-Benjamin, USAD was playing its part in disproving the racist view that Africans could not organise themselves. It had 'a strong faith in the Negro and other races', believed 'in the introduction of Christianity and democracy to parts of Africa where they do not already exist', and seems to have been supported by British commercial and humanitarian interests and the weekly British journal *West Africa*. One of USAD's main concerns was student accommodation. As the hostel issue had not been resolved, the Union helped to find lodgings for new students, and encouraged African parents who were unfamiliar with British conditions to contact it for advice at Student Movement House in London.[4]

The Union saw itself as a literary and social club, hoped to publish its own journal, and in its early years was probably popular for its dinners and dances, as much as for its fortnightly debates on religion, sociology and literature. It declared itself to be apolitical and explained: 'a premature participation in politics does not seem likely to serve the best interests of the average student. For one thing students generally are apt to solve political problems before they have fully understood them'. However, there is every indication in the pages of *West Africa* that USAD was also deeply involved in all the major political debates of the day.[5]

Ladipo Solanke and the Empire exhibition

A Nigerian USAD member, Ladipo Solanke, who had come to Britain in 1922 to study law at University College, London (UCL), soon began to make a name for himself as a spokesman for the growing number of West African students who now resided in the country.[6] In March 1924, he wrote to *West Africa* to complain about an article entitled 'Empire Making in Nigeria', which had appeared in the *Evening News*. This article had credited the colonial government with abolishing 'cannibalism' and 'black magic' within twenty years, and had made use of a recent speech by the Nigerian Governor, Sir Hugh Clifford, in which he had apparently referred to areas of Nigeria in which 'human meat was sold openly in the markets in quite recent times'.[7] According to Solanke, the *Evening News* article was a great distortion of Clifford's speech, and would mislead the British public just before the opening of the Empire exhibition at Wembley, which was being held as a morale booster for the British public, following the devastation of the First World War. It would 'do serious harm to those of us from Nigeria who are now in London for educational purposes'. He also added that there were no records of cannibalism in Nigeria, and called on the newspaper to give more prominence to the facts.[8] The vice-president of USAD, the Nigerian law student A. K. Soetan, wrote to *West Africa* in support of Solanke's letter. He pointed out that such racism undermined what he saw as the good work of colonial administrators and missionaries in Africa, and he agreed with Solanke that the offending article had appeared at a most unfortunate time. Soetan argued that prejudice on the basis of skin colour should cease, and pointed out that Japan's rapid development refuted racist notions of non-European inferiority.[9]

The article in the *Evening News* was followed by similarly derogatory articles in the *Sunday Express* and *Saturday Review*, which ridiculed the West African section of the British Empire exhibition. The article in *Saturday Review* entitled 'A Day at Wembley', was an attempt at a humorous sketch. One paragraph contained a number of petty racist comments, for example about what was seen as the absurdity of Gold Coast 'natives' in European dress. The second, and even more offensive article was entitled 'When West Africa Woos'. It appeared alongside a cartoon, and was introduced with the words: 'One of the features of Wembley is a West African village ruled by a native princess. Below she tells the story of love as it is made in Akropong'.[10]

USAD immediately passed a resolution denouncing the articles, which it sent to the Colonial Secretary, J.H. Thomas. In particular the students protested against articles and photographs which 'hold up to public ridicule citizens of countries whose money has been voted in large sums for the purpose of the exhibition'. The Union suggested that the Colonial Office, 'should impress on the Exhibition authorities the necessity either for keeping intact the proper privacy of West African workers concerned, or for seeing that those permitted to see them in their village in the walled city are capable of the decencies of ordinary conduct'. It made clear that it would be sending copies of the resolution to the West African newspapers, 'together with any reply the Colonial Office may care to make'. It also intended to send a copy of the resolution to the Prince of Wales, the President of the British Empire exhibition, the West African governors, and Lord Beaverbrook, the proprietor of the *Sunday Express*.[11]

Colonial Office officials were reluctant to take any direct action on the matter, arguing that the Colonial Office could not control the press, and not wishing to enhance the credibility of USAD, or any other student organisation, which might lead to inundation with 'fancied grievances where none exist'. Eventually the Governor of the Gold Coast, Sir F. Guggisberg intervened to bar the activities of the press in the Gold Coast village, and the publicity council of the exhibition also took steps to prevent the publication of further derogatory articles.

The protest by USAD was therefore highly successful, and marks a turning point in the political activities of West African students in Britain. The students' protest was of a much more assertive nature, and they had also received substantial support from *West Africa*, which printed the USAD resolution, and carried a front-page editorial demanding action to protect 'British West Africans from such outrages'. In fact *West Africa* publicised details of the whole campaign, and thereby elevated the importance of USAD and the West African students.[12]

The British Empire exhibition focused a great deal of attention on West African affairs, as well as bringing large numbers of West African celebrities to Britain. USAD and APU, as well as individual students such as Solanke, made the most of the situation, as can be seen from the numerous meetings, letters to the press, and other activities which took place during 1924. USAD followed up its protest campaign with a series of meetings featuring many of the West African notables then in the country, including Dr James Aggrey and Dr C.C. Adeniyi-Jones, a member of Nigeria's Legislative Council.[13] The meetings became a forum for a wide ranging debate over the future of West Africa, the issues facing West African students, and the need for West Africans in Britain to form their own independent organisations.

The students' political consciousness was also influenced by events in West Africa. Britain's four colonies were largely administered according to the principles of 'indirect rule', that is to say that Africans were governed through the agency of their own institutions and rulers backed up by the British army under the direction of colonial governors and the Colonial Office. In addition, the colonies had executive and legislative councils, which had largely advisory powers, made up of British officials and commercial interests. In the early 1920s new constitutions, which allowed the election of a few African representatives to the legislative councils, were introduced in Nigeria in 1923, Sierra Leone in 1924 and the Gold Coast in 1925. Elected members had virtually no power and represented a very limited electorate, but the new constitutions did stimulate local elite politics and in some cases the formation of new political parties such as the Nigerian National Democratic Party (NNDP), founded by Herbert Macaulay in 1923. In 1920 the National Congress of British West Africa (NCBWA), which included representatives from all four of Britain's West African colonies was founded. The NCBWA was an important, but relatively short-lived, forum for the discussion of the common concerns of the West African merchants and professionals. It pledged loyalty to the Empire but also agitated for political, social and economic reforms. Its ultimate aim was dominion status for a West African political entity; and here it resurrected ideas of a West African state which had earlier been part of the thinking of Africanus Horton and Edward Blyden. Such notions of West African 'nationhood' reflected the extensive connections and commercial interests which existed amongst western-educated and wealthy West Africans at this time, and indeed throughout the colonial period.[14] The founders of the NCBWA, J.E. Casely Hayford and R. A. Savage had themselves been students in Britain, and when a NCBWA delegation visited Britain in 1920 a number of meetings were held with the West African students.

The Nigerian Progress Union (NPU)

In this changing political climate it was the Nigerian students in London, led by Ladipo Solanke, who first decided to form their own organisation. Solanke had found that like many West African students in Britain he was living in poverty and thoroughly miserable. According to his diary, he was soon in debt and spent the whole of the summer of 1924 teaching Yoruba to other students, in order 'to get my daily bread'.[15] He evidently disliked the corrupting influence of life in London, and what he referred to as the 'characteristic features' of some of his Nigerian friends, whom he described as lacking in morals, 'polygamous by nature' and 'practising polyandry among the white girls'. He concluded that such vices must be avoided and that students should live a 'high moral life' if they were to become successful politicians and leaders of the African 'masses'. It also appeared to Solanke that many Nigerian students were unconcerned about their own cultural traditions, and he lamented the fact that when he had delivered a lecture on traditional Yoruba institutions to the student union at UCL, only two Nigerians had attended.[16]

Solanke first emerged as a prominent student activist during the protests concerning the British Empire exhibition. In addition to his letters to the press, he had proposed that USAD adopt a resolution to 'begin a campaign to suppress the every day ridicule against the Blacks in this country', and he regularly scoured the pages of the press for instances of offensive reports. Following the publication of his protest letters in the *Evening News* and *West Africa* he received encouragement from an unexpected quarter. Amy Ashwood Garvey, the estranged wife of Marcus Garvey, had seen the protest letters and wrote to congratulate him. They became friends and, largely due to Amy Ashwood Garvey's enthusiasm, went on to form the Nigerian Progress Union (NPU).

The NPU was founded by thirteen Nigerian students in London in July 1924, in order 'to promote the general welfare of Nigerians from an educational not political point of view'.[17] From this time onwards Solanke, the leading figure in the NPU, was destined to play a major role in West African student politics until his death in 1958. The philosophy guiding the formation and direction of the NPU owed as much to the ideas of Marcus Garvey as it did to those of his estranged wife, but it also reflected the ideologies and policies of the emergent West African nationalist organisations such as the NCBWA and the NNDP. Solanke viewed Nigeria as a possible 'mighty Negro Empire or Republic', a country 'full of immense possibilities' and 'undeveloped resources and wealth'. However, according to the thinking of the NPU, this potential greatness could not be realised, not because Nigeria was a British colony, but because its education system was inadequate or 'not national enough'. The NPU was particularly concerned that the Nigerian 'has been taught to hate all his national institutions and customs and brand them all as fetish while most of them are in truth and fact good'. The students also complained that Nigeria had no university college and that the education of women was being totally neglected. The Union therefore aspired: 'to solve the social, industrial, economic and commercial problem of Nigeria from the platform of Education of the masses of the Nigerian peoples; co-operating of course, with the Government, Missionaries and other bodies that have hitherto been bearing the brunt of the whole burden'.[18]

The emphasis on education was certainly not a new idea, but clearly coincided with the thinking of Amy Ashwood Garvey, who had formulated her own plans for mass vernacular education in Nigeria. In her view education was more important than politics: 'The Negro as a race is not yet ripe for political emancipation. You must educate him before he will be able to understand anything about politics'.[19] Certainly the NPU was also influenced by the opinions of Marcus Garvey and aspired 'to foster the habit of self-help, self-sacrifice, self-control and self-knowledge'. Solanke, who was later to correspond and work with Garvey, claimed that he and the Universal Negro Improvement Association (UNIA) had, 'aroused in us in a material way our race consciousness although we may disagree with some of the methods of that great Negro organiser'.[20]

Solanke's 'Open Letter to the Negroes of the World', addressed to both West Africans and African-Americans, indicates that he and the NPU were in the process of developing their own political opinions, based on what they considered to be the most pressing problems in the British colonies in West Africa, and particularly in Nigeria 'the mighty home of the American and West Indian Negroes'. There was not much questioning of colonial rule itself, although there was concern that, as had occurred in East and South Africa, land might be seized by 'British capitalists', such as Lord Leverhulme. But education was equally, if not more important, if the masses of West Africa were to be in a position to exploit their own natural resources. For this purpose, argued Solanke, education could not be in the hands of the British government or missionaries; West Africans must establish their own 'Tuskegees', assisted by the co-operation of their 'brethren in America', to produce trained specialists of all types. Ironically this was the policy favoured by the British government, and in 1923 the Colonial Office had sent one of its own 'specialists', Hanns Vischer, to the US to visit Booker T. Washington's Tuskegee Institute, in order to learn something of how 'Negro Education' was organised, and how its principles might be applied in the African colonies.[21]

In 1925, as a result of an introduction by Amy Ashwood Garvey, Solanke's 'Open Letter' and other articles concerning NPU were published in the African-American journal *The Spokesman*. These articles show that Solanke and the NPU were confident enough to present their views to an audience in the United States as well as in West Africa. Solanke argued that first and foremost it was up to West Africans themselves to raise the finance necessary for the education of the masses, only then might they call for the assistance of their 'brethren' in the USA. His 'Open Letter' concluded with the view that:

> The time has come now when the Negro at home and the Negro abroad

should find their way out to understand each other better with a view to co-operating for the final emancipation of the whole of the Negro race educationally, industrially, politically and commercially.[22]

Solanke also directed his appeals at traditional leaders and the emergent nationalist forces in West Africa, calling on them to unite to give 'a helping hand for progress'. In one letter to Herbert Macaulay he explained: 'Neither the Government nor the (commercial) European Industrialist are strong enough to constitute our formidable or unconquerable foe if we really unite and co-operate'.[23] Solanke and the NPU also developed links with other leading Nigerian political figures. Patrons included Dr C. Adeniyi-Jones, whose two daughters were members of the NPU; J.H. Doherty, 'Merchant Prince of Lagos', Dr Henry Carr, ex-Resident of Lagos, and Chief Richard Henshaw of the Calabar National League.

The politics of the NPU was influenced by the development of nationalist politics in southern Nigeria, as well as by the formation of the NCBWA. Solanke had a concern with 'the masses', which was uncommon in West African politics at the time, but he also stated that 'political agitation should be left to only a few who love and understand it'. Solanke even went as far as to speak of 'national independence' in West Africa, but at the same time thought that 'responsible government' was unlikely for another thirty years. In a number of published articles he was critical of the NCBWA's declared programme, which was centred around moderate political reforms, and which, from the NPU standpoint, did not focus sufficiently on education. In one article which referred to the NCBWA he explained:

> ... about nine-tenths of the Congress programme should be devoted to educational purposes and the remainder to other activities, political or otherwise, because at present 'politics', strictly speaking, do not exist in West Africa and our problem lies wholly in the educational rather than the political field'.[24]

Solanke and the NPU soon came to the attention of the Colonial Office, and their activities were also monitored by the authorities at UCL, who wrote to the Colonial Office, concerned that the Union's activities were 'a concealed form of political propaganda'. Subsequently Solanke officially informed the Colonial Office of the formation of the NPU and began to try to enlist its support for 'the foundation of a much needed hostel in London for all African students'.[25] The Colonial Office concluded that the Union was idealistic and harmless, but officials were not entirely dismissive, being increasingly concerned with the dilemma of exactly how to deal with the presence of students and other Africans in Britain. The Empire exhibition highlighted the problem of accommodating temporary African visitors and notables, who might be subjected to the colour bar or some other form of discrimination. The 'insensitivity' of the press had added to the Colonial Office's problems, and the whole occasion, far from promoting the Empire, served rather to highlight its inequalities, and to stimulate African students in Britain to become involved in more organised political activity. Indeed Solanke was to claim in future years that it was the treatment of Africans and their media coverage at the Empire exhibition, which spurred him to attempt to organise West African students in Britain.[26]

During the 1920s many more West Africans were able to afford the passage to Britain, or arrived as stowaways, hoping to advance themselves as students or by other means. West African seamen also often found themselves stranded in Britain. Some Africans became totally destitute within a few weeks of landing, and then attempted to find some charitable institution which could support them. The CWAE was one such body that was forever trying to solicit support from the Colonial Office, to help it cope with the ever-growing numbers of what were referred to as 'destitute natives'. The problem for the Colonial Office was that it was almost impossible to control the influx of these Africans, something which gave officials cause for concern.

Representatives of those concerned with the welfare of African students were not slow in making clear to the Colonial Office the difficulties which accompanied the increasing number of Africans in Britain. A Cambridge don complained that many African students were not up to the required standard and therefore could not finish their courses. He felt strongly that something should be quickly done about the problem, 'because it will be a very serious thing if negroes begin to hang around London in the way that Indian students have done for many years with great detriment to themselves from every point of view'.[27] In 1923, the CWAE issued an *Open Letter to African Parents*, warning of the problems confronting young students in Britain, and the difficulties of finding suitable accommodation and schools. It was therefore evident to all those concerned about the welfare of African students that some action had to be taken. The Colonial Office was now increasingly in favour of a scheme of control and supervision, and made some attempts to limit the numbers of students leaving West Africa. The problem for the Colonial Office was how to avoid antagonising the students and nationalist opinion in West Africa. It was feared that ill-considered measures could force students to go to the United States for their education, where they might 'fall into the hands of Marcus Garvey and the like'.[28]

The founding of the West African Students' Union (WASU)

In 1925, Dr Herbert Bankole-Bright a member of the Legislative Council of Sierra Leone and the NCBWA, and a former medical student at Edinburgh University visited London. His presence in the country, and influence on the students, were to lead directly to the formation of the West African Students' Union. In August 1925, at a meeting of West African students in London, Bankole-Bright urged the students to forge a unity that would mirror that established by the NCBWA in West Africa. Although there were four existing organisations in London: APU and USAD in which West Africans often played a leading role, the NPU and a newly formed Gold Coast Students' Association (GCSA), Bankole-Bright argued that the students might be more effective in realising their aims by forming a single West African organisation, run on similar lines to the Indian Students' Union in Britain.[29]

Solanke had himself considered forming such an organisation as early as 1923, when as a member of USAD he had proposed a motion that 'the Union be incorporated in the Congress of West Africa', and that USAD together with the other existing unions 'be incorporated into one or establish one union called the United Africa Society or Central Committee of Students of African Descent'.[30] Nothing came of these proposals but Solanke continued to seek support for his idea with other students, and according to one account, he also approached the president of the NCBWA, J.E. Casely Hayford, who gave the plan his blessing.[31] Solanke's own explanation for the founding of the WASU involved divine revelation during a dream. The dream contained a political message:

> that until Africans at home and abroad, including all persons of African descent, organise and develop the spirit of the principles of self-help,

unity and co-operation among themselves, and fight it out to remove the colour bar, they would have to continue to suffer the results of colour prejudice, and remain hewers of wood and drawers of water for the other races of mankind.[32]

Solanke later claimed that henceforth he devoted his life to these ideals. Significantly the dream focuses on the removal of the colour bar and colour prejudice rather than direct opposition to colonial rule. However, it is clear that Solanke and the other students viewed the two issues as inseparable.

Not surprisingly, Bankole-Bright's proposal sparked off a heated debate amongst the students. Some of those most closely connected with USAD naturally fiercely defended that organisation. Many of the arguments centred on the fact that the aim of the new organisation was: 'To afford opportunity exclusively to West African students in Great Britain and Ireland to discuss matters affecting West Africa educationally, commercially, economically and politically, and to co-operate with the NCBWA'.[33] Solanke and his supporters were branded 'segregationists' who wished to put West African unity before Pan-African unity, and who wished to separate themselves from those 'Europeans' such as the SCM, who had been influential within the USAD, and thereby damage 'race relations'. While the 'segregationists' replied that they wished to be self-reliant and solve their own problems, and that USAD and APU had achieved little. When the proposal to form the West African Students' Union was finally put to the vote it was unanimously supported by all those present. J.B. Danquah became WASU's first president, and Solanke became secretary-general, a post he was to hold for the next twenty-five years.[34]

WASU was established with the following aims:

1. to provide and maintain a hostel for students of African descent;
2. to act as a bureau of information on African history, customs, law and institutions;
3. to act as a centre for research on all subjects appertaining to Africa and its developments;
4. to promote through regular contacts a spirit of goodwill, better understanding and brotherhood between all persons of African descent and other races of mankind;
5. to present to the world a true picture of African life and philosophy, thereby making a definitely African contribution towards the

progress of civilisation;
6. to promote the spirit of self-help, unity and co-operation amongst its members;
7. to foster a spirit of national consciousness and racial pride amongst its members;
8. to publish a monthly magazine called *Wasu*.[35]

The controversy surrounding the founding of the WASU continued for some time. But despite protests from some, most of the West African students felt a need for the new organisation, not just as African students in Britain facing the problems of racism and the colour bar, but also as a means to advance the political interests of the West African colonies. The students were clearly aiming for a more political organisation which might agitate for and emphasise the needs of the future 'United West Africa' which was increasingly evident in their thinking.[36]

Wasu and West African nationalism

Wasu, the journal of the Union, was launched in March 1926, and in the first 'Editorial Notes' made clear its aims:

> We issue out into the world to-day. We are the offspring of the enthusiasm and vision of youth anxious for their own and their country's advancement. Of our parentage we are insufferably proud because of its courage and its belief in its mission. *Wasu* is our name, which is derived from Yoruba, one of the languages of Nigeria, the original home of most of the peoples of West Africa. As our name indicates, we have been brought forth to preach; and the first message we have to declare in general to all Negroes, and in particular to those of British West Africa is the saving one of co-operation. Africans everywhere have recognised the need for closer association in the common endeavour, of the peoples of West Africa, and individual writers in this impression have essayed to indicate means whereby co-operation could be effected.[37]

The journal also made clear its aim to explain the concerns of West Africans to the world at large:

> About no other people or country has there been so much misconcep-

tion as about the African and his land. Many attempts have indeed been made to get at the 'back of the black man's mind'; but they have all met with the kind of success inevitable in the case of such attempts undertaken by people not fitted to do so. Wasu now comes forward to help in exposing that mind, and in interpreting some of the riddles therein.[38]

As well as preaching co-operation and explaining the apparent riddles of 'the black man's mind', *Wasu* set out to stress the need for West African progress and development. Solanke and WASU strongly supported the NCBWA's demand for compulsory education in West Africa and there were many *Wasu* articles on education, and the importance of developing more educational facilities in West Africa. Students welcomed the new college at Achimota in the Gold Coast, which was even seen by some as the 'nucleus of the West African nation', but lamented the fact that it employed so few African teachers. Some articles stressed the need for African students in Britain to undertake more research into 'native medicine' and other aspects of traditional culture. Others debated the relative merits of studying law and medicine, and commented on the lack of science graduates. Above all else, the first six editions were all concerned with the concept of 'West African nationality'; how such nationhood might be realised, and with the related issue of re-evaluating, and presenting African history and culture from, what today might be called, an Afrocentric perspective.

The idea of a West African nationality did not find sudden expression in the 1920s. Certainly Blyden, and before him Horton, had attempted to develop this concept, which above all reflected the strivings of the emergent West African bourgeoisie to develop their own polity, a striving which had been encouraged by the Select Committee of the House of Commons which in 1865 had recommended self-government for Britain's West African colonies. By the end of the nineteenth century, the rise of imperialism and the military 'pacification' of West Africa thwarted any further moves towards self-government. However, the idea of a united West Africa remained, and to some extent was further developed, by the addition of various elements of cultural nationalism, which comprised the main ideological response of the West African merchants and professionals to the overt racism which accompanied the 'new imperialism' and 'scramble for Africa'.[39] The founding of the NCBWA, a consequence of the political stirrings of the embryonic bourgeoisie in West Africa, led to a further development of the idea of West African nationhood.

As a consequence of WASU's concern with the concept of the West African nation, and the development of the cultural, political and economic unity of this 'nation', *Wasu* featured many articles on West African history, languages, marriage customs, and traditional political institutions. Many of these, reflecting the composition of WASU, focused on the culture of the Yoruba people of Nigeria. Solanke, and to a lesser extent Julius Ojo-Cole, took the lead in writing essays and poems which stressed the greatness of the Yoruba past, and even claimed that it was the Yoruba who had played the major part in founding all the great kingdoms of West Africa.[40] There were also articles which called for the development of a West African religion, which might be based on the tenets of the Ethiopian Orthodox Church. Others, perhaps encouraged by the views of the African-American writer Alain Locke, encouraged a synthesis of traditional cultures on the basis that: 'as many African cultures as we are able to assimilate, so large an area shall we be capable of consolidating into the West African Nation which is our aim to establish'. According to *Wasu*, Africa would make its contribution to the future of civilisation because it 'is the richest continent in racial types and harbours in its tolerant climate the greatest conglomeration of men of all shades of colour, customs and cultures'.[41]

The notion of West African nationhood was encouraged by Casely Hayford, the first patron of WASU, when he addressed the Union in 1926. His speech, entitled 'Nationalism as a West African Ideal', outlined many of the principles which were to influence the Union in the early years of its existence. In particular, Casely Hayford stressed the important role of education, both European and American, and of the students themselves, whom he referred to as 'the flower of African intelligence'. It was their duty, he said, to correct any wrong impressions about their 'race'. He strongly opposed the views of some British politicians and colonial officials, who attempted to denigrate the 'educated African', or create divisions between them and their less educated compatriots, as part of the policy of indirect rule. A strong believer in self-help, Casely Hayford called on the students in Britain to play their full part in helping the NCBWA to attain West African nationhood.[42]

The students readily took on this role and saw their task as 'helping to create a healthy national sentiment throughout the whole of West Africa'. But they also saw West African unity as important for the whole continent, as the basis for Pan-African unity. As WASU's president explained:

> You cannot make a nation of Africa, but by securing unity in West Africa, and by securing African rights in the western portion, you thereby raise the general standard of African welfare and lay down an ideal of life which the African in the east and south will strive to realise. If Africans are to survive, West Africa must become a nation; it must unite under the sentiment of national progress.[43]

In *Wasu* West Africans were encouraged to travel throughout West Africa and learn each other's languages and customs, so as to strengthen and develop the idea of nationhood. A 1928 editorial declared:

> We members of the WASU believe that the study of our African customs and institutions together with the adoption and reverent preservation of our African idiosyncrasies leads to the formation of a national character which is the corner-stone of nationhood.[44]

The students also showed some concern for the economic development of West Africa, and called for West African merchants to work together and establish 'inter-colonial enterprises' for their mutual benefit. They deplored the reliance of the colonies on single crops and argued that economic power had to be the basis for increasing political autonomy. As J.B. Danquah, the Union's president explained: 'Until West Africa determines to rise into a position of economic pre-eminence, all talk of progress and power sounds hollow and purposeless'.[45]

However, many of the students and their compatriots in West Africa still felt that continued co-operation with Britain was vital to attain the progress and development of the West Africa colonies. They could see no other way forward, and although they were determined to be ultimately self-reliant, they also looked to British 'trusteeship' to assist colonial development. There was clearly a contradiction here which reflected the precarious position of the emergent bourgeoisie itself. It was as yet too weak to end colonial rule and in some ways directly benefited from and was a product of the colonial system. But it was constantly thwarted in its attempts to assert itself politically, economically and socially and was therefore compelled to struggle against the conditions imposed by colonialism and sometimes colonial rule itself.

WASU's members produced two other major publications dedicated to West African nationhood, Solanke's *United West Africa at the Bar of the Family of Nations*, and de Graft Johnson's *Towards Nationhood in West Africa*. Joseph William de Graft Johnson was a leading member of USAD as well as a member of WASU, and a sub-editor of *Wasu*. *Towards Nationhood in West Africa*, which was published in 1928, was the end product of a series of lectures delivered to youth organisations in Britain, and was subtitled 'Thoughts of Young Africa Addressed to Young Britain'. Like Solanke, and the other West African students, he aimed to write a historical defence of Africa and Africans and of the doctrine of 'the equality of the races', and to argue the case for eventual African self-government. He naturally defended the role of the so called 'educated natives', whom he regarded as the best interpreters of African views and needs, and he vigorously opposed the views of many colonial officials that they were 'an obstacle to government'.[46] His *Preface* gives some idea of West African students' aspirations at the time:

> The hope and desire of Africa is the same throughout the length and breadth of the continent. It is concentrated in the great yearning for freedom, for emancipation from the yoke of the centuries. The youth of Africa everywhere, is assailed by the alluring thoughts of a free Africa, of an Africa that owning no foreign burden, but stepping into her rightful place as a unit in the powerful army of the human family, will emerge from the darkness of the past and assume her obligations and responsibilities as a respectable and respected member of society... Young Africans are co-operating for the cause of Africa. In their two organisations, the USAD and the WASU they are correlating lines of thought and action. They have laid siege to the citadel of England's nobleness of mind and soul, and there are hopes, great hopes, that the future will see the African better understood and appreciated, and given his due right of recognition in the Comity of Nations.[47]

Solanke's work, published in 1927, aimed to bring the 'Negro into European consciousness'. It was dedicated to 'all the Native Rulers and Youths of West Africa', and was written as a defence both of African history and civilisation, and of the modern strivings of Africans from the continent and diaspora. Solanke gave a rather glowing account of Africa's history before the fifteenth century, and highlighted the importance of Moorish Spain to the European Renaissance, and the role of the slave trade in the development of Europe and underdevelopment of Africa, and as the basis of modern racism.[48] As far as modern Africa was concerned, Solanke lamented the fact that what he referred to as 'anti-national' education had split the educated African from the traditional rulers, and he argued that 'the Family of Nations' (missionaries, merchants and colonial officials) should play its part in developing education and religion which reflected the national characteristics which existed in West Africa. He also hoped that colonial officials would act more impartially; help the traditional rulers, stop regarding 'educated Africans' as the enemy, and not always side with the capitalist concerns, which he said were always scheming to get hold of African land. Solanke therefore encouraged unity, not only between the traditional rulers and the intelligentsia, but also between the latter and colonial officials.[49] His most positive pronouncements concerned WASU itself, which he described as 'a training ground for practical unity and effective co-operation', and a means to assert 'West African individuality' in Britain. Clearly *Wasu* had a part to play in this process, so too did the successful organisation of an African students' hostel, which would be an excellent example of self-help.[50]

The student hostel and the colour bar

The controversial issue of establishing a hostel or club was one of the main aims of WASU, just as it had been an objective of the NPU and USAD. As well as being an example of self-help, Solanke argued that a hostel would help to dispel the racist notion that Africans were unable to manage their own affairs. It was also needed as a 'home from home'; a place where West Africans could eat and present to others their 'delicious and most palatable dishes'.[51] The Colonial Office and others concerned about the welfare of African students were also interested in the idea of a hostel, as it became clear that African students would continue to arrive in Britain. The Colonial Office was particularly concerned about those students who were financially or educationally ill-prepared when they came to Britain. Those who 'dropped out' or failed to gain admission to colleges might drift around London or come under the influence of what officials considered bad company. Even more worrying were those who formed liaisons with British women, some of whom subsequently became pregnant, and then burdened the Colonial Office with the problem of their offspring.

There was also the more general problem of the colour bar and racism in Britain, which was having an extremely untoward effect on West Africa's future leaders. At a Colonial Office conference in 1927, officials concluded that in order to exert their influence, some sort of centre or hostel should be provided for African students in London. Major Hanns Vischer, secretary-general of the International Institute of African Languages and Cultures and a former Director of Education in Northern Nigeria, was given the task of liaison with WASU, USAD, and other African students. Officials were well aware that their dilemma could not easily be resolved. Because of the virtual non-existence of higher education in West Africa, and the gradual expansion of secondary education, more and more West Africans were likely to end up in Britain. It was grudgingly recognised that these students could not be kept out, nor their movements rigidly controlled once they arrived, but something might be done to 'look after them properly' during their stay in Britain.

The most important issue was who would assume control of a student hostel: the students and other Africans, the Colonial Office or various humanitarian interests? In August 1928, J.A. Doherty, the WASU president, appealed to supporters in West Africa for funds for a hostel. He claimed that 'The Colonial Office has expressed its readiness to undertake the whole responsibility', but that in his view, it should be WASU's members who initiated such a project. Solanke too made an appeal for assistance to set up 'a central home in London for African students' to the traditional rulers and intelligentsia of West Africa, and received some encouragement from one of WASU's patrons in West Africa, Nana Sir Ofori Atta, an influential leader of traditional rulers in the Gold Coast Legislative Council, who visited Britain in 1928.[52] Solanke felt that such a hostel would unite the students and promote West African nationhood, and would cost around £4000, a quarter of which he expected to raise from fund-raising in Nigeria, and proportionately less from the other colonies. Following several meetings with Vischer who talked of the hostel as 'a veritable home to which your people will look as something belonging to themselves and not as a charity',[53] Solanke concluded that the Colonial Office was willing 'to render all possible assistance to further the scheme'.[54]

The question of a hostel in London was again assuming some importance because of the 'colour bar' and other instances of racism and discrimination, which were becoming ever more frequent. There were government attempts to control and limit the entry of colonial workers into Britain such as the Coloured Alien Seamen Order of 1925, and one Chief Constable had even argued for legislation to ban sexual relationships between black men and white women.[55] WASU had as one of its aims the promotion of 'inter-racial understanding', and throughout the 1920s it vigorously opposed any discrimination or signs of racism, and sent Solanke, de Graft Johnson, and other WASU members to speak at meetings and conferences throughout Britain on the subject. In *Wasu* the achievements of the students themselves, and often those of other Africans and African-Americans, were regularly presented to counter any notions of inferiority, and to promote the progress and advances of the 'Negro Race'. One letter sent to the *Wasu* from a former colonial official who had served in Sierra Leone argued: 'Without us, the Negro perishes so far as concerns his advance to the form of civilisation of the greatest value to mankind'. The letter, which extolled the virtues of the British empire, concluded that it would be 'a sad day for the Negro' if the slogan 'Africa for the Africans' was ever realised.[56] Such correspondence gives some idea of the problems which the students had to face, even from those who would have considered themselves sympathetic. Indeed it is noticeable that even in 'A Student's Romance', a serialised short story which appeared in *Wasu*, racism was featured as a normal part of student life in Britain.[57]

The number of blatant examples of racism reported in the press were once again troubling not only the students, but also representatives of the Colonial Office. In October 1928 *West Africa* reported the case of Ekundayo Akerele and Adetokunbo Ademola, two Nigerian law students who had successfully appealed against a conviction for a breach of the peace. This was alleged to have occurred when they were abused by an English woman, who was subsequently found to have been lying about the whole incident.[58] The following summer, attention focused firstly on David Lloyd George's use of the word 'nigger' during an election speech, and then on the colour bar operating in various London hotels, which had excluded, amongst others, the future WASU patron Paul Robeson.[59] Naturally such incidents, and the concern expressed by some MPs that racial prejudice damaged imperial interests, put greater pressure on the Colonial Office to find solutions, and provided ammunition and support for the students' demand for a hostel, which might protect them against such indignities.

According to Colonial Office information, there were in 1929 about 125 African students at universities in Britain, most of them originating from West Africa. It was estimated that there were about forty in London, thirty two in Edinburgh, and the rest at Oxford, Cambridge, Newcastle and Bristol universities. The vast majority of these students were also self-financing, which as far as the Colonial Office was concerned, meant that they were even more difficult to supervise and control. Vischer was in contact with both USAD and WASU throughout 1928 and 1929, and reported that the students often referred to the colour bar and the problem of accommodation at their meetings. He concluded that 'Those who come into contact with these African students here or in Africa will, I think, agree with me that in the majority of cases they feel very bitter against us as a result of their experiences in England'. This state of affairs was felt to be even more regrettable, because as Vischer pointed out, 'these men on their return to Africa are most likely to occupy important positions in their own community', and because as another official confirmed, they were also subjected to the 'racial prejudice prevailing amongst the majority of Englishmen and women' in West Africa.[60]

Vischer suggested that the Colonial Office concentrate on WASU, because in his view: 'These people if properly handled, can do more to keep their fellow countrymen out of trouble in this country than we shall ever be able to do'. WASU should be encouraged with its plans to open a hostel, but at the same time the Colonial Office should also play its part in forming a hostel organising committee, although it would be unwise for them to become openly and officially involved. Instead Vischer would work unofficially to organise such a committee, composed of retired colonial officials, missionaries, and various commercial interests, which would help to organise and raise the finance for the hostel. The Colonial Office planned to include two students on the organising committee and to seek the involvement of the colonial governments in West Africa. In 1929 however, Solanke made it clear to the Colonial Office that WASU were 'the prime movers in the affair', that the hostel must be organised by the students on the basis of self-help, and that therefore it had been decided to despatch him to West Africa on a fund-raising trip. All further meetings with any Colonial Office representatives were to be suspended until he returned. Solanke still tried to get official backing for his West African mission, but the Colonial Office immediately alerted all the West African governors, and advised them to carefully monitor his fund-raising activities.[61]

Student organisations and politics

The latter half of the 1920s witnessed significant developments in the organisation and activities of West African students in Britain. The political revival in West Africa and the formation of the NCBWA influenced not only the founding of WASU, but also stimulated a general increase in student activity and organisation. The Colonial Office was generally contemptuous of student claims to represent public opinion in West Africa. But the students continued to campaign, demanding, amongst other things, that Africans' land rights be respected, and the repeal of unpopular and oppressive legislation.[62]

Even after the founding of WASU, the NPU continued to function, while USAD underwent something of a revival under the presidency of R.S. Blay and was perhaps the most active of all the student organisations during this period.[63] It held regular weekly meetings, often with a West African focus, on a range of subjects, and its members (who were often also WASU members) were regularly in demand as public speakers. USAD was also concerned about the issue of education in West Africa, and in 1926 together with APU, it petitioned the Colonial Secretary over the lack of government scholarships for West Africans, at a time when such scholarships were awarded to students from the West Indian colonies and British Guiana.[64] The Colonial Office did not wish to encourage any more African students to come to Britain, nor to develop educational facilities in West Africa. It was against the granting of scholarships, because in its view the level of education in West Africa was 'not high enough'. It was accepted that awards might be granted in the future, 'but not unless some arrangements could be made for the supervision of the students while in this country'.

In addition to WASU and USAD, one of the other main African student organisations which emerged in the mid-1920s was the GCSA, which was founded by R.S. Blay and aimed: 'to promote and protect the Social, Educational and Political interests' of the Gold Coast, and to 'encourage common understanding, co-operation and unity among the Gold Coast students in Europe'.[65] The GCSA shared its membership with the other student organisations, and included amongst its officers several students who were also officers or members of WASU and USAD.[66] The GCSA seems to have been more of a social organisation than anything else, and may have been initiated by Blay in part to rival the NPU. Although Nigerians also initially dominated WASU, by 1926 both the president and the vice-president of the Union were from the Gold Coast.

There were also a number of other African student societies and organisations in colleges and cities throughout Britain, such as Oxford and Cambridge and at some Scottish universities. Clearly a great amount of debate and discussion took place during this period, especially in London, where the three main African student organisations were also constantly in contact with visiting West African politicians and other leading personalities. The students also managed to develop a number of international links during this period. J.B. Danquah and WASU president E.O. Asafu-Adjaye, were both invited to attend the World YMCA Conference in Finland in 1926, where they met and conferred with, amongst others, the South African Max Yergan, at that time a member of the executive committee of the World Student Christian Federation.[67] WASU also established contacts in the United States, the Belgian Congo, South Africa and the Caribbean, and some attempts were made to strengthen these ties during this period.[68]

The students also continued their campaigns against racism. In 1929, J. A. Doherty a former president of the Union, had taken the lead in exposing the attempts of a Mr Singer, described in *Wasu* as 'an English capitalist', to organise an 'African Village' as part of an exhibition in Newcastle. In particular, Doherty and WASU were opposed to any repeat of the incidents which had occurred at the 1924 Empire exhibition, and to the exploitation of some two hundred people from North Africa who had been organised to live in the village. The *Manchester Guardian* reported that WASU 'strongly object as educated Africans to making a show of native life in such a way as to draw attention to the more backward side of African life'. WASU also felt that such an exhibition was likely 'to arouse feelings of racial prejudice leading to antagonism between the black and white races'. Because of the possibility that the Africans involved might have been recruited from French colonies, a letter of protest was also sent to Paris.[69] This case was also reported by *The Times* and involved the Indian communist MP Shapurji Saklatvala, who raised the whole matter in the House of Commons. Saklatvala questioned whether such an exhibition could be useful to British trade, pointed out that it would 'only be making an exhibition of the wretched way in which citizens are living', and called on the Secretary to the Overseas Trade Department to take steps to make sure that the exhibition did not 'bring the Negro population into contempt or ridicule'.[70]

During the 1920s Solanke and WASU were also in contact with James Maxton of the ILP, Reginald Bridgeman and the League Against Imperialism (LAI) and Norman Leys of the Labour Party, who had sat in on some of WASU's executive committee meetings, written an article on Kenya for *Wasu* and perhaps most importantly had loaned the Union money for the proposed hostel. As a result of its links with Saklatvala and Bridgeman, WASU was also in touch with the Communist Party of Great Britain (CPGB). Through these contacts and Solanke's friendship with Jomo Kenyatta a link had also been established with the Profintern's International Trade Union Committee of Negro Workers (ITUC-NW), which was presided over by the African-American communist James Ford.[71]

It seems that Ford had been in contact with Solanke since at least early 1929. In February of that year Solanke had responded to an earlier communication which had included ten copies of the ITUC-NW's *Negro Worker*. After thanking Ford, and promising to send *Wasu* in return, Solanke, concerning *Negro Worker* added:

> I have read it and found it to be most interesting indeed. It is also a great eye-opener because it is full of valuable information which hitherto our union has not been aware of. I therefore thank you in the name of our WASU of Great Britain and Ireland. I shall distribute the copies forwarded to me among the members. There is nothing like co-operation between all organisations of the world, especially among Negro organisations with a view to defending their rights and liberty.[72]

However at the Second World Congress of the LAI in 1929, Ford specifically mentioned the Union and Solanke's *United West Africa at the Bar of the Family of Nations*. In his speech 'The Negro's Struggle Against Imperialism', Ford said of WASU:

> Our good friends here also have some hazy ideas about the liberation of Africa. The Secretary of the Union in one pamphlet advocates that 'our good friends' (capitalists) of Germany, England, America and France can help the Africans by lending their money for the uplifting of West Africa. Does he think that this is a struggle against imperialism; has he not enough of British imperialism in West Africa; is he so naive as to think that capitalists from these countries have any other design but the subjugation of the African people, or does he think that these shrew capitalists are simple fools?[73]

WASU and Marcus Garvey

One of the most significant of WASU's contacts in the 1920s was

Marcus Garvey, the founder of the Universal Negro Improvement Association (UNIA), who was one of the most influential Pan-Africanists at this time. Solanke met Garvey in 1928, when the latter visited Britain to strengthen the London branch of the UNIA, which had been established four years earlier. It is not clear how they met, or whether Solanke's friendship with Garvey's estranged wife played any part in their meeting. When Garvey returned to Jamaica at the end of 1928, he placed the UNIA headquarters in West London at WASU's disposal, and the two men continued to correspond for several months.[74]

From their letters it is clear that Solanke received some finance from Garvey, and attempted to secure more by persuading him that the students were a greater 'weapon' than the newly re-formed London UNIA. Solanke told Garvey that he was already carrying out propaganda work for his cause amongst other Africans, and suggested that he might be sent to Africa on Garvey's behalf 'in a secret mission to organise in every country'. Garvey's financial support for WASU was used to impress the students, and it seems that at one time, Solanke planned, or claimed that he planned, to establish the Union as the nucleus of the UNIA in Britain. In his letters to Garvey he was always extremely critical of the UNIA members in London, such as the Sierra Leonean born merchant Robert Broadhurst, a leading member of APU. Solanke also claimed that he had contacted 'various eminent persons', including 'several members of the Independent Labour Party' in order 'to exploit these men to further our own Race interest'. But it appears that he might also have been trying to exploit his relationship with Garvey too, partly for financial reasons, but also in order to use Garvey's name to strengthen the work of WASU. It was for this reason that Solanke asked to be sent an initialled walking stick, to identify him as Garvey's representative when he went to West Africa on WASU's behalf. There were at this time some supporters of Garveyism in West Africa, even amongst the representatives of the NCBWA. Garveyism was clearly seen as a threat to Empire, and by 1923, with Colonial Office approval, Garvey's *Negro World* had been banned by the colonial government in Nigeria.[75] However, Garvey's message of racial pride and self-reliance did corresponded with the aspirations of the students. Solanke himself speaks of 'the indirect effects of Garveyism' on the students, a result of Garvey's 'labour in the interest of the race'.[76] Nothing more is known of the relationship between Solanke and Garvey, but they certainly remained in contact, and in 1936

West African Student Organisations 1923–30

Solanke contributed an article on 'Life and Conditions in West Africa' to Garvey's *The Blackman*.[77]

By the late 1920s then, West African students, whose numbers had increased significantly during that decade, were making their voices heard on a range of important issues, and had established a number of significant political contacts.[78] They had established their own active organisations, which agitated not only on behalf of the students' interests in Britain, but also on behalf of the developing national aspirations of the West African colonies. The next decade would lead to even greater student participation in political affairs, and greater links with diverse political interests both in Britain and internationally.[79]

Notes

1. *Glasgow University Students' Handbook* (1930/31) p149.
2. *West Africa*, 25 February 1922, p133.
3. *West Africa*, 25 October 1924, p1179.
4. *Ibid.*
5. *Ibid.*
6. Ladipo Solanke (1886-1958) came to Britain after studying at Fourah Bay College in Sierra Leone. He was a law student at UCL from 1923-1927.
7. 'An Outrage', *West Africa*, 22 March 1924, p247.
8. *Ibid.* To put such matters into perspective Solanke referred to an 1884 report of cannibalism amongst shipwrecked British sailors, and an alleged incident around the same time concerning a woman from Essex who had been sold by her husband.
9. 'Africans and Britons', *West Africa*, 10 May 1924, p445.
10. *Sunday Express*, 4 May 1924.
11. USAD to the Colonial Secretary, 14 May 1924, Public Records Office (PRO) CO 554/64/23120. Also 'Manners Makyth Empire', *West Africa*, 10 May 1924 and 'When West Africa Protests', *West Africa*, 17 May 1924, p484.
12. See e.g. 'The West African Students' Protest', *West Africa*, 24 May 1924, p505. *West Africa* was owned by Elder Dempster, the main British monopoly concern in West Africa.
13. J.E. Kwegyir Aggrey (1875-1927) was a leading Gold Coast scholar who had been educated in the United States. He was the only African on the two Phelps-Stokes Education Commissions to Africa, and was appointed assistant vice-principal of Achimota College in the Gold Coast. He was

widely seen as a role model by many West Africans and by the colonial authorities.
14. M. Crowder, *West Africa Under Colonial Rule*, Hutchinson, London 1972, pp419-28.
15. H. Adi, 'The Nigerian Progress Union', *ASACACHIB Newsletter*, April 1994, p8.
16. *Ibid.*
17. *Ibid.* p5. The motto of the NPU was *Sol Omnibus Lucet* – 'The sun shines for all'. The aims of the NPU included securing a hostel in London; fostering 'the habit of self-control, self-sacrifice, self-knowledge and self-help'; promoting African literature, customs and institutions, the education of 'the masses' in Nigeria; establishing 'national schools' throughout Nigeria; and sending Nigerian students abroad to train in 'necessary professions for the progress of Nigeria'.
18. *Ibid.* p10.
19. *Ibid.* p13.
20. L. Solanke, 'Open Letter to the Negroes of the World', *The Spokesman*, June 1925, p15.
21. See Appendix, and regarding Vischer, PRO CO 554/161/8864, Colonial Office memo, 26 November 1923.
22. L. Solanke, 'The Why of the NPU', *The Spokesman*, April-May 1925, p26.
23. H Adi, *op.cit.*, p7.
24. L. Solanke, 'West African Land and Self-Development', *West Africa*, 4 April 1925, p311.
25. The NPU claimed that it had thirty members but branches throughout Britain as well as in Nigeria.
26. Quoted in P. Garigue, 'The West African Students' Union: A Study in Culture Contact', *Africa*, 23/1, January 1953, p56.
27. P. Giles to Colonial Office, 8 August 1923, PRO CO 554/161/8864.
28. Reverend E.W. Thompson to Colonial Office, 2 October 1925, PRO CO 554/67/47017.
29. G. Olusanya, *The West African Students' Union and the Politics of Decolonisation, 1925-1958*, Daystar, Ibadan 1982, pp6-7.
30. L. Solanke, 'Diary for 1920', pp59-60, Solanke Papers (SOL) 35.
31. Garigue, *op.cit.*, p56.
32. *Ibid.*
33. Olusanya, *op.cit.*, p19.
34. *Ibid* p7 and *West Africa*, 15 August 1925, p1007. Many of the twenty one founder members were law students. Dr J.B. Danquah (1895-1965) subsequently became one of the Gold Coast's leading nationalists, founder of

the Gold Coast Youth Congress and United Gold Coast Convention (UGCC) and a member of the Legislative Council. He later became an opponent of Nkrumah and died in prison.
35. *West Africa*, 15 August 1925, p1002.
36. See e.g. the letter from O. During in *West Africa*, 24 October 1925, p1377.
37. *Wasu*, 1/1, March 1926. On the various other meanings of the word 'wasu' see G. Olusanya, *op.cit.*, pp16-17. The first volume of the journal included nine editions, the last one appearing in December 1932, although originally the intention had been to produce a quarterly journal.
38. *Wasu*, 1/1, March 1926.
39. See J. A. Langley, *op.cit.*, p110.
40. See e.g. L. Solanke, 'Unity and Co-operation among West African Ancients as disclosed by history and tradition', *Wasu*, 1/5, September 1927, p18; 'A Glimpse of Yoruba Civilisation', *Wasu*, 1/3, March 1927 p16 and 'The Introduction of Civilisation in West Africa', *Wasu*, 1/2, December 1926, p7.
41. 'Editorial', *Wasu*, 1/8, January 1929, p6.
42. *Wasu*, 1/2, December 1926, p23.
43. *West Africa*, 27 September 1926, p49.
44. 'Towards West African Nationhood', *Wasu*, 1/6-7, August 1928, p1.
45. 'The President's Letter', *Wasu*, 1/1, March 1926, p2.
46. In part de Graft Johnson's book was a response to some of the unenlightened views on racial discrimination that were in evidence at the Annual Conference of the British Federation of Youth in 1927, and which also appeared in the BFY journal *The Youth*.
47. J.W. de Graft Johnson, *Towards Nationhood in West Africa – Thoughts of Young Africa Addressed to Young Britain*, Frank Cass, London 1971, pvi.
48. L. Solanke, *United West Africa (or Africa) at the Bar of the Family of Nations*, African Publication Society, London 1969.
49. *Ibid.*, pp50-53.
50. *Ibid.*, p64.
51. *Ibid.*, p66.
52. *West Africa*, 7 July 1928, p789. Ofori Atta was also the brother of WASU president J.B. Danquah.
53. *West Africa*, 14 July 1928, p920.
54. 'Presidential Letter', *Wasu*, 1/7, p2 and 'An Appeal', *Ibid.*, p32.
55. P. Rich, *Race and Empire in British Politics*, Cambridge University Press, Cambridge 1990, pp127-28. On the effects of this Order see T. Lane, 'The Political Imperatives of Bureaucracy and Empire: The Case of the Coloured Alien Seamen Order, 1925', *Immigrants and Minorities*,

July/November 1994, 13/2&3.
56. *Wasu*, 1/2, December 1926, p42.
57. *Wasu*, 1/3-4, March-June 1927, p21.
58. *West Africa*, 20 October 1928, p1425. Sir Adetokunbo Ademola was at that time a twenty-one year old law student at Cambridge University. He later became Chief Justice of Nigeria and a Privy Councillor, and was knighted in 1957.
59. *Ibid.*, 15 June 1929, p785. This expression was also widely used by the press and the BBC. Also *Ibid.*, 31 August 1929, p1165 and 26 October 1929, p1446.
60. H. Vischer memo, 9 January 1929, PRO CO 323/1025/60050.
61. See Solanke to Vischer, 28 September 1929, *Ibid*.
62. A.J. Harding memo, 5 April 1926, in PRO CO 554/71/3 PRO CO 55417113, also *West Africa*, 20 March 1926, p327.
63. R.S. Blay, a law student, became an important supporter of WASU when he returned to the Gold Coast. He was later a founder member of the UGCC.
64. PRO CO 55417113, also *West Africa*, 20 March 1926, p327.
65. GCSA Minute Book, 1934-40, SOL.
66. J.B. Danquah was at one time president of WASU and vice-president of USAD; he was also a member of the GCSA.
67. Sir E.O. Asafu-Adjaye (1903-76) was a law student at London University. He subsequently became Minister of Local Government and Minister of Trade and Industry in Nkrumah's first cabinet and was Ghana's first High Commissioner to Britain. He was knighted in 1960.
68. *Wasu* was also read by African students in France and the Union's activities reported in the Comité de Défense de la Race Nègre's, *La Race Negre*, Langley, *op.cit.*, p304.
69. *Wasu*, 2/1, January 1933, p18.
70. *Ibid*.
71. The ITUC-NW was founded at a conference in Hamburg in 1929. It included representatives of workers in Africa, the Caribbean and the US.
72. Solanke to Ford, 22 February 1929, SOL 78. In 1933 Solanke was warned to discontinue his association with *Negro Worker* after a copy he had sent to the editor of the *Nigerian Daily Telegraph* was discovered in a raid by the Nigerian police.
73. J. Ford, *The Negro's Struggle Against Imperialism – A Report to the 2nd World Congress of the LAI* (Provisional International Trade Union Committee of Negro Workers, 1930) p22.
74. See the report of the Assistant Commissioner, Special Branch, 19 June

1929, PRO CO 533/384/9/15540. According to this report both Solanke and Kenyatta were living in Garvey's house and both were members of the UNIA.
75. See J.A. Langley, 'Garveyism and African Nationalism', *Race*, XI/2,1969, pp157-71.
76. Solanke to M. Garvey, 25 November 1928, 20 December 1928 and 6 January 1929, SOL 42.
77. R. Lewis, 'The Last London Years, 1935-1940', in J.H. Clarke (Ed) *Marcus Garvey and the Vision of Africa*, Vintage Books, New York 1974, pp334-35.
78. Official estimates of student numbers are unreliable, but in 1927 the Colonial Office calculated that there were forty-five West African undergraduates in Britain and one hundred and twenty-five African university students in total.
79. At the present time little can be said about women students from West Africa. Initially the WASU appears to have had no women members, although a number of women were at that time students in Britain. They tended to be training as midwives or nurses or to be studying subjects such as domestic sciences at institutions such as Portway College in Reading. But they seem to be noticeably absent from the activities of the main student organisations, although a number of women, including the Sierra Leonean Emma Smith, were active in the APU, and three Nigerian women, Doris Williams and the daughters of Dr Adeniyi-Jones, were connected with the NPU.

The Search for a Black United Front 1930–39

In 1929, following Solanke's departure on his fund-raising mission to West Africa, the Colonial Office decided to press ahead with its plans to establish a student hostel, and a small *ad hoc* committee headed by Hanns Vischer was set up to make all the necessary preparations. However, the Colonial Office was reluctant to openly proclaim its intention of competing with WASU's plans in order to have some control over the students through the organisation of its own hostel. This meant that the committee had to appear to be independent. The Colonial Office even decided to exclude church and missionary societies from the committee, as they feared that bodies such as the Student Christian Movement, which was already formulating its own independent plans for a hostel, might attempt some 'spiritual uplifting' which would antagonise the students, or expose the hand of the Colonial Office.[1]

There was also the tricky problem of raising sufficient finance for the scheme. Cadbury Brothers, Rowntree, and other monopolies with a financial interest in West Africa including the major banks, were approached for funds, as was the CWAE. It was hoped that the West African governments would also contribute. However, as the effects of the Depression intensified, the Colonial Office found its task increasingly difficult, not least because of the need to maintain a veil of secrecy over the whole scheme. Some news of the Colonial Office's plans eventually did leak out, but the students, who were alarmed by reports that attempts were afoot to exert some control over their activities, were assured that nothing concerning the proposed hostel would be settled until Solanke returned.[2]

The colour bar

The need for some provision for the students was daily made more obvious by the widespread operation of the colour bar. In Glasgow for example, despite the opposition of the Glasgow Students' Representative Council, 'non-European' students were denied reduced fees at the city's dance hall. At Edinburgh University one racist student was reported to have claimed 'We have been watching for a suitable moment to launch our attack on the coloured students for some time'.[3] While in London, the problem of racism remained one of the most pressing problems confronting the students. In *West Africa*, a Sierra Leonean student claimed that students were forced to live with English women because of the difficulty of finding accommodation, as well as for financial reasons, and that this situation then led to unwanted pregnancies and neglected children.[4]

The president of WASU, Dr Okunade Ajibade urged that letters on the issue of the colour bar should be written to the West African press. He explained that: 'In such articles reference may be made to the difficulty of getting a house for rent, whereas in Africa, our people ignorant of these things part far too quickly with their land.' He complained that 'In one breath we are being asked to buy Empire goods but we cannot find rooms in Hotels to lay our heads.'[5] Ajibade continued his protests against the colour bar, even leading a deputation to see MPs in the House of Commons. He gained the support of the newly formed West Indian Students' Association and Indian and Ceylonese students and was in contact with the Jamaican Dr. Harold Moody, the future founder of the League of Coloured Peoples (LCP), which was formed in 1931 to promote the welfare and interests of the 'coloured races'. Ajibade called for Solanke to try and get the public and political leaders in the West African colonies to agitate and pass resolutions against the colour bar, and send them to the colonial governors and the British government.[6]

Another organisation formed to encourage 'racial co-operation' at this time was the West African National Association (WANA). Founded by A.K. Kpapkpa-Quartey, who was originally from Accra in the Gold Coast. The WANA had the aim of establishing a residential club for Africans in London. Even though nothing came of its plans, the membership of this innocuous organisation were carefully monitored by the Colonial Office and even by the Special Branch.[7] Yet another organisation formed at this time was the League of Africans, which included several Ethiopian members. Its first president was Alex Ansah Koi, a medical student from the Gold Coast and its treasurer Jomo Kenyatta.[8] The League's Pan-African aim was to 'promote mutual understanding and to maintain sincere friendly relationships among the Native races of South, East, and West Africa, Egyptians and other Native races of North Africa.'[9]

The colour bar and other forms of discrimination led to greater student demands for a hostel, but many were still wary of the idea of co-operation with official bodies, and some cautionary tales appeared in the West African press warning that there were 'attempts to enslave African manhood in London'. Colonial Office officials were fully aware of the effect of racism on West African students and other black people in Britain, but the Home Secretary claimed that he was powerless to take any action. The issue of accommodation and the attitude of hoteliers, especially in London, were major concerns, particularly as the Residential Hotels and Caterers Association declared their continued support for the colour bar.[10]

The problems connected with the colour bar were highlighted by the success of O.A. Alakija, an executive committee member of the LCP, and president of WASU, in a court case against a London hotel keeper who had refused him accommodation. Oluwole Ayodele Alakija was a graduate of Jesus College, Oxford, studying for the bar at the Middle Temple. In early 1932 he successfully sued New Mansion Hotels, Lancaster Gate, London, for the sum of £55 for breach of contract. The hotel had refused to allow him to occupy his room because he was an African. O.A. Alakija was the son of the Chairman of the Nigerian Printing and Publishing Company, and a nephew of the Alake of Abeokuta, one of Nigeria's most important traditional rulers. He was described to the court as obviously 'a gentleman who was entitled to expect accommodation at any London Hotel which had accommodation to offer.' The court awarded Alakija the costs of the case and £12 in damages.[11]

Not surprisingly the verdict was well received by the African students, their well-wishers, and organisations such as the LCP. However, the nature of the case caused some anxiety amongst those who were doing everything they could to minimise such incidents, which could 'poison the mind of the West African against the British'.[12] The Alakija case and other incidents not only highlighted the question of discrimination and the colour bar in Britain, it also focused some attention on the situation in the West African colonies; the lack of educational facilities, the discrimination faced by African professionals, and indeed the nature of colonial rule itself. The effects of the Depression were clearly showing, as one WASU member expressed it, that colonial 'trusteeship' was 'a business concern which pays a greater dividend to the trustees than to the wards'.[13]

Racism was also an issue of international concern at the time, and many of the African and West Indian students took part in the protest movement over the Scottsboro case in the United States, (where eight African-American youths were falsely accused of raping two white women, and initially sentenced to death). In the London School of Economics alone over 800 students and teachers signed a petition condemning the judgement of the American courts. WASU members had shown a keen interest and one of the most active, Cobina Kessie, was a vice-president of the Scottsboro Defence Committee initiated by the Negro Welfare Association (NWA).[14] The struggle against racism was therefore also bringing the students into closer contact with some of the most radical political organisations in Britain, such as the communist-led NWA and the LAI, the very forces which the Colonial Office wished to steer them away from.[15]

Privately the Colonial Office was forced to admit that racial prejudice was far worse in Britain and in British universities, than elsewhere in Europe, although some officials attempted to exonerate the university vice-chancellors from any blame, by arguing that colonial students were not welcomed to the universities because they 'tend very often to be a centre of communist or seditious political propaganda.' The Colonial Office did however decide to investigate the whole question of the colour bar, as it was recognised that future leaders were being alienated from the Empire by their experiences in Britain. The Colonial Secretary stated that he was sympathetic to the problems which Africans and others were facing, but that 'the difficulty seemed to him to lie in the unfortunate colour prejudice of certain classes of the population, especially in London.' Naturally the Colonial Office was unable to explain the origin of such prejudice, and did not conclude that it was in any way connected with colonial rule, or openly racist laws in Britain such as the Coloured Alien Seaman Order.[16]

Solanke and WASU in West Africa

During the three years which Solanke spent in West Africa, WASU in Britain suffered from a lack of leadership, internal disputes between students from the Gold Coast and those from Nigeria and the non-appearance of *Wasu*. However, in West Africa over 20 branches of the Union had been established throughout the Gold Coast, Nigeria and

Sierra Leone, as well as one in the Belgian Congo. Solanke's presence in West Africa also stimulated a lively debate in the local press over the question of the students' hostel, racism in Britain and other topical issues. There was some opposition to the hostel idea from ex-students, but Solanke had persuasively explained that the proposed hostel would be for the use of African visitors to Britain as well as students, and would 'also serve as a bureau of information on matters concerning Africa (and Africans) and as a centre where African students can easily come into contact with respectable persons of the British Isles.'[17]

Solanke was backed by *West Africa*, which gave full support to his mission and his appeal for funds. The Governor of the Gold Coast, in a speech to the Liverpool Chamber of Commerce, applauded Solanke's efforts and appealed to the Chamber of Commerce not to ignore the African students and to offer them assistance.[18] The West African press also gave full coverage of Solanke's progress from area to area and colony to colony, including the amount of money he was able to collect. WASU's mission was therefore significant not only for the money which was raised, but also because Solanke was able to strengthen the links between the students in Britain and their compatriots in West Africa, both the intelligentsia and 'traditional rulers'. It was generally from these two sections of society that WASU branches in West Africa were formed, often around a nucleus of former Union members who had returned from Britain.[19]

The formation of the West African branches not only enhanced the credibility and strengthened the effectiveness of WASU as a pressure group in Britain, it also helped to develop the conditions for the emergence of the future nationalist organisations in West Africa. As Olusanya has pointed out, 'the various Youth Movements which sprang up in the 1930s – the Nigerian Youth Movement and the Gold Coast Youth Conference – drew their membership mainly from the local branches of the WASU.' WASU continued to assist the development of the anti-colonial movement in West Africa throughout the 1930s, and was one way in which an important network of anti-colonial organisations in the West African colonies and in Britain was established. Solanke's mission also led to the propagation of WASU's aims and ideals amongst the youth of West Africa, who would have been present at the various fund-raising events, which took place in the principal secondary schools of the region, such as King's College, Lagos.[20]

The Colonial Office and Aggrey House

In March 1932 Moody and the LCP announced that they hoped to open their own hostel within six months. At this time nearly all the members of the LCP's executive committee were West Africans and WASU members, including Alex Ansah Koi, the LCP vice-president. In some ways the LCP could claim, just as WASU did, that it too represented West African student opinion.[21] How the West African members of the LCP managed to cope with their increasingly divided loyalties is not clear, although some defections from WASU's ranks resulted from the split between Nigerian and Gold Coast members, which also polarised the Union's relations with the GCSA. The Colonial Office's hostel committee, and Hanns Vischer in particular, recognised that Moody would be a great asset for their scheme. They therefore managed to get the LCP to drop any plans they may have had for a hostel, and co-opted Moody onto their committee. As Moody and the LCP were now involved in the Colonial Office's plans, it was decided that the hostel would now be established for 'all coloured people', and not just for Africans.

Solanke's return to Britain in 1932, and the fact that he had collected over £1300 towards WASU's hostel, interrupted the plans of the Colonial Office and Vischer's committee. The latter decided to go ahead and organise their 'club', which they hoped would be a meeting place between 'black and white', and 'a door to the English home and English life'. The committee had purchased a ten year lease on premises in Doughty Street, next to the Dickens' Museum, which was to be known as Aggrey House, after the Gold Coast scholar Dr J.E. Kwegyir Aggrey. Vischer knew that WASU wanted a hostel of its own, but since the co-opting of Moody, he had seen an opportunity to bypass Solanke and WASU, despite previous agreements to work with them. Moody on the other hand, who clearly recognised his own importance to Vischer's plans, was angling to become the dominant force in Aggrey House.

Even before Vischer and Moody could open Aggrey House, WASU announced that it had found premises in Camden, and immediately launched an appeal for furniture in both Britain and West Africa. In the spring of 1933 *Wasu* reported that Solanke and 'an African lady', Olu Obisanya, the future Mrs Solanke, had been busily preparing the hostel, and had received visits and congratulations from Vischer and Moody. The hostel officially opened on 9 March 1933, and received its first resident, Prince A.A. Ademola. *Wasu* was soon to include the written congratulations of two of the hostel's other early residents, who commented on the excellent African atmosphere and cuisine.[22]

The opening of the African students' hostel by WASU clearly provoked the intense disapproval of Vischer and the Colonial Office. It was also feared that Aggrey House would be unable to attract African students and sufficient finance. Vischer was especially concerned that WASU seemed to have secured the support of *West Africa*, the West African press, and Cadbury Brothers, since in his view WASU's aim was 'definitely to work for complete political and financial independence of British West Africa'.[23] In response the Colonial Office decided to co-opt Albert Cartwright, the editor of *West Africa* on to the Aggrey House committee. During 1933, for whatever reason, there was hardly any mention of WASU, its hostel, or West African students, in the pages of *West Africa*.

The truth about Aggrey House – WASU and communist influence

WASU was still facing some complex internal problems. By the beginning of 1933 the disputes centred around Solanke, who was criticised for his extravagant spending while in West Africa, and the high-handed way in which he was attempting to run the newly opened hostel. By October of that year, after many heated and stormy meetings, it was proposed that Solanke should be suspended as general-secretary. This proposal was eventually agreed and a commission was elected to undertake all his former work.[24] Within a few weeks Solanke had been reinstated, but the dispute smouldered on with many of the Gold Coast students involved. As a result a number of students resigned and withdrew into the GCSA and the LCP. This dispute Solanke saw as an attempt to destroy WASU, and he blamed Moody, the LCP, and 'British Imperialists' such as Vischer. Most of the branches in West Africa seem to have stayed loyal to Solanke, although the branch in the Belgian Congo did not, while in Britain he retained the support of Ansah Koi, Cobina Kessie and most of the Nigerian students. This dispute came precisely at the time when the West African students needed to be most united, as they started their campaign against Aggrey House.

It was the attitude of WASU to Aggrey House which now caused the Colonial Office most concern. In March 1934, WASU published a small pamphlet: *The Truth about Aggrey House – An Exposure of the Government Plan for Control of African Students in Great Britain.* It was claimed that the Colonial Office had decided to establish a hostel because 'of the difficulties experienced at the hands of Indian and Egyptian students of the past decade over whose thoughts and actions in this country the Government had little control and who on returning home battled against the oppression of the Imperial Government.'[25] WASU also argued that it had been prepared to work with the Colonial Office. However, according to the Union, the Colonial Office had become concerned about the 'rousing of National consciousness among the younger elements in West Africa', and 'concluded that WASU could not be used in its scheme to bring African students in London under its control.' The students' publication suggested that the Government would:

> take due precautions that it keeps under control and watches closely the actions of every West African student in England; will see that no West African possesses any opinion contrary to the prolonged existence of capitalist oppression in the Colonies and will utilise the taxes extorted from West Africans to keep their youth in perpetual subjection.[26]

WASU therefore issued an appeal:

> We appeal to every lover of freedom to help us check this scheme of Imperialism which would strangle the very thought of its subjects and control their every action and opinion.
>
> We appeal to all Africans, students or otherwise, to wash their hands of this scheme, in whatever innocent guise it might be represented – a scheme which would destroy their individuality and nullify their souls. We beg them to work unceasingly for the independence of their thought and actions which is a necessary preliminary to the greater independence.[27]

WASU made sure that it enlisted support in the campaign against Aggrey House and the Colonial Office. In March 1934 the Union held a protest meeting, inviting representatives of the Society of Friends, the Federation of Student Societies, the National Council for Civil Liberties (NCCL), the Society for International Students, the New India Political Group, and the communist-led NWA and LAI.[28] John

Fletcher of the Society of Friends, who was a member of the Aggrey House Committee, spoke at the meeting, but was unable to convince the audience that the Colonial Office did not mean to use Aggrey House in some way contrary to the interests of the students. They argued that unless the 'entire control and management of Aggrey House was to be in the hands of the students', the scheme would remain 'a device for promoting British imperialism' and for the control of their 'freedom and liberty'. They reasoned that Aggrey House 'could never be used for any revolutionary propaganda, nor even for any ordinary criticisms of the Government if such criticisms should become regular, systematic and effective.' Many saw Aggrey House as a repeat of attempts made by the Government since 1913 to control the political activities of Indian students, and pointed out that some invited speakers had been banned by the authorities from the Indian students' hostels. Those present decided to organise a boycott of Aggrey House, and to develop the campaign 'to assure that the present African hostel should be continued under the complete control of African students and others of African descent resident in London.' This body became known as the Africa House Defence Committee (AHDC).[29]

Ladipo Odunsi, the secretary of AHDC and the other WASU members established a close working relationship with the LAI, NWA and NCCL during this time. The AHDC also received support from Norman Leys, one of the Labour Party's 'colonial specialists' and Kingsley Martin, editor of *New Statesman and Nation*, Professor John McMurray of UCL, the Countess of Warwick and the Earl of Listowel, who all agreed to act as vice-presidents of the Committee. The NCCL continued to help WASU with legal advice on a range of issues throughout the 1930s, and used WASU as a source of information concerning events in West Africa, which it wished to publicise in Britain. The NCCL, NWA and the LAI gained increasing influence amongst the students and in West Africa itself during the 1930s. Through sympathetic MPs they were able to raise a number of questions on West African issues in Parliament. It also seems that they were in part responsible for the more radical phraseology employed by the students during this period.[30]

The LAI called for 'Complete freedom for African peoples and peoples of African descent' and 'Possession by Africans of African lands and administration.' From 1934 it was administered from Britain by Reginald Bridgeman, a former colonial official who was a close supporter of the Communist Party of Great Britain (CPGB), and until

1937 it was through this organisation that the CPGB carried out much of its anti-colonial activities.[31] Bridgeman had been in contact with WASU since the late 1920s, but became a regular visitor at WASU functions during the 1930s and represented the LAI on the AHDC. The LAI viewed Aggrey House as a centre of 'imperialist propaganda' where the Colonial Office could monitor the activities of West African students.[32] The LAI aimed to establish contact with students from colonial countries and interest them in the League's work 'even if they do not openly identify with it.' It wished to 'break down the belief so carefully encouraged in the colonial countries that all Englishmen without exception are united in support of British imperialism.' Colonial students were encouraged to challenge any speeches made in defence of colonial policy in Britain, and with the guidance of the LAI to 'make anti-imperialist contributions to the press of their own countries.'[33]

It is not difficult to see the appeal that the LAI had for many West African students. Apart from the financial assistance which it might have offered, political support was just as important. The LAI and its affiliates supported WASU's fight against Aggrey House and the colour bar, and most importantly called for the complete independence of the West African colonies. At its annual conference in 1933 the LAI passed a 'Resolution on the Struggles of the Negro Workers'. The concluding part of this resolution gave a comprehensive view of its international political platform.

> This Conference emphatically protests against the arrest, charge and sentence of the nine Negro Boys in Scottsboro and demands their unconditional release. It also condemns the continued oppression of the Negro peoples, and pledges itself to give the fullest support to the struggles of the Negroes workers in Africa and the West Indies for complete freedom and self-determination. It calls upon the British workers to demand the withdrawal of all British troops from the colonies and to work with the workers and peasants of the West Indies and British Guiana in their present struggle for complete independence. The Conference further pledges itself to fight for the abolition of colour restrictions in Britain and the colonies, and to demand the right of coloured workers to become members of trade unions on a basis of equality with the white workers; to struggle against the reserve and compound system and the expropriation of lands of the natives, and for the return of all lands to the peasants; to fight against the alien registra-

tion scheme which deprives coloured British born seamen of the right of British nationality.[34]

WASU had been in contact with the NWA since at least 1933, and probably from its founding in 1931. The NWA was an affiliate of the LAI chaired by Bridgeman. The treasurer was H.P. Rathbone and the secretary the Barbadian communist Arnold Ward, who was also a member of the editorial board of *Negro Worker*. The NWA was based in London and included amongst its aims 'To work for the complete liberation and independence of all Negroes who are suffering from capitalist exploitation and imperialist domination and to co-operate with all peoples who are struggling against all forms of colonial oppression.' The NWA involved itself in a range of issues: it campaigned in support of trades unions in the Caribbean, against the colour bar in Britain and in 1933 was instrumental in forming the Scottsboro Defence Committee.

WASU's campaign and supporters therefore caused some consternation in the Colonial Office. WASU's anger was now directed against the Colonial Office itself, rather than Moody or anyone else, and worst of all, from the Colonial Office's point of view, it appeared that the whole affair had driven the students into the arms of the communists, and thus defeated the attempts to closet them away from such subversive influences.

West African politics in Britain

Throughout 1934 the Aggrey House campaign continued to gain momentum. WASU had taken the step of linking their struggle in Britain with those in West Africa, by passing a resolution which condemned both the attempts to control African students in Britain, and the proposed introduction of new sedition laws in the colonies. The Union saw both as attacks on their struggle for self-determination, and as the concern of 'every friend of liberty'.[35] The students made similar statements in the *New Statesman and Nation*, while the Colonial Office found that Solanke had written to the Archbishop of Canterbury on several occasions, asking for money and 'His Grace's Blessing', and enclosing a copy of *The Truth About Aggrey House*.

In May 1934 the GCSA also passed a resolution demanding that the legislation recently introduced in the Gold Coast should not be ratified by the British government. The growing radicalisation of West African students in Britain was therefore due not only to their experiences and contacts in Britain, but also as a result of their involvement with events in Africa itself. Solanke, for example, wrote:

> In our own case, I may say at once that we are just starting the A.B.C. in the lessons of British Imperialism in West Africa. The Criminal Code of Nigeria, the system of Indirect Rule (from British Imperialist point of view), the Sedition Bill on the Gold Coast, the Criminal Code in Gambia, and last but not least the Aggrey House versus African hostel issue in London, are all mere elementary lessons in British Imperialism in West Africa.[36]

The Aggrey House dispute allowed WASU to step up its calls for support from West Africa. The WASU hostel was seen as 'a symbol of West African Nationalism...a miniature West African Federal State under the management of a miniature West African Federal authority popularly known as WASU', as well as a centre for all those of African descent and of Pan-African unity.[37] Financial donations for the hostel were made by branches and individuals in West Africa, despite the Depression, and by supporters in Britain such as Paul Robeson. Starting in 1933 the Union also instituted its own WASU Day celebration in October each year. This celebration based around the aim of 'West African Nationhood' grew in significance and was used to raise both political awareness and finances in Britain and in West Africa. The political aims of the Union remained those of reform leading to a greater measure of self-government, but essentially along the lines mapped out by the British government. The students saw themselves as being able to speed up the reform process, so that a self-governing West Africa might be able to take its place within the British Commonwealth.

During 1934 two delegations, the Gold Coast and Ashanti Delegation, headed by Nana Ofori Atta with J.B. Danquah as secretary, and the Aborigines' Rights Protection Society Delegation, consisting of S.R Wood and Tufuhin Moore arrived in Britain from the Gold Coast. Both had been sent to protest over proposed legislation, especially the introduction of the Sedition Bill. The West African students did all they could to assist the two delegations, and in particular the members of the ARPS delegation, who remained in Britain for some time. The treatment of this delegation by the British government (they waited nearly two years before their petition was heard) and the introduction of the 'iniquitous bills' themselves, served to strengthen the anti-colonial sentiments of West African students in Britain. Agitation over the Sedition Bill also strengthened the links between West African organisations in Britain and in Africa, and these organisations and radical and left-wing organisations in Britain such as the NCCL and the LAI, and led to a general exchange of political ideas.[38] Indirectly the whole episode helped to make the students more aware of the importance of British public opinion and the need to establish firmer links with MPs. The campaign over the introduction of the Sedition Bills in West Africa was turned into a major political campaign by the LAI and NCCL, and during the 1935 General Election the ARPS delegation even campaigned in the constituency of the Secretary of State for the Colonies, Malcolm Macdonald, and may have played some part in his electoral defeat.[39]

WASU and Aggrey House

Colonial Office reports show that WASU's propaganda against Aggrey House was extremely effective, and that officials were not sure how to reply. The AHDC continued with its campaign and resolved that the students would take all steps to resist Colonial Office control including 'a complete boycott of Aggrey House by all students of African descent in London'.[40] The boycott put further pressure on the Colonial Office but its effectiveness was hindered by the continuing rift between the leaders of the LCP and WASU and the refusal of the LCP and GCSA to support the boycott, as well as by WASU's internal problems. Eventually the Colonial Office offered the students official recognition and some government support for their hostel in order to bring the boycott to an end. However Vischer was forced to admit that 'Many Africans and West Indians at present frequent the society of Communists and go to doubtful places of entertainment', the twin evils which the Aggrey House scheme had been designed to prevent.[41]

When Aggrey House was eventually formally opened in October 1934, it was in the worst possible circumstances, £3000 over its original budget, and in full rivalry with the WASU hostel. By the beginning of 1935, it was fully operational, with a resident secretary, Ivor Cummings, and housekeeper, both from Sierra Leone. Almost half of its fifty members were from West Africa, the rest mainly of Caribbean origin, but including a few from East and South Africa. Nevertheless, according to Vischer, Aggrey House had a remarkable effect on some Africans. 'I have often seen Kenyatta Johnstone there', he wrote, 'meek and mild and very happy, and I am sure that the influence of Aggrey House on him and other wild lads from Africa of similar disposition cannot be overestimated.'[42] Indeed Aggrey House soon became an important centre for meetings and other social gatherings, and little by little the boycott was eroded. Even the *Daily Express* and its columnist 'William Hickey' wrote approvingly of Aggrey House and its work for the furtherance of 'racial harmony'.[43]

WASU's dire financial situation forced it to turn to any quarter for support, and *Wasu* appealed to its readers for badly needed finances. WASU continued to suffer from major internal problems, partly brought about by Solanke's reluctance to publish a full financial account of his fund-raising mission to West Africa, and also due to disputes over the running of the hostel. These disputes had led to all but one of the Gold Coast students leaving the Union, despite a meeting of reconciliation called by Nana Sir Ofori Atta, during his visit to Britain in 1934.[44] The splits and ill-feeling were then made worse when Aggrey House opened. A committee was established to look into all the problems and criticisms concerning the management of the hostel and the running of the Union, including the non-appearance of *Wasu* for over a year, due to lack of funds. No immediate solutions were found and the ill-feeling between many Gold Coast students and the GCSA, on the one hand, and WASU, on the other, continued. However WASU called on all its members to unite and pointed out:

> At present only a few have the foresight to see the possibilities latent in WASU and the Hostel. It is not enough for us to fight in the colonies for freedom. It is of the utmost importance that in the heart of the Empire we own and man a Hostel which will fight our cause *on the spot* and give the lie to traducers of the race whenever they say that we have not the capacity to manage our own affairs. It is for this reason that the white man of the imperialist school is doing his utmost to ruin the movement. If owing to lack of support from our people or from any cause whatsoever this Hostel is closed, the hands of progress will be put centuries backwards.[45]

Nevertheless, WASU's financial problems continued to mount, a circumstance which seems to have forced the Union to reach a compromise agreement with Vischer and the Colonial Office at the end of 1935. It was agreed that Vischer should help to put the Union on a sound financial basis, chair a committee of reorganisation, in his personal capacity, and secure the financial assistance of the West African governments. Vischer hoped to use the WASU hostel to supply further bedrooms to supplement Aggrey House, and felt that if the hostel could be reorganised, and financed, it could perform a useful function. Other officials at the Colonial Office however, had different ideas. They were concerned about WASU's politics and wanted it made clear 'that the club is not used for political purposes West African or other.' Vischer's approach was more subtle, as he explained:

> We cannot expect that any students club, not even places like Aggrey House, will prevent its members from discussing political questions, but I am convinced that such discussions are not likely to result in political activities of an undesirable nature as long as they are carried on in an atmosphere such as we have already been able to establish at Aggrey House and will no doubt be able to introduce and maintain in WASU hostel.[46]

WASU, for their part, were clearly relieved to have some support, from whatever quarter and Vischer was applauded as 'The Man of the Hour'. The CWAE had also offered a possible loan, if the Colonial Office managed to secure funding from the West African governments. Solanke and WASU continued with their policy of conciliation and moderation and efforts were made to establish co-operation between the WASU hostel and Aggrey House, as well as between WASU and the Colonial Office. Even the United Africa Company, which had made a £40 donation to the WASU hostel, was now praised in *Wasu* as a company whose primary concern might be trade, but who had 'directly or indirectly contributed through their method of trading, much toward the progress of civilisation among the masses of the native inhabitants of British West Africa'.[47]

Clearly WASU had been forced to compromise over the principle of self-help, because of its financial and other difficulties. It seemed as if despite the earlier AHDC, and pledges of support from the NCCL and LAI, the militancy of WASU and its apparent pro-communist leanings, which so alarmed the Colonial Office, as a consequence of the Depression it was still the Colonial Office on whom the students were being forced to rely. In order to maintain their hostel it seemed that

WASU was now even prepared to sacrifice its independence. But Solanke and many other WASU members did not feel that there was anything contradictory about accepting money from those they might refer to as 'British Imperialists'. They believed that they were entitled to support especially from taxes collected in West Africa, and there were few signs that as a Union they were likely to change their opposition to colonial rule.

The invasion of Ethiopia

The visit of the two delegations from the Gold Coast had helped to focus the attention of the students on the need for greater unity, especially between the two principal West African student organisations, WASU and the GCSA, but the dispute remained unresolved. During the next few years a number of further attempts at reconciliation were made, but it was not until 1938 during the period of the Gold Coast cocoa hold-up, and after the opening of WASU's new hostel, that the majority of Gold Coast students began to renew their membership of WASU. The period when WASU was suffering from splits and financial difficulties was also the period of some of the most significant political events in the history of modern Africa, including the Italian invasion of Ethiopia in 1935.

The Italo–Ethiopian war was one of the first episodes of the Second World War, an early example of how the appeasement policies of Britain and France would be applied, and the ineffectual nature of the League of Nations and the concept of 'collective security'. Amongst ordinary people throughout the world however, there was universal condemnation of the Italian invasion and the organisation of wide scale protests. Especially amongst Africans, African-Americans and people of the Caribbean, Ethiopia had long been seen as a symbol for the whole of Africa and for all black people. The invasion was often viewed as something of a 'racial war' and as 'the betrayal of the black race' by the League of Nations. It served to intensify sentiments not only of anti-colonialism but also of anti-fascism amongst millions of people throughout the colonial world.[48]

In Britain the Italian invasion led to an intensification of political activity amongst all the black organisations. Even before the Italian invasion the Trinidadian C.L.R. James had formed the International African Friends of Abyssinia (IAFA) in 1934 with the aim 'to assist by all means in their power in the maintenance of the territorial integrity and political independence of Abyssinia'.[49] The LAI and LCP also organised protest meetings, *The Keys* published a series of articles, and there were demonstrations of support for Ethiopia by Africans in Cardiff, Liverpool, Edinburgh and other cities. The Italian invasion had a great effect on the students and opposition to the Italian invasion created the conditions for greater unity between many of the black organisations in Britain.[50]

WASU was involved in many of the initial protest meetings in Britain and was also in contact with the Paris-based Comité de Défense de l'Independence National de l'Ethiope.[51] In July 1935 *Wasu* published an article – 'The League, Italy and Abyssinia' which made clear the position of the Union. Regarding the League of Nations the article stated that events had proved that as the Union had always suspected it was 'most ineffectual', while in an uncompromising conclusion it declared: 'Perhaps it is as well that the whole of Africa be brought into subjection by the white man, so that when the day of reckoning comes, there will not be a single country in that continent to afford him an asylum.'[52] For WASU the Italo-Ethiopian war had indeed become a 'racial war'. But it served to heighten their opposition to all forms of colonialism practised by the European powers, and especially the alleged 'benevolent trusteeship' of the British government. In the August 1935 issue of *Wasu* the Union stated:

> We are constrained to call the attention of our people to the fact that the western powers are not in Africa for the African's good. The claims of humanity do not enter into their dealings with us, in spite of assurances to the contrary. Repeatedly, whenever their interests clash with ours it is theirs that prevail. We hope that this recent perfidy of the British Government will open the eyes of those who are still unaware of the ruthlessness of imperialism.[53]

In the same month WASU passed a resolution which it sent to the Foreign Secretary: 'That this union views with horror alarm and indignation the contemplated aggression of Italy on Abyssinia and it most strongly protests against it.'[54] The Union claimed that despite world public opinion the European powers had done nothing to stop Italian aggression. They argued that Britain should take the lead in this respect, as the eyes of all those in the colonies were on the Government to save

'European civilisation' from what it called the 'disgraceful destruction' which might ensue from Italy's actions. For WASU as for many others the Italian invasion was a moral as well as a political issue, as an article in *Wasu* expressed it, 'Politically and religiously the West has been weighed in the balance and found wanting.' As far as the students were concerned the whole matter was an example of 'The spiritual bankruptcy of the West'.[55] In September 1935 WASU held the first of a series of weekly religious services at the Hostel which combined religion and nationalist politics, and were designed to 'invoke divine intervention' in the Italo-Ethiopian dispute. A month later an Ethiopian Defence Fund was established to raise money in defence 'of the people of Ethiopia against the present Italian aggression. The Fund, which was started following an address to the Union by Amy Ashwood Garvey, was to be administered by an all-female committee.[56]

It is clear that the invasion of Ethiopia and the effects of the Depression led to an intensification of the activities of many organisations and individuals in West Africa, and also led to something of a radicalisation in their political thinking. For the West African students in Britain this was also the case, although WASU's radicalism did not include all the students and could not be sustained indefinitely, it is possible to see a marked change of attitude, especially as a result of Britain's appeasement of Italy. In part, WASU was no doubt influenced by organisations such as the LAI and the IAFA, with which it was in contact, which maintained a strong anti-imperialist stance throughout. At the same time it is clear that the Union must have been swept leftwards by their experiences with Aggrey House, world events themselves, and the need to reflect changing public opinion in West Africa. In November 1935 *Wasu* commented:

> The nations who met at Geneva and condemned the aggression of Italy subscribe to a form of society based on the exploitation of the many by the few for the enrichment of the latter, and in such a society war is an integral part. What Italy is doing today the other 'great' nations had done in the past. When it is not a war of aggression, as in the case of Italy, it is a war (euphemistically called 'struggle') of a more subtle, but none the less ruthless nature between the classes – those who exploit and those who are exploited – within the nation.[57]

For WASU the Ethiopian war showed the necessity for greater unity – for a 'Black United Front' against what they saw as the common front of European imperialism. It was no doubt this view which led them to declare 'The Ethiopian disaster may yet prove a blessing in disguise if it succeeds in uniting the black peoples of the world.' However, the unity which WASU and others sought was not so easy to attain. As mentioned above it was difficult even for the union to work with the GCSA during this period, and it was still necessary for Solanke and WASU to appeal to Moody, the LCP and other West Indian students for greater solidarity. Nevertheless the invasion of Ethiopia did at least create the basis for much greater unity.[58]

WASU's campaign over Ethiopia was also handicapped by some of the statements made by the Ethiopian legation in London, the hostile press campaign launched by some supporters of the Italian invasion, and those who sought to create divisions amongst the growing 'Black United Front', by arguing as *West Africa* did that West Africans had nothing in common with Ethiopians.[59] The question of the Ethiopians' links with other Africans, with what was seen as their racial identity, was a subject that did create some doubt in the minds of the West African students in Britain. In 1936 whilst he was in London, Haile Selassie was interviewed by H.O. Davies, at that time the president of WASU.[60] The interview was reported in *West Africa* and Davies was able to relate that the idea that the Ethiopian rulers looked down on other darker-skinned Africans was just Italian propaganda. However, the Emperor did confirm that he did not regard himself as a black African, and that the Ethiopians were 'a mixed Hamito-Semitic people'.[61] The Emperor's words, which included rather fulsome praise for the British government, did not encourage greater enthusiasm amongst the students. Seeds of doubt had been sown, and although the campaign and the relief fund continued the students were no longer so keen.

The colonial question

Even though WASU's protests might have become somewhat muted, Italy's attempt to gain 'a place in the sun' at Ethiopia's expense did provoke a great amount of criticism. The whole colonial system came under the spotlight and the British Empire was forced to justify its existence. Italy's demands for African colonies and its method of securing them, were surely not that different to Britain's. If Britain benefited from its possession of colonies, the jealous rivalry of other European powers could be more easily understood.

From early 1934 Lord Rothermere had argued that the former German colonies, administered as League of Nations mandates by Britain and France, should be returned to Germany. By 1936 questions were being asked in Parliament concerning a possible transfer of colonies to Germany in the context of Britain's attempts at appeasement. The colonial question became a major political issue in Britain as economic and political competition amongst the great powers intensified.[62] The major political parties in Britain expressed their opposition to any transfer of colonies, although there was some uncertainty about the Government's position. The public were also opposed to such a move, yet stories kept appearing in the press suggesting, for example, that parts of the Gold Coast, Gambia and Nigeria might be transferred to Germany. *West Africa* demanded that such reports cease, while an article in the *Manchester Guardian* pinpointed the main issue by stating in regard to Britain's position: 'If it is good for us to be a colonial power it is good for Germany; if it is bad for Germany it should be bad for us.'[63]

Not surprisingly, past German rule in Africa as well as Nazi ideology, were also elements in the debate and were compared with Britain's own record. Unfortunately from the British government's point of view the debate occurred at a time when the Sedition Ordinances introduced in West Africa were being discussed in Parliament. There was some alarm at the impact these ordinances would have, and the unfavourable comparisons that would be made with the lack of democratic rights in Italy and Germany. Britain, it was feared, could not be said to be any more moral than the fascist dictatorships.[64] German demands for colonies also led to an examination of Britain's claims over African territories. What exactly was a 'protectorate', and what was the nature of the 'treaties' which had been signed by African rulers? Some commentators even argued that if there were not a place for Germany within the colonial system, the whole system needed dismantling. By the end of 1938 the rumours of a transfer of west Cameroon, incorporated in Nigeria, as well as other areas of West Africa, were so strong that WASU called a public meeting in protest, which was chaired by Eleanor Rathbone MP, at which the main speaker was the Labour Party's future Colonial Secretary, Arthur Creech Jones.[65] As a result of this meeting, which was attended by over seventy students including those from the Gold Coast, a resolution was adopted and sent to both Prime Minister Chamberlain, and the Foreign Secretary, opposing any plan to hand over colonies to Germany.

> Whereas we Africans, apart from those most terrible experiences which we and our people had once suffered under the German rule before the Great War in the Camerouns, Togoland, and the German South West Africa, have recently studied very carefully what Germany's administrative policy means as disclosed in Herr Hitler's book entitled 'Mein Kempf' from which we find inter alia, that in so far as we Natives of Africa are concerned, Germany does not and shall never regard nor treat us as human beings.

The resolution concluded: 'We prefer to continue to remain under His Majesty's Government protection and tutelage until we are able to stand for ourselves within the British Commonwealth of Nations.'[66]

The British government subsequently stated that no such transfer would take place, while at the same time promising a greater development of educational facilities in the colonies, and a move towards self-government. This statement says something of the difficult position facing the Government. On the one hand attempts were being made to reach a colonial agreement with Italy and especially with Germany; at the same time Britain did not want to give up its colonies and was concerned that nationalist unrest in Africa and elsewhere might undermine these attempts, especially if war with Germany broke out.[67] From such statements the students drew the conclusion that their aspirations might be better realised under British imperial rule, rather than that of Nazi Germany. But they also realised that they were in a more favourable position, especially following WASU's official recognition, to demand political reforms in the colonies.

Indeed shortly after the declaration of war in 1939 the Colonial Secretary received a deputation from WASU, LAI, NWA, NCCL, LCP and other organisations, which had the support of Arthur Creech Jones who had asked for the meeting on their behalf. The aim of the deputation seems to have been not only to embarrass the Colonial Office; they wished to discuss deportation, sedition, undesirable literature, trades union and other legislation in Sierra Leone, as well as alleged flogging and torture in the colony, but also to highlight the contradictions in Britain's war aims. How could a country that was allegedly fighting for freedom and democracy, deny this freedom and democracy to its own colonial subjects?[68]

The cocoa hold-up

West African students in Britain were also extremely active in the campaign against cartelized cocoa purchasing and the fall in cocoa prices, which particularly affected Nigeria and the Gold Coast. What has been called 'the largest demonstration of rural discontent in West African colonial history' – the 1937 cocoa hold-up – developed out of several attempts by farmers in the Gold Coast and Nigeria to raise the cocoa prices paid by mainly British buying companies, by halting cocoa production and a boycott of imported goods. On several occasions the farmers had sought ways of bypassing these companies and selling direct to the international market. Indeed in December 1937, the Gold Coast Farmers Union had written to Solanke to complain that UAC and Cadbury had formed a buyers' pool to purchase cocoa at the lowest possible prices. The farmers asked WASU to find them alternative buyers.[69]

The cocoa hold-up was seen by Solanke and WASU as the perfect opportunity to re-establish some unity between students from the Gold Coast and Nigeria, and especially between WASU and the GCSA. Solanke also wrote to Nana Sir Ofori Atta, the Asantehene, and J.B. Danquah, urging greater unity between the two colonies during the crisis. He asked Danquah to use his influence with the GCSA, so that there might be more co-operation between the two organisations. For their part the GCSA sent a letter of support to the leaders of the hold-up and became affiliated to the Gold Coast Youth Conference.

WASU held a public meeting in support of the cocoa hold-up in April 1938. It was the first occasion on which the Union had been openly connected with the two Labour MPs Arthur Creech Jones and Reginald Sorensen, the former chaired the meeting, the latter was the main speaker. This meeting was the occasion not only for declarations of solidarity with the West African cocoa producers, but also for further criticism of the entire colonial system which had created the conditions for cartelized cocoa purchasing. WASU's links with members of the Labour Party grew out of the MPs' contacts with the LAI and NCCL as well as a more general concern for colonial matters following the labour disturbances in the Caribbean. Both sides saw advantages in developing the relationship and WASU began to meet regularly with a number of MPs and send them proposals, some originating in West Africa, on a variety of colonial matters. There seems little doubt that through such contacts WASU was able to exert some influence on the thinking of certain sections of the Labour Party.

One important consequence of the cocoa hold-up was the increased co-operation between WASU and the GCSA. The dispute between the two student bodies had smouldered on, in spite of repeated attempts at reconciliation. For WASU and Solanke in particular the inclusion of the Gold Coast students was vital, not only for West African unity in general, but also so that WASU would not be seen as just a Nigerian organisation. This was especially important in the Union's relationship with the Colonial Office and other official bodies in Britain. The divisions between the students weakened the union's bargaining position, and undermined its position as a pressure group representing West African interests in Britain. Perhaps most importantly, at a time when WASU was looking for financial assistance, it needed to be seen as a united organisation. By mid 1938 many of the Gold Coast students had returned to WASU. This was partly as a result of problems within the GCSA and also because WASU had been able to open a new and more luxurious hostel.

The WASU hostel

WASU's indebtedness, and therefore the need for some source of finance to ensure the hostel's survival, meant that for a time the Union was prepared to take almost any measures which might encourage official patronage. This did not find favour with some of the Union's staunchest members and Solanke found it necessary to justify what was widely seen as a change of course. In order to gain some support for its demands for official finance WASU also called on its friends in West Africa for support in the legislative councils and organised its own fund-raising socials and dances.

Eventually the Colonial Office decided to let the West African governments decide whether they would lend support to WASU. In the meantime the Union had, despite some misgivings, attempted to strengthen its links with John Harris and the CWAE. During his visit to the coronation in 1937, the Alake of Abeokuta, a patron of WASU and other West African representatives held a meeting with Harris. As a result of this and other meetings it was agreed that the CWAE would lend WASU £750 to buy a new hostel. In 1937, following a vigorous campaign, the Nigerian government agreed to make a yearly grant to WASU of £250. The Alake would donate a further £100, while it was hoped that the remaining £400 would be supplied by the West African governments. The Union also issued its own appeal for funds, and did everything to curry favour with the Governor of Nigeria, Sir Bernard Bourdillon, who eventually became one of WASU's patrons. Two years later the Gold Coast government awarded the Union a grant of a further £100.[70]

At the end of 1937, Hanns Vischer returned to his role as WASU's hostel fund treasurer, and money was donated from the UAC, Cadbury Brothers and Barclays Bank and a number of prominent and wealthy individuals. By 1938 the hostel appeal had raised over £1500, so that the loan from the CWAE was no longer necessary, it now being possible to purchase freehold premises in Camden Square. Unfortunately, WASU and the CWAE agreed that the latter should hold the building 'in nominal trust', while WASU would manage the hostel, but according to an official report, the trust deed 'was found to contain the provision that WASU were merely tenants, at will, of the Trustees, who were given very wide powers of control.'[71] Thus began a major disagreement between WASU and the CWAE as to who were the rightful owners of the hostel, which subsided only slightly with the death of Sir John Harris in 1940. One of the important legacies of this dispute was that WASU's financial position improved considerably since they paid neither rent nor any mortgage for the new hostel.

The new WASU hostel was opened in July 1938 by Lady Simon, the wife of the Chancellor of the Exchequer.[72] It ended a very difficult period in the Union's history, when it was suffering not only from internal divisions but also from severe financial problems, which for a time threatened to force the closure of the hostel. Vischer as a representative of the Colonial Office was still attempting to bring about a reconciliation between the WASU hostel and the rival Government sponsored Aggrey House. He had persuaded the Colonial Office that WASU would be a useful addition to Aggrey House, as it represented so many West African students in Britain; and, if the two institutions merged, this would justify continued West African government spending on Aggrey House. At the same time Vischer pointed out that it was important that the Colonial Office did all it could to get WASU 'into the Aggrey House scheme on the side of the Government otherwise I fear it will again be used as a centre of anti-government activity and intrigue.'[73] As he explained, he was anxious to keep in touch with WASU because of his concern with 'the renewed activity of certain undesirable political extremists who seem to be very busy with young Africans of late.'[74]

Political influences

How far were Vischer's fears justified? As mentioned above, since the late 1920s WASU had been in contact with a number of 'left-wing' organisations and individuals, both in Britain and throughout the world. The 1930s was a period when the members of WASU and other students from the colonies, increasingly came into contact with the politics of anti-imperialism, anti-fascism, and socialism. The very fact of colonialism however, and the position of colonial students in Britain; the problem of discrimination and racism in accommodation, admissions to higher education, and employment, meant that many of them were forced to view life and politics afresh, from a more radical standpoint. For this reason they were often drawn towards the more radical and left-wing organisations and individuals, who were most likely to support them, be sympathetic to their plight, and be opposed to colonialism. At the same time left-wing organisations such as the LAI were eager to exert influence over the young colonials so as to encourage radical political change in the colonies. From the early part of the century it was precisely this relationship, with all its potential dangers for the Empire, which Colonial Office officials and other defenders of the Empire feared. They therefore did their best to shield colonial students from such subversive influences and from the more unpleasant aspects of life in Britain, and to provide the students with facilities and contacts which might encourage political moderation and support for the Empire. The aim was to groom a class of future leaders who would be sympathetic to Britain. However, very often this proved a difficult task. Not only were the colour bar and discrimination prevalent in Britain, but also, because of the very nature of colonialism, events occurred in West Africa and in Britain, which would continue to fuel the nationalist sentiments and activities of West African students and propel them towards an increasingly radical critique and solution of their problems. During the 1930s new anti-imperialist organisations were to develop from within the African and Caribbean communities in Britain such as the International African Service Bureau (IASB), which with such individuals as George

Padmore and Isaac Wallace Johnson, created a new Marxist and anti-imperialist as well as a Pan-Africanist political milieu which held great attractions for many West African students.[75]

Padmore was in contact with WASU from at least 1933. He continued to write to Solanke as the editor of *Negro Worker*, and was already in contact with various nationalists in West Africa. Padmore wrote to Solanke asking for copies of *Wasu* and other West African papers, so that he could keep in touch with West African affairs. Amongst other things he stated:

> All the young African friends made a great impression on me. I now feel that despite all our difficulties and the terrible plight of our fatherland, there is a future for Africa. The youth of today are waking up. We who are getting old must encourage and stimulate them to hold up their heads as equal of all. Once the black youth has the spirit of pride and self-respect all the forces of reaction are of no avail. For you may crush a man's body but the spirit goes marching on. It is the spirit of a people that counts.[76]

When Padmore settled in Britain in 1935 he maintained links with both WASU and the GCSA. It was also at that time that he joined forces with C.L.R. James and others, firstly in the IAFA and then from 1937 in the IASB formed, 'to assist by all means in our power the uncoordinated struggle of Africans and people of African descent against the oppression from which they suffer in every country.' For this purpose the IASB established its own journal, the *International African Opinion* which aimed to 'be the mouthpiece of the black workers and peasants, and those intellectuals who see the necessity of making the cause of the masses their own.'[77]

The IASB's various publications were no doubt read by many West African students, who by these means were put in touch with the thinking of Padmore, James, Wallace Johnson and others on a wide range of topics including the labour disturbances in the Caribbean, the future of the South African protectorates, and the lack of political rights in various African colonies. The IASB's membership included Solanke's old friends Kenyatta, who had been honorary secretary of the IAFA, and Amy Ashwood Garvey, who was one of the vice-presidents of the Bureau. The Nigerian Babalola Wilkey was also a member until his expulsion in early 1939. Perhaps most significantly, the first general-secretary of the IASB was the Sierra Leonean I.T.A. Wallace

Johnson, and its treasurer another West African, Robert Broadhurst, while the Bureau's executive committee also included the Nigerian Louis Mbanefo, a member of WASU and the LCP.

Wallace Johnson emerged as one of the main political organisers in West Africa during the 1930s, and was the secretary of the West African Youth League (WAYL), perhaps the most radical and active of all the anti-colonial organisations of this period. He achieved greater fame with the publication of his article 'Has the African a God', for which he was arrested and charged with sedition by the colonial authorities. Indeed Wallace Johnson's outspoken views seem to have bothered both Solanke and the GCSA. Solanke quarrelled with Wallace Johnson following the latter's criticism of the Alake of Abeokuta's support for indirect rule, whilst amongst the membership of the GCSA there was some reluctance to affiliate to the WAYL, following Wallace Johnson's arrest.

The activities and publications of the LAI and NWA and the Marxist-oriented Pan-Africanism of Padmore clearly had some influence on West African students in Britain. All around them anti-colonial political discussion would have taken place and the leading figures in this debate all leaned towards the left. From the early 1930s WASU was also in close contact with Paul Robeson, who in 1935 was given the Yoruba title of Babasale of the Union. It is difficult to judge what influence Robeson had on the students, although clearly he would have been unlikely to discourage their growing radicalisation. The Union and other West African students also had links with Nancy Cunard, and Ade Ademola, O.A. Alakija, and others contributed to her *Negro Anthology*. Cunard had at one time been connected with the NWA, and her stand in opposition to racism and for the rights of black people no doubt won the students' respect.

By the late 1930s to be at least sympathetic to Marxism and left-wing organisations would not have appeared so strange to many West African students. WASU for example, in addition to the organisations already mentioned, was also in contact with the British Committee of the World Congress against Anti-Semitism and Racism, the League for the Boycott of Aggressor Nations, the Students' World Committee against War and Fascism, the British Youth Conference on Democracy and War and the Irish Republican Congress. As a result, Special Branch and even MI5 monitoring of the students and other Africans remained considerable during this period, although 'communist' was a label applied to those holding a wide range of political views. Some members of WASU, and Solanke in particular, remained suspicious of and sometimes hostile to communism and the Soviet Union.[78]

It is however difficult to judge how much the members of WASU were politically influenced by the events and personalities of this period. During 1938 and 1939 *Wasu* did not appear, but the last two editions of 1937 express some of the differences in political thinking, that evidently existed between the members. In one article the journal stated that WASU's nationalism was not 'rabid nationalism'.

> Ours is based on justice. We have never claimed anything for ourselves which we do not concede to others. We do not believe in the parrot-cry, 'Africa for the Africans', but rather Africans for Africa – a great difference. It is when the opportunity is denied to us to show what we could do for Africa that our ambition finds outlet in narrow nationalism. As Lord Hailey pointed out, it is up to our rulers to meet us 'in the right spirit' and guide our legitimate aspiration 'into fruitful and constructive channels'.[79]

The same edition also contained an article applauding Nnamdi Azikiwe and Wallace Johnson for the publication of the latter's 'Has the African a God'; an article on the Egba Native Administration which was presented as 'proof of the wisdom of the System of Indirect Rule and a credit to the British Statesmanship'; and an article by Louis Mbanefo on 'Unity and Co-operation among the Paramount Chiefs in Nigeria', in which he referred to the 'reactionary tendencies of the Indirect Rule system'. Just this one edition of *Wasu* is enough to show that despite external political influences, the students still expressed diverse political opinions, and Solanke in particular was determined to keep the Union's anti-colonialism within constitutional limits.[80] WASU chiefly functioned as a pressure group for a West African nationalism which was itself in an embryonic form, but also as a conduit between West Africa and Britain, which allowed a constant exchange of information and ideas, some of them presenting radical solutions to the colonial problem.

Pan-Africanism and the Gold Coast Students' Association

The GCSA[81] was subject to similar political influences as WASU and other students, although as a smaller, less prominent organisation it appears to have maintained a more moderate stance, at least until the late 1930s.[82] At the time of the Aggrey House dispute some members of the Association strongly supported Aggrey House and were members of the LCP. The GCSA met and supported both of the delegations from the Gold Coast sent to protest against the Sedition and other ordinances, but some members were cautious about involvement with those considered too radical such as Wallace Johnson.

By 1938 the GCSA appeared to have forgotten some of its caution: Padmore was invited to give a talk entitled 'Africa a pawn in European politics'; the Association affiliated to the Gold Coast Youth Conference, and sent a letter of support to the leaders of the Gold Coast and Ashanti cocoa hold-up. Even the organised debates held by the GCSA appear to have become more stridently political. For example, in October 1938 Desmond Buckle proposed the motion 'that this Association refuses to fight for the British Empire'. A month later he opposed and defeated a motion proposed by William Ofori Atta 'that the salvation of the Gold Coast lies in close co-operation with the British Labour Party'.[83]

By this time Desmond Buckle had emerged as the leading figure in the GCSA and had been elected as both its secretary from 1936-7 and president from 1937-8. Buckle had received some of his secondary education in Britain and had subsequently begun a degree in medicine at London University. He did not complete his studies however, and during the 1930s he played an increasingly active role in the GCSA and in the NWA. In early 1939, for example he wrote to the GCSA asking 'members of our association to take more interest in public meetings concerning Negro Welfare and asking for donations on behalf of the Negro Welfare Association.' As a result of this appeal Arnold Ward was invited to give a talk to the GCSA about the work of the NWA. Buckle was also involved in organising the Conference on African Peoples, Democracy and World Peace, which was held in July 1939 in London. Indeed the GCSA was listed alongside the LCP, NWA, and Coloured Film Artistes Association, as the main organisers of this conference, the purpose of which was 'to show how the British people can ... safeguard their own liberties, extend the boundaries of democracy to embrace the peoples of Britain's colonial empire and, by so doing, lay the foundations for true freedom and lasting peace in the world.'[84]

The activities of 'certain undesirable political extremists' continued to be of concern to the Colonial Office. Both WASU and the GCSA it seems, were just sufficiently in contact with such subversive influences to warrant very careful handling by the Colonial Office. But even the officials at the Colonial Office were uncertain about how significant these influences might be, with some concluding that West African student politics was 'mostly talk'. There were similar differences of opinion expressed at the First West African Governors Conference, held at Lagos in August 1939. On that occasion Sir Bernard Bourdillon, who perhaps of the four governors had most contact with the students, felt that there was much 'latent good' in WASU, and expressed the view 'that to reject it would merely antagonise students already susceptible to communistic influences'.[85]

Following the report of the Colonial Students Committee, established by the Secretary of State for the Colonies in 1937, the Colonial Office hoped to use the Victoria League and similar bodies to introduce West African students to respectable families in Britain, who could divert them away from 'subversive influences'. Initially this policy appeared quite successful. A Colonial Office report of 1940, for example, listed over 60 West African students who were regularly in touch with the Victoria League. These included a number of members of the GCSA who were all members of Aggrey House. Included in this list was the name of Desmond Buckle, at this time described in rather glowing terms, but who in the future was to be held responsible for the forced closure of Aggrey House.[86]

WASU and GCSA were based in London but were both in contact with West African students in other parts of Britain. In 1936 a GCSA was formed in Edinburgh, following a break with the Edinburgh African Association which was led by Solanke's friend and future WASU president E.A. Shanu.[87] During the 1930s WASU also co-operated with the handful of West African students at Trinity College, Dublin, who had formed the Association of Students of African Descent (ASAD). The Dublin students declined Solanke's offer to constitute themselves a branch of WASU, but they often co-operated on particular issues and some joined on an individual basis, so that from 1935 the Union styled itself WASU of Great Britain and Ireland. In 1939 ASAD proposed a conference to unite all students of African descent throughout the British Isles, but it seems that the war prevented any further development of this idea.[88]

During the 1930s WASU also established links with organisations around the world. It had contacts throughout Africa, the United States, Europe, the Caribbean, and South America. In the United States for example, WASU had made contact with W.E.B. Du Bois' *Crisis*, the African International Trading Association, the African Patriotic Students' Club, the United Ethiopian Students' Association and the Congress of the African Peoples of the World. The Union organised its own agents in the United States as sellers of *Wasu* and even established a Harlem branch of the Union as early as 1934. In addition to these contacts WASU also had a readership and had appointed agents for its journal in Trinidad, Jamaica and Brazil.

The outbreak of the Second World War presented WASU and other West African students with further opportunities to reach their avowed goal of 'West African full Nationhood'. The war years were to show that whatever the political influences on the students during the 1930s, they were still determined to advance what they saw as the interests of West Africa. By the late 1930s with their new hostel, links with MPs, and increasing official recognition, as well as close contact with the emerging nationalist movements in West Africa, WASU in particular seemed extremely well placed to take advantage of the changes which the war years would bring.

Notes

1. 'African Students in the UK' in PRO CO 323/1078/70238 also 'African Students' Club' in CO 554/86/4364/B.
2. 'London Club for African Students' in PRO CO 554/85/4319.
3. *West Africa*, 9 May 1931 p552, and *Wasu*, 6/1, January 1937, p3. For a contemporary account of racism see Nancy Cunard's 'Colour Bar' in *Negro – An Anthology*, Frederick Ungar Pub. Co., New York 1970, pp342-45.
4. *West Africa*, 14 February 1931, p156.
5. Ajibade to Solanke, 1 September 1929, SOL 56/3.
6. Ajibade to Solanke, 12 November 1929, SOL 56/6. The LCP included amongst its prominent West African members Ansah Koi, the League's first vice-president, Stephen Thomas, the League's secretary and his sister Stella Thomas, the first African woman to qualify as a barrister.
7. See 'London Club for African Students' in PRO CO 554/86/4364/A.
8. Dr A. Ansah Koi subsequently became president of WASU and in 1951 was a minister in Nkrumah's first cabinet.
9. *West Africa*, 26 December 1931, p1606.
10. A National Union of Students' survey found that only 1 per cent of hoteliers were willing to accept 'Coloured guests'.

11. *West Africa*, 5 March 1932, p209 and A. Ade Ademola, 'Colour Bar Notoriety in Great Britain', in N. Cunard *op.cit.*, p346-47.
12. *West Africa*, 12 March 1932. A similar point was made by Harold Moody in a letter to the Colonial Secretary. Moody to Sir Cunliffe Lister, 31 March 1932, PRO CO 323/1199/91261 pt.1.
13. E.N. Jones, 'What is wrong with West Africa? A diagnosis', *West Africa*, 19 September 1931, p1152.
14. Cobina Kessie, a law student, was editor of *Wasu* and a member of the GCSA. He was subsequently a member of the Coussey Committee on constitutional reform in the Gold Coast and a leading member of the UGCC.
15. For an example of the anti-racist activities of the LAI see N. Cunard *op.cit.*, and *West Africa*, 4 June 1932, p570.
16. In 1932 the Colonial Secretary publicly explained the unfortunate effects of the colour bar and reminded his audience of the economic importance of the colonies. *West Africa*, 4 June 1932, p570.
17. *Nigerian Daily Times*, 25 July 1930. See also G.O. Olusanya, *The West African Students' Union and the Politics of Decolonisation, 1925-1958*, Daystar, Ibadan 1982, pp24-5.
18. *West Africa*, 25 October 1930, p1512.
19. WASUs patrons in West Africa included some of the most important traditional rulers including the Asantehene, Nana Sir Ofori Atta, the Emir of Kano, the Oni of Ife and the Alake of Abeokuta. Even the Union's anniversaries were celebrated in the region's main cathedrals, a fact that did not go unnoticed by the Colonial Office.
20. G.O. Olusanya, *op.cit.*, p101.
21. There was a West Africans membership of the LCP throughout the 1930s. The League continued to maintain an interest in West African affairs and in 1938 established a branch in Sierra Leone.
22. *Wasu*, 2/2, April 1933, p11. The hostel served an extremely important function as a 'home from home' for African students and visitors. West African food, music and even traditional games were available. G.O. Olusanya *op.cit.*, pp26-7.
23. Vischer to Ezechiel, 18 February 1933, PRO CO 323/1243/11751/1. The following year WASU constitution declared that the aim of the Union was: 'To propagate Nationalism in West Africa such nationhood being based on the conception of West Africa as one political unit.'
24. One of the significant differences between Solanke and his opponents was whether the Union should be a social or political body. Eventually the politicians won the day.

25. *The Truth About Aggrey House – An Exposure of the Government Plan for the Control of African Students in Great Britain*, WASU, London 1934 (see Appendix). Also *Wasu*, 3/1, March 1934 p3 and *West Africa*, 3 February 1934, p109 and 20 January 1934, p48.
26. See Appendix.
27. *Ibid.* The Colonial Office and others speculated about the author of this publication and concluded that WASU was 'under Communist influence'. Clearly the LAI exerted some influence over the writing of *The Truth* and the subsequent campaign.
28. 'WASU Campaign Against Aggrey House', Herbert Macaulay Papers, Box 18 File 7.
29. *Ibid.* Africa House was the name given to WASU hostel. G.O. Olusanya, *op.cit.*, pp28-9.
30. On these contacts see S. Rohdie, 'The Gold Coast Aborigines Abroad', *Journal of African History*, 6/3, 1963, pp389-411.
31. CPGB member Ben Bradley played a leading role in the LAI. From 1937, following the demise of the LAI, the CPGB began to take a more direct interest in the African colonies. In that year its Colonial Committee produced the *Colonial Information Bulletin*, which was issued fortnightly until the outbreak of war, and contained articles on Britain and the Caribbean as well as Africa.
32. *Colonial News*, 1/2, April 1934, p6. For further details on the LAI see S. Howe, *Anticolonialism in British Politics – The Left and the End of Empire 1918-1964*, Oxford University Press, Oxford 1993, pp71-7.
33. Report of the International Secretariat of the LAI, 1934. Bridgeman Papers, DBN 24/21A.
34. LAI 1933 Annual Conference, Bridgeman Papers, DBN 25/21A.
35. The Sedition Bill or Criminal Code Amendment Act became law in the Gold Coast in 1934, despite the fact that all the African members of the Legislative Council voted against it. Amongst other things the Act gave the Governor the power to prohibit the import of any newspaper, book or document considered undesirable. The Act was clearly aimed at political and especially communist literature. Possession of such literature could be punished by imprisonment for three years for a first offence and seven years for a second. Similar laws in Gambia and other colonies prohibited publications such as *Negro Worker*, Nancy Cunard's *Negro Anthology* and anything produced by the LAI. As part of its campaign the AHDC wrote to the African members of the legislative councils urging them to prevent 'public money' going to Aggrey House.
36. L. Solanke, 'The New Year Open Letter to the Educated Youths in West

Africa', 1 January 1935, SOL 59/4.
37. L. Solanke, 'WASU Day Oration', 25 October 1934, SOL 59/4. African visitors to the hostel included Prof. Z.K. Mathews, Hastings Banda and Nnamdi Azikiwe, who presented a series of lectures to WASU members.
38. S. Rohdie, *op.cit.*, p402.
39. A notable example of joint West African/British political co-operation, the campaign slogan was 'Justice for African People'. See 'Shall British Subjects Plead in Vain for Justice', NCCL, 1935. The NCCL also launched an appeal and organised legal defence for the Sierra Leonean activist Isaac Wallace Johnson following his conviction for sedition in 1936. See 'An African Sedition Prosecution', NCCL, 1936.
40. *West Africa*, 5 May 1934, p473. The boycott was formally proposed by C.L.R. James at that time a member of the LCP.
41. Vischer memo, 4 September 1934, PRO CO 323/1281/31474.
42. Vischer to A. de Wade, 8 July 1935, PRO CO 323/1342/6652 pt.2.
43. The Colonial Office did eventually receive significant financial support for Aggrey House. Donations were received from United Africa Company, Anglo-American Corporation, and GEC amongst others. One of the largest contributions, some $12,500, was from the Carnegie Foundation in the United States.
44. *Wasu*, 4/2, August 1935, p19.
45. *Wasu*, 4/3, September 1935, p35.
46. Vischer memo, 3 July 1936, PRO CO 847/7/2.
47. *Wasu*, 5/2&3, June/July 1936, p28. With Vischer as honorary treasurer of WASU Hostel Fund, finance was offered to the Union from many quarters including the UAC and Barclays Bank.
48. S.K.B. Asante, *Pan-African Protest: West Africa and the Italo-Ethiopian Crisis, 1934-1941*, Longman, London 1977, p41.
49. *Ibid.* p45. See also P. Esedebe, *Pan-Africanism – The Idea and Movement 1776-1963*, Howard University Press, Washington D.C. 1982 pp115-23. The IAFA executive committee included J.B. Danquah, S.R. Wood and G.E. Moore from the 1934 Gold Coast delegations to Britain and others such as George Padmore who would go on to found the International African Service Bureau (IASB) and the Pan African Federation (PAF).
50. The best known student reaction to the invasion was that of Kwame Nkrumah who in 1935 journeyed to London from the US. According to his own testimony,

> At that very moment it was almost as if the whole of London had suddenly declared war on me personally. For the next few minutes I

could do nothing but glare at each impassive face wondering if those people could possibly realise the wickedness of colonialism and praying that the day might come when I could play my part in bringing about the downfall of such a system. My nationalism surged to the fore; I was ready and willing to go through hell itself, if need be, in order to achieve my object.

K. Nkrumah, *The Autobiography of Kwame Nkrumah*, Thomas Nelson & Sons, Edinburgh 1957, p77.

51. This organisation was founded by Tiemoho Garan-Kouyate from the French Sudan, who was to become a member of the executive committee of the IASB. See Asante, *op.cit.*, pp42-4.
52. *Wasu*, 4/1, July 1935, p3.
53. *Wasu*, 4/2, August 1935, p21. The perfidy of the Government presumably refers to the various agreements made with the Italian Fascists and the attempts to exclude the representatives of Abyssinia from the bodies of the League of Nations.
54. WASU to the Foreign Secretary, 31 August 1935, SOL 72/4.
55. *Wasu*, 4/5, November 1935, p71.
56. *Ibid*. p70. It is important to point out that besides Mrs Olu Solanke who acted as matron at WASU hostel, the Union had a number of active women members during the 1930s including: Ibidun Doherty, who was amongst the representatives of the Union in talks with Aggrey House and Titi Folarin who was the Union's honorary treasurer. The women members were also responsible for organising many of the fund-raising and social activities of the Union, but on occasions held their own meetings. See *West Africa*, 18 March 1939, p337.
57. *Ibid*.
58. See e.g. *The Keys*, 7/1, July/September 1939, p7.
59. Quoted in Asante *op.cit.*, p55.
60. H.O. Davies, who was a student at the LSE, was one of the founders of the Nigerian Youth Movement and a leading nationalist politician. Subsequently he was Nigeria's first QC, and in 1964 Minister of State for Industry.
61. *Ibid*., p60.
62. In 1937 the Nigerian government actually donated £75,000 from its balance of trade surplus for 'imperial defence'. *West Africa*, 6 March 1937, p253.
63. *West Africa*, 19 September 1936, p1300.
64. *West Africa*, 8 August 1936, p1082. During this period there was a much

greater interest in African affairs in Parliament, partly provoked by the questions of Labour MPs such as Creech Jones and Reginald Sorensen.
65. It seems that this issue was first brought to WASU's attention by the ITUC-NW. Similar protest were organised by the LCP and other organisations. According to one report many of the students strongly disagreed with the views expressed by Creech Jones. *West Africa*, 3 December 1938, p1679.
66. WASU to the Prime Minister and Foreign Secretary, 29 November 1938, SOL 77/6. The meeting also received messages of support from West African students in Edinburgh and Dublin. The resolution was also sent to the governments of France and the United States. The protests continued for some time. In early 1939 a WASU delegation met MPs at Westminster to deliver further resolutions from the Nigerian Youth Movement and Cameroun Union. *West African Review*, January 1939, p45.
67. This was the period following Lord Hailey's *Africa Survey* and the major labour rebellions in the Caribbean, when plans for 'colonial development' were already being discussed in the Colonial Office.
68. PRO CO 267/673/32254/8. Throughout the 1930s Moody and the LCP organised protests against the colour bar in Britain and the most oppressive features of colonial rule in Africa and the Caribbean. On Creech Jones' lobbying of the Colonial Office see P.S. Gupta, *Imperialism and the British Labour Movement 1914-1964*, MacMillan, London 1975, p264.
69. WASU received donations from both UAC and Cadbury, two of the biggest firms in the buyers' pool It seems that after the Union's protest meeting the donations stopped.
70. In all these manoeuvrings Solanke showed that he was a skilled politician. Having secured the patronage of Bourdillon to obtain much needed finance, he intended to use the relationship to secure protection for WASU's Nigerian branches and continually badgered the NYM and other nationalists for demands that could be put to the Governor of Nigeria.
71. 'Report on WASU Hostel submitted by Dr R.B. Wellesley Cole', The Advisory Committee on the Welfare of Colonial People in the United Kingdom (ACWUK) No. 34, December 1942.
72. This occasion showed how much official recognition the Union now had. The Union was subsequently visited by several of the West African governors and other VIPs.
73. Vischer to Downie, 4 January 1937, PRO CO 847/7/2.
74. Vischer to Sir John Shuckburgh, 4 August 1939, PRO CO 554/119/3.
75. However, as Obafemi Awolowo remarked, many students stung into political action by the colour bar in Britain renounced politics in order to

'further themselves' when they returned to West Africa. *West Africa Review*, January 1939, p17. George Padmore (1902-59) was editor of *Negro Worker* until his expulsion by the Comintern in 1934. He then became a leading figure in Pan-African politics in Britain.

76. Padmore to Solanke, 21 February 1934, SOL 2/2.
77. *International African Opinion*, 1/1, July 1938.
78. Police reports were sometimes as concerned with the sexual activities of the students as they were with their politics. See e.g. PRO CO 323/1517/7046.
79. *Wasu*, 6/2, 1937 p22.
80. *Ibid.*, pp23, 28, 31.
81. The aims of the GCSA were: 'To bring together all students who claim to be of Gold Coast Nationality; to encourage common understanding, co-operation and unity among the Gold Coast students in Europe; to help the members of the Association in times of difficulty according to the Association's discretion; to promote and protect the social, educational and political interests of the country.
82. In 1936 the GCSA had just twenty-six members; WASU claimed over two hundred, while the Colonial Office in 1938 estimated around sixty.
83. W. Ofori Atta was subsequently a founder member of the United Gold Coast Convention, and was imprisoned by the colonial authorities following the riots in the Gold Coast in 1948. See GCSA Minute Book, SOL 78.
84. PRO CO 323/1679/5. Earlier in 1939 the same organisations had organised a meeting on the theme 'Colonies and Peace'.
85. 'Report of the Proceedings of the First West African Governors' Conference', PRO CO 554/119/3.
86. Colonial Office minute, February 1940, PRO CO 859/20/8.
87. *West Africa*, 27 June 1936, p893. An African Races Association still existed at Glasgow University during this period.
88. According to H.O. Davies the 1938 Nigerian Youth Movement campaign against the possible transfer of parts of Nigeria to Germany was occasioned by the arrival of an ASAD cablegram in Nigeria. H.O. Davies, *Memoirs*, Evans Brothers, Ibadan 1989, pp96-7.

The War Years 1939–45

The declaration of war by the Government in September 1939 radically changed the circumstances of the students in Britain and conditions in the West African colonies. The war, ostensibly fought for freedom and democracy and in opposition to the theories of racial supremacy, actually made the students and their organisations more significant, as they were able to expose and capitalise on the hypocrisy of the 'democratic' Allied war propaganda. The Government entered the war and enlisted the support of its colonies. As a result, during the course of the conflict, it was forced to justify the war effort and explain in some detail the meaning of such phrases as self-determination. Colonial rule was increasingly explained not just as trusteeship, but also as 'partnership', with the understanding that after the war, major changes would be made to Britain's colonial empire. But the colonies were not just enlisted in a general sense. Men and women from Africa, the Caribbean and elsewhere were recruited to come to Britain and serve in the forces and in the war industries. A major propaganda campaign was mounted to counter the effects of racism and the colour bar, and everything was done to persuade colonial subjects that the war was worth fighting, and that there was equality within the empire. As such equality clearly did not exist, some attempts were made to appease anti-colonial sentiments and to encourage a sense of partnership. In Britain the West African students were seen by the Colonial Office as important barometers of colonial opinion, who should, wherever possible, be appeased and courted. As it became more evident that changes would have to be made in the colonies after the war, the ideas and aims of the probable future leaders and opinion-formers assumed an even greater significance.

Even before the war the issue of self-government in West Africa had been discussed in Britain, although only a few demanded immediate independence.[1] West African demands had generally centred around greater participation in the political process, particularly securing the majority of elected representatives in each of the four legislative councils; greater access to government office, and a greater role in the colonies' economies. Some West Africans in Britain went further. In February 1939, for example, William Ofori Atta, the vice-president of the GCSA, made a speech denouncing what he saw as the hypocrisy of trusteeship, and claimed that the abolition of the colonial system would be a great step towards the removal of the major causes of war. In March 1939 an organisation calling itself the Africa Economic Union published a booklet entitled *Colonies: What Africa Thinks*, written by WASU member Cobina Kessie. Kessie also called for an end to colonial rule and its replacement with a 'commonwealth of free peoples' who would enjoy representation at Westminster.[2]

WASU and most other West African students declared themselves in support of the war which was viewed as being fought 'for suppression and abolition of force and aggression, and in the defence of freedom, liberty and democracy'. They pledged their allegiance to the Allies and what Solanke referred to as 'that mighty and most marvellous institution popularly known as the British Commonwealth of Nations'.[3] Indeed Solanke went much further and declared that British rule was far preferable to colonial rule by Nazi Germany. As he explained during the war, 'WASU have found that the English are the best of all the other European "SHARKS" in Africa ... We Africans must cast our lot with theirs in order to be saved'.[4] However, alongside the press and public opinion in West Africa, WASU demanded that loyal subjects be treated as such and be assured that they were fighting for freedom and democracy not just for Britain but also for the colonies. Along with other organisations it now felt it was in a stronger position to make demands which the Colonial Office and the Government could not completely ignore. From the start of the war Solanke continually urged the nationalists in West Africa to take the opportunity to make constitutional demands even though these were essentially minor political reforms. WASU continued to play this important role throughout the war years, until the development of mass nationalist movements in West Africa.[5]

The war and the colour bar

Racism and the colour bar had remained one of the most important issues affecting the students and other black people throughout the

1930s.[6] Once war was declared the colour bar became an even more significant issue. In September 1939 the Rev. E.N. Jones (Laminoh Sankoh) a leading member of WASU, and a former editor of *Wasu*, was dismissed from his post as a stretcher bearer with the Air Raid Precautions (ARP) medical services in Paddington.[7] At about the same time two other black men were also dismissed, allegedly because both residents and other stretcher bearers had complained about their presence. WASU immediately took up the case of E.N. Jones, which it viewed as a clear example of racial discrimination and, in the first instance, protested to Paddington Borough Council, and then informed the Home Secretary, the Colonial Secretary, as well as its influential friends in Parliament. The students highlighted the evil of the colour bar during wartime, especially at a time when colonial subjects were being asked to risk their lives in defence of the Empire.[8] A large amount of publicity was generated by the case and other related incidents. Three Indian ARP wardens had also been dismissed in Paddington, an incident which led to over 50 others signing a letter of protest. Articles appeared in the press and questions were raised in Parliament by Reginald Sorensen, while Creech Jones and Lord Listowel both raised the matter with the Home Secretary. However the issue was not resolved satisfactorily, in spite of the public outcry and the support which WASU received from the MPs, *West Africa* and others.[9]

These were the first of many cases of racial discrimination during the war years which further alienated large sections of the students and other black people in Britain, as well as those in West Africa and other colonies. They also continued to cause consternation amongst those in the Colonial Office and elsewhere who were conscious of the effects of such incidents in the colonies. In 1940 J.L. Keith of the Colonial Office stated that 'prejudice against coloured persons is widespread in this country', a situation which was obviously at odds with government declarations that the war was being fought against the evils of racism. An interesting aspect of Colonial Office work during the war years was the attempt to find a solution to the problem of racial discrimination.[10]

During the first few months of the war other protests were made to the Government concerning the colour bar. A deputation from the LCP visited the Colonial Secretary to demand an end to discrimination and equal admission for all to the armed forces and the colonial civil service, and there were protests by leading figures in British churches, including the Archbishop of Canterbury. In November 1939 the Prime

Minister was compelled to make a speech in which he declared an end to all racial discrimination in the armed services.[11] Further pressure was applied to the Government to openly declare its war aims by the LCP, WASU and others, something which it persistently refused to do. WASU and the press in West Africa hoped to persuade the Government that its war aims should include the promise of representative government to West Africa.[12]

Aggrey House

Although during the war years WASU enjoyed a much closer and more amicable relationship with the Colonial Office, it still sought to use every opportunity to further its own and what it saw as West Africa's interests. During the early war years, it was again events at Aggrey House which provided a *cause célèbre*, which united the students and embarrassed the Colonial Office. Officials became increasingly concerned about the political discussions which went on at the Government sponsored Aggrey House. In early 1940 Vischer complained, 'From all I can see and from all I hear Aggrey House is becoming known as a centre for subversion and definitely anti-allied propaganda'. The plans of the Colonial Office to maintain some political influence over colonial students seemed to be in jeopardy. Vischer concluded that, 'I cannot help feeling that there are some responsible people behind all this, whose object seems to be to embarrass the authorities'.[13]

In theory, Aggrey House was administered by four trustees operating through a management committee which included representatives of the members' 'house committee'. In practice however the Colonial Office remained in control. In April 1940, the differences between the members and trustees of Aggrey House, which had been simmering for some time, boiled over into a major dispute. One of the members was expelled for 'immoral conduct' with a woman on the premises. Following the house committee's annual general meeting he had been re-admitted, but this decision had been opposed by the trustees and subsequently led to a dispute with the members. Because the Colonial Office viewed Aggrey House as a 'centre for subversion', the trustees were encouraged to close it, which they did in May 1940. The closure led to a protest campaign, led by Desmond Buckle, the chairman of the house committee. Articles appeared in

West Africa, the *Evening Standard* and the *Daily Worker* and were a considerable annoyance to the Colonial Office, which took the precaution of sending its own version of events to the Ministry of Information, so that they might combat any 'hostile propaganda' which appeared in the colonial press.[14] The members began, but did not continue, legal proceedings to reopen Aggrey House, a further embarrassment for the Colonial Office, which privately admitted that the closure was neither legal nor constitutional. Publicly the trustees maintained that 'it was a moral issue' which led to the closure, while at the Colonial Office J.L. Keith admitted: 'It was thought better to raise the moral rather than the political issue but one of the objects of closing the Club is to get rid of a generally undesirable House committee'.[15]

From the Colonial Office viewpoint Aggrey House had a number of weaknesses. Some officials, such as Vischer, had no confidence in John Fletcher, one of the trustees, who Vischer described as 'very unreliable' and someone who 'encouraged political talk at the Club'. J.L. Keith criticised the constitution of Aggrey House, which he claimed gave too much power to the members. Many at the Colonial Office believed that it was older non-student members 'who are very politically-minded, and have given the discussions at the club a very communistic tone'. The Colonial Office was convinced that at the core of the dispute were the activities of two people in particular, the Barbadian Peter Blackman and Desmond Buckle from the Gold Coast. Both were members of the NWA and of the CPGB, but were also both members of the LCP. The Colonial Office was particularly concerned because the protest campaign over Aggrey House affected all black students, and because as a result there was 'a great deal of disaffection and disloyalty among these students at the present time and there are signs that they are being influenced by German propaganda'.[16]

The Colonial Office requested that MI5 monitor the activities of Buckle and Blackman, but at the same time began to think of how it could organise a new and more successful student centre to take the place of Aggrey House. There was no immediate solution to this problem and because of wartime conditions and the influx of colonial service personnel and volunteers over the next few years, the Colonial Office was forced to rely increasingly on WASU, which now controlled the only hostel and social centre for 'persons of African descent' in the capital. Naturally the Union took full advantage of this situation and in a press release in May 1940 did all it could to extol the virtues of its Africa House, and to point out that because of strictly enforced rules no 'Moral Issue' could arise there.[17]

The Colonial Office considered how it might continue its work with colonial students in the light of the difficulties over Aggrey House, which was eventually reopened, but boycotted by most students. Solanke and WASU vigorously denied they were in any way involved in a boycott, but took every opportunity to create further difficulties for the Colonial Office and to expose the fact that Aggrey House was 'a Government Institution for Government purpose'.

While Aggrey House remained closed, WASU's Africa House occupied a unique position in the capital, and the Colonial Office was anxious to stay on friendly terms. It tried to avoid discussion with the Union over political matters, and in letters explained that WASU was not to be encouraged to advise the Colonial Secretary 'on questions of policy or on matters which are the concerns of the Colonial governments'.[18] However, it is clear that the members of the Union were not likely to give up their 'activities in the field of constructive politics'. As *Wasu* explained in 1941: 'The members of WASU being aware of their future responsibility as potential leaders of thought and action among their people in West Africa, often meet to study and deliberate over not only the economic but also the political problems of the Country on Constructive lines'.[19]

West African politics

Throughout 1939 and the early years of the war WASU stepped up its involvement in West African political and economic affairs and paid particular attention to the land and agricultural problems of the West African colonies.[20] The Government appointed Leverhulme Commission had investigated the same issue during 1938-9 and the Union instructed Solanke and N.A. Fadipe to carry out their own research 'with special reference to Nigerian Land Tenure'.[21] In early 1939, the Union asked the Labour MP Leslie Haden-Guest, a member of the Leverhulme Commission, to give his impressions of West Africa at two WASU meetings. As a result of these meetings, the students passed resolutions which were sent to the Government and to supporters in West Africa, insisting on the preservation of communal land tenure in West Africa. WASU made it clear that it condemned 'the system of any European-owned plantation and it is strongly opposed

James Africanus Beal Horton.

Prince Bandele Omoniyi, author of *A Defence of the Ethiopian Movement*.

Top: West African and Caribbean members of the Union of Students' of African descent, 1927. (By permission of the British Library. Taken from 27/8/97 edition of West Africa.)

Bottom: The Nigerian Progress Union – Amy Ashwood Garvey seated, second row, 1925.

Chief Ladipo Solanke, founder of WASU (courtesy Olu Ogunbiyi).

150,000 Employees of the Government of Nigeria on strike!

THEY DEMAND A MINIMUM LIVING WAGE OF 2s-6d PER DAY

A Public Meeting under the auspices of the West African Students' Union & other Organisations will be held in Conway Hall, Red Lion Square on Sunday July 15th 1945 at 2.30 p.m. when the labour conditions in Nigeria which have led to the strike will be discussed.

All are cordially invited.

West African Students Union, 1 South Villas N.W.1.

WASU poster, 1945

WASU MAGAZINE

Published by the West African Students' Union of Great Britain and Ireland

VOL. XII. No. 5.   SUMMER, 1948

CONTENTS

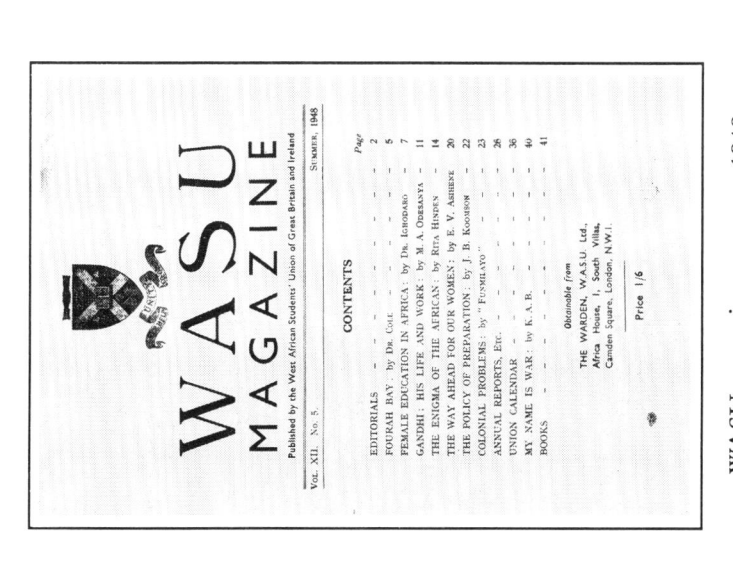

	Page
EDITORIALS	2
FOURAH BAY : by Dr. COLE	5
FEMALE EDUCATION IN AFRICA : by Dr. IGBOBAKO	7
GANDHI : HIS LIFE AND WORK : by M. A. OGESANYA	11
THE ENIGMA OF THE AFRICAN : by RITA HINDEN	14
THE WAY AHEAD FOR OUR WOMEN : by E. V. ASHERVE	20
THE POLICY OF PREPARATION : by J. B. KOOMSON	22
COLONIAL PROBLEMS : by "FUNMILAYO"	23
ANNUAL REPORTS, ETC.	26
UNION CALENDAR	36
MY NAME IS WAR : by K.A.B.	40
BOOKS	41

Obtainable from
THE WARDEN, W.A.S.U. Ltd.,
Africa House, 1, South Villas,
Camden Square, London, N.W.1.

Price 1/6

WASU magazine, summer 1948

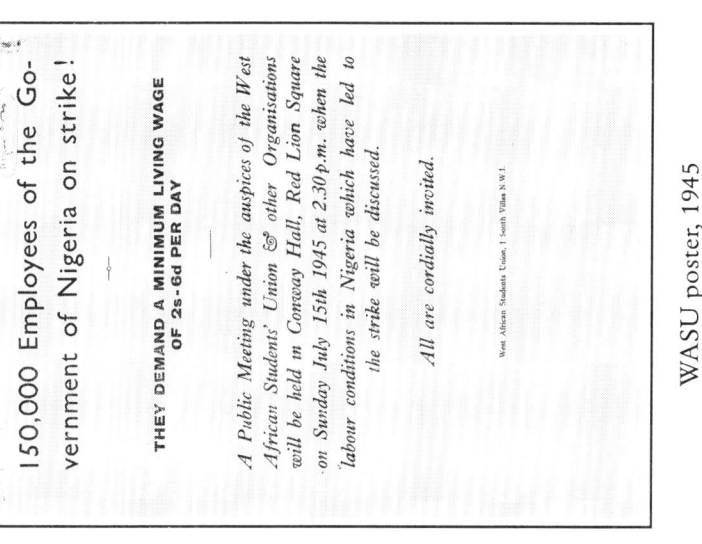

Top: The president and vice-president of the Nigerian Union, Olu Akinfosile and Ms A. Adenubi speaking to Nnamdi Azikiwe at a reception in 1957 (courtesy of West Africa).

Bottom: WASU members and friend c. 1946. Nkrumah seated extreme right, Wallace Johnson seated second from left.

to any sale of freehold estate in land'. It subsequently established a standing committee to research and report on economic, political and social issues in West Africa.[22]

In April 1940 WASU sent a thirty-six page memorandum to the Colonial Office which called for an increase in the prices paid for primary products, such as cocoa and groundnuts, in the West African colonies. The Union's view, which was also widespread in West Africa at the time, was that the Government was deliberately suppressing these prices at a time when prices of imported goods were rising. At the same time, in Parliament, the Government was questioned on the matter by Arthur Creech Jones and Reginald Sorensen. WASU also received support from ASAD in Dublin and the NCCL, while the GCSA sent its own resolution of protest to the Colonial Office. The WASU memorandum provoked some controversy amongst trading interests in Britain, such as the Liverpool Chamber of Commerce, and in the pages of *West Africa*. The Colonial Office, although reluctant to recognise WASU as representing West African opinion, was now compelled to issue a full response, which maintained that it was actually safeguarding the interests of the farmers at a time of a glut in the international market.[23]

WASU's concern with such issues is evidence of its links with the farmers' organisations in West Africa, as well as campaigning organisations in Britain. The correspondence between Solanke and Fadipe, who drafted the memorandum, shows that they were concerned not only with price controls, but that they also wished to secure for the producers the right of direct sale to Britain, thereby bypassing the monopolies such as UAC and Cadbury, from whom the Union still received grants. Farmers' organisations urged WASU to bring their complaints before Parliament. These included not only price controls and reductions, but also export quotas and other economic restrictions which they wished to see removed. WASU was to be widely used, by both individuals and organisations in West Africa as a 'bureau of information', and to petition Parliament through its links with sympathetic MPs. In 1938 the Union received over 500 letters of enquiry and many of these enclosed petitions or asked for help and advice. The following year over 1000 letters were received, half from West Africa, and a quarter asking for information on business opportunities in Britain. WASU was clearly very much more than just a students' union.[24]

WASU: an anti-colonial pressure group

The change in WASU's status is most clearly seen in its relationship with Government ministers and the Colonial Office. As part of its plan to gain Colonial Office support the students invited the (Labour) Under-Secretary of State for the Colonies, George Hall, to visit Africa House. The invitation seems to have been initially suggested by Sorensen and was perhaps viewed sympathetically in the Colonial Office because of the complimentary remarks made about the Union's hostel, following a visit from the Governor of Nigeria, Sir Bernard Bourdillon. Following Hall's visit to WASU in August 1940, the new Secretary of State for the Colonies, Lord Lloyd, made history by visiting Africa House. His visit was widely reported in the press and was seen as a great success by Colonial Office officials. In part the visit aimed to stem the disaffection amongst the students caused by events at Aggrey House. These events had left WASU in a strong position, which Solanke was trying to exploit by encouraging opposition among the students to Colonial Office attempts to reopen Aggrey House. The visit of Lord Lloyd only strengthened the Union's position and it used the occasion to present him with a lengthy address outlining student demands for greater democracy in West Africa, and for more Government finance for Africa House.[25]

The Colonial Office was prepared to grant some of WASU's requests for finance, but wished to use its patronage to put pressure on the students to co-operate over Aggrey House. However, there was less sympathy for the second part of WASU's address, which dealt with political demands for West Africa. The students presented Lord Lloyd with seventeen points for his 'consideration and recommendation', and stated that they believed that these represented 'the views, the feelings and the prayers of not only the members of WASU but also of our people in West Africa'.[26]

The Union's main political demand was for 'Dominion Status' for the West African colonies and for a rapid movement towards full adult suffrage in most colonies and protectorates in the region. In addition the Union advocated the development of the various 'Native Administrations' with a view to ultimately creating a 'Commonwealth of the West African Tribes to take its position as an independent unit in the British Commonwealth of free Nations'. The other demands included African majority representation on the legislative councils, and representation on the executive councils in the colonies; greater access for Africans to higher administrative posts; the same civil liberties as existed in Britain, including trade union rights; the introduction of compulsory elementary education and of military education in schools and colleges. The Union also advanced a number of social and economic demands including the establishment of agricultural and credit banks; an end to 'foreign combines' strangle-hold on the economic life of the native inhabitants'; preservation of African land tenure, and improvement of health and social services.[27]

There seems little doubt that the Union's demand for dominion status was prompted by a speech by Colonial Secretary Macdonald in February 1940, in which he had promised dominion status to India and later perhaps for other colonies. In the same month Cobina Kessie had controversially proposed that WASU should demand self-government for the West African colonies and fifty per cent Africanisation of government posts within five years, and form an organisation in Britain to work for this goal. It is therefore possible that the Address was very much a document of compromise.[28]

In its Address to Lord Lloyd the Union attempted to put pressure on the Colonial Office to make some declaration concerning the future of the West African colonies. One senior official thought that demands for dominion status were 'of course for the most part preposterous' but admitted that the Colonial Office had been considering changes in the African representation in the legislative and executive councils, in the higher ranks of the Colonial Service, and changes to the system of indirect rule. Officials maintained that WASU must be treated as a student body and not as a political one, and therefore could not expect a reply. However they recognised that they were in a difficult position, since Lord Lloyd had accepted the Address and because WASU had already been acknowledged as a political body when the Colonial Office had replied to its memorandum on price controls.[29]

The following year WASU was again able to exert pressure on the Colonial Office officials and government ministers. During the early part of 1941 the Union was visited by Sir Douglas Jardine, Governor of Sierra Leone, Sir Alan Burns, Governor of the Gold Coast, Sir Hanns Vischer and others, who were all subjected to the students' demands, while the Union also intensified its campaign for more funding from the West African governments. One of the most important visitors to Africa House in 1941 was the Deputy Prime Minister, Clement Attlee. His visit was widely reported in the press and was notable for his statements in support of increasing self-government in

Africa, which were a direct response to determined questioning by WASU. In its welcoming statement the Union asked what West Africa might gain after the war in recognition of its support for the Allies. In response Attlee stated:

> We in the Labour Party have always been conscious of the wrongs done by the white races to the races with darker skins. We have always demanded that the freedom which we claim for ourselves should be extended to all men. I look for an ever-increasing measure of self-government and political freedom in Africa and for an ever-rising standard of life for all the peoples of Africa. Out of this horror of war and destruction we shall come to a world of peace, security and social justice, not for one people, nor for one continent but for all the peoples of all the continents of the world.[30]

Attlee also commented on the Atlantic Charter recently signed by Churchill and Roosevelt, and announced to the students 'You will not find in the declarations made on behalf of the Government any suggestion that the freedom and social security for which we fight should be denied to any of the races of mankind'. The students were impressed. Attlee also stated that he was glad 'To see how, with the passing of the years, the old conception of Colonies as places inhabited by inferior people, whose function was only to serve and produce wealth for the benefit of other people, has made way for nobler and more just ideas'. The students commented that in the light of such 'sacred assurances', they were looking forward to advances throughout West Africa in recognition of war-time loyalty. Only a week later, Prime Minister Churchill shattered such hopes when he explained that references to self-determination in the Atlantic Charter, applied to Europe and not to the colonies.[31] It was in the midst of such controversy that WASU's Conference on African Problems took place at the end of August 1941.[32]

The conference was an important occasion in the evolution of the Union's political thinking and resulted in a number of significant resolutions concerned with political, educational, social, and economic reforms and the question of land rights and ownership. The main political resolutions echoed those presented to Lord Lloyd the previous year, and in general were concerned with introducing or extending representative democracy in the colonies. The Conference looked forward to 'a full-fledged Responsible Federal National Government as the ideal, legitimate, ultimate form of Government for West

Africa'.[33] The Conference also proposed the creation of a West African University, changes and modernisation of marriage and divorce laws; recommended greater economic development and planning; greater African involvement in the colonial service and a host of other reforms which would lead West Africa forward to self-government.[34] In addition to WASU members, conference speakers and participants included Dr Rita Hinden of the Fabian Colonial Bureau (FCB), Margery Perham, Sorensen and Bridgeman.[35]

Solanke sent copies of the conference resolutions to the West African press, legislative council members, traditional rulers, the West African governors and the various nationalist organisations. He thought that the resolutions were a way 'to educate people' and that 'special mass meetings' might be held in West Africa to 'register the people's views'. In a letter he explained:

> Our aim is to submit to the Government with intelligent co-operation of our people at home, constructive suggestions and demands for improvement in our present welfare at home. We intend to co-operate with the Government in the task of solving our various problems both at home and abroad ... What is uppermost in our minds (is) to see that all our Native Administrations in Nigeria are thoroughly democratised on modern lines with a view to making it possible within the next ten years to set up a United Nigeria under whatever form of democratic government may suit our cause then.[36]

Colonial Office officials also took a great interest in the conference resolutions, although they were careful not to encourage WASU to consider itself a representative political body. Officials found that the resolutions were 'interesting and perhaps significant', and 'in many ways encouraging'. Certainly there was a growing trend within the Colonial Office which viewed WASU's political aspirations with some sympathy, especially as they increasingly echoed official thinking. The discussions within official circles concerning post-war colonial policy were shifting attitudes and presenting the students with more favourable opportunities to present the views of nationalist opinion. The view of the Colonial Office is best summed up by F.J. Pedler (later chairman of the UAC) who wrote regarding WASU resolutions on Nigeria:

> The memorandum is interesting and seems mostly quite reasonable. The part on indirect rule in particular contains a lot of good stuff and most

of its conclusions are almost the same as those which Lord Hailey has drawn from his recent enquiries - not excluding the criticism of 'the autocratic and feudalistic form of government in the Northern Provinces'. It is most interesting to find this expression of educated, and mostly coastal, opinion supporting the native administration policy and arguing 'that the form and character of the native administrations in Nigeria be adopted as a model for all other native administrations wherever they may be established in West Africa'.[37]

The level of Colonial Office agreement with the WASU conference resolutions was clearly a step forward for the students, but perhaps emphasises how moderate their demands were. In November 1941 Sir Donald Cameron, the ex-Governor of Nigeria, paid a visit to Africa House and stated that he too was generally in agreement with the conference resolutions. WASU was also receiving continual support from Sorensen, Creech Jones and Listowel in Parliament.[38] Many sympathetic MPs agreed with Creech Jones that 'the voice of Africa must be heard and listened to in all development and reconstruction work', and with Listowel who stated: 'I am sure that this is the moment to draw up plans for the future of Africa, even if they cannot be put into operation until after the war'. In a letter to Solanke, Rita Hinden also recognised the wartime changes in 'the official attitude towards the Colonies', and urged the students to take advantage of them by pushing for the implementation of new Colonial Office policies.[39] In part this review of colonial policy had commenced during the late 1930s and had then received added momentum both from the rebellions in the Caribbean and the Report of the Moyne Commission, and the publication in 1938 of Lord Hailey's *An African Survey*. The outbreak of war meant that colonial policy had to be tailored not only to avoid disturbances in the colonies, but also to encourage support for the war effort. At the same time there was a need for changes to counter German propaganda and to prepare for the end of the war, when the colonial question would again come under close scrutiny. In addition, the economic and other needs of Britain might be assisted by development in the colonies, a fact which led in 1943 to the appointment of Lord Swinton as Minister Resident for West Africa. It was with regard to such issues that colonial policy was altered during the war, the first major change being the Colonial Development and Welfare Act of 1940. The loss of important colonies during the war years such as Malaya, Singapore and Burma, and pressure from the United States meant that colonial policy was constantly being redefined during these years. Not only were there these external pressures but also internal critics and reformers such as Lord Hailey and Sir Alan Burns. The result was a definite shift in policy at least some way towards increasing self-government and Africanisation.[40]

The Parliamentary Committee

There is evidence therefore that WASU enjoyed some official recognition, and was becoming accepted as a representative for certain West African interests; as such it was increasingly acting in the role of advisor to the Labour Party and the wartime coalition government. Whether or not WASU directly influenced the members of the FCB or the Government, it now found itself representing views which were not far removed from those expressed in official circles, and which therefore were not seen as a threat to the Empire. At the heart of this empire and with important contacts and supporters built up over many years, WASU was in an ideal position to take advantage of the changes in circumstances. In the autumn of 1941, following the successful conference, the Union established a regular fortnightly study group led by Robert Gardiner.[41] The study group aimed to keep the students informed of the latest economic, political and cultural developments in West Africa, through the presentation of researched discussion papers. As *West Africa* commented, these would also include useful information for the press, Colonial Office and general well-wishers, as well as providing vital information for WASU's friends in Parliament. While Gardiner saw the study group as fulfilling a crucial role of training 'well-informed men who can transform the aspirations of our age into ideas' and who could provide an African interpretation of events for the outside world.[42]

WASU was now also in a position to call on its supporters to put pressure on the Government. Solanke was able to involve the Anti-Slavery Society, the FCB, and MPs Creech Jones, Ben Riley and Sorensen in support of the demands of the Nigerian Civil Service Union for better conditions and salaries during 1941. As a result the basic salary of African clerks was raised and the Government agreed to appoint an independent commission for a comprehensive review of salaries and conditions of African civil servants. Sorensen was the most active of WASU's parliamentary supporters, asking a variety of questions concerning the West African colonies at every opportunity. Creech Jones and other sympathetic MPs also took part in the important House of Commons debate on colonial affairs at the end of November 1941, urging the Government to make those constitutional changes which the students and others were demanding.[43]

Throughout the war years WASU forged a close working relationship with those Labour MPs who were linked in some way to the FCB, the organisation whose membership provided many of the Labour Party's 'colonial specialists'. Solanke's regular meetings with Sorensen resulted in questions being raised in Parliament, and also directly with the Colonial Office, on all the issues of concern to the students and various interest groups in West Africa. In early 1942 the students began to discuss the idea of a West African Parliamentary Committee, which in a more organised way would act as a pressure group, bringing West African affairs and the deliberations of the Study Group before Parliament. However, WASU maintained that the Committee would be independent of the FCB, and 'would be free to determine its own policy while the WASU would from time to time present to the Committee through its representatives its own decisions on different questions and present from the very outset its own fundamental policy as regards West Africa's present and immediate future'.[44] The Parliamentary Committee was eventually launched in August 1942 and chaired by Sorensen, with F.O.B. Blaize, later a leading member of the National Council of Nigeria and the Cameroons (NCNC) as the first secretary. Its main aims were:

a) To consider current West African problems
b) To consider matters relating to the future of West Africa
c) To make such representations as are possible
d) To secure contact between bodies and persons concerned with West African democratic progress

The formation of the Committee again shows how influential WASU had become. It now had a formal link with representatives of the Labour Party, although other MPs were also welcome to join the Committee, and the means to work as an effective parliamentary pressure group in the heart of the Empire.[45]

Self-government now

In April 1942 WASU sent a new resolution to the Under-Secretary of State for the Colonies, Harold Macmillan stating:

> In the interests of Freedom, Justice and true Democracy and in view of the lessons of Malaya and Burma, as well as the obvious need of giving the peoples of the Empire something to fight for, WASU in Great Britain strongly urges the British Government to grant to the British West African Colonies and protectorates INTERNAL SELF-GOVERNMENT NOW, with a DEFINITE GUARANTEE OF COMPLETE SELF-GOVERNMENT WITHIN FIVE YEARS AFTER THE WAR. We are convinced that only a realistic approach and generous gesture on the part of the Imperial Government Now can save the Empire from collapse.[46] (capitals in original)

It appears that Gardiner, Solanke and some others within WASU ranks had adopted a more cautious approach to the question of self-government and had opposed the resolution. Other West Africans in Britain, such as the Edinburgh Africa Association, were concerned that they had not been consulted before such a resolution was submitted to the Government, while the newly formed West African Students' Club at Cambridge felt compelled to inform the Union: 'We feel convinced that Internal Self-Government is not our immediate need, and we would not therefore support any demands for immediate Internal Self-Government for the West African dependencies'.[47]

In West Africa the resolution also met with a mixed reception. One student at Fourah Bay College, wrote to Gardiner that:

> Some of us here especially the Gold Coast students have been following with interest the activities of WASU in England on behalf of West Africa. We were particularly struck to hear of your recent resolution to the British Government asking for immediate self-government and complete independence within five years after the war. That same spirit which stirs you up to these exploits animates us also and some of us have been considering how best we can support your move and thereby help towards the upliftment of our country.[48]

While in an editorial, Azikiwe's *West African Pilot* criticised the resolution for being vague, disagreed about the time factor, and suggested that the entire statement be clarified. There followed a frank exchange of opinions between WASU and Azikiwe, but the whole episode shows the diversity of opinions which existed amongst West Africans.[49]

In the pages of *West Africa* and the *West African Review* the resolution sparked off a further debate, but WASU reaffirmed its position:

> We stand firmly by our Resolution. We are convinced that we deserve it and should get it. We say again that freedom is indivisible and should not be denied to us. The 'NEW WORLD' should be one of Justice, Freedom and a Better Life, not only for Europe but for other peoples as well; and West Africa demands a share in the amenities of that 'New World' for the making of which she is sacrificing so much in this war in monetary contributions, valuable war material, even forced labour, and what is more, the precious lives of so many of her sons in the Army and Air Force.[50]

The Colonial Office declined to respond, but Sorensen arranged for Harold Macmillan to visit Africa House for discussions with WASU. F.J. Pedler of the Colonial Office also paid a visit to the Union and reported how the members did not seem to him 'to be in any way unreasonable on the political side'.[51]

The Colonial Office perception of WASU was that they were less of a threat than they had been during the 1930s. Indeed the Union's policy of increasingly relying on Government finance and the change in the Colonial Office's attitude to social and political reforms in West Africa, may have led some officials to underestimate WASU's influence. However, Solanke wanted, as J.L. Keith remarked, the best of both worlds for the Union - financial support *and* political independence from the Government. Solanke and the Union had performed this juggling act for many years. One WASU Annual Report declared:

> West Africa is ripe for INTERNAL SELF-GOVERNMENT... Furthermore the more adequately the people of West Africa finance WASU the more efficient and the more stable will its independence become and the more able will its hands be strengthened to fight for the independence not only of itself but also of the whole of West Africa for the betterment of all our people in that country.[52]

However in *Wasu* the Report was followed by the publication of a letter from the United Africa Company, which included a cheque for

100 guineas. The letter curiously and paradoxically stated that the value of the Union lay in the fact that it was financed and managed by Africans!

WASU stayed on the offensive throughout their second annual conference at the end of August 1942, which was chaired by Sorensen and addressed by Creech Jones, Haden-Guest, Rita Hinden, Arthur Lewis, and Kenneth Little, as well as members of the Union. The resolutions of the previous year, including the demand for immediate internal self-government, were reaffirmed, and a number of calls were made to the Government to openly state its war aims and to clarify former declarations regarding the Atlantic Charter. Individual papers were presented regarding education, economic and social problems, colour prejudice and land tenure, and following discussion appropriate resolutions were adopted.[53]

Once again it is interesting to note the significant role played by the Labour Party during this conference. Sorensen in his opening remarks declared that the war was being fought for a democracy that was indivisible. He stated, 'Accepting democracy as our criterion, we reject racial domination and economic exploitation alike and proceed to discover how best in the West African colonies it can be advanced and its political problems solved'.[54] R.W. Beoku-Betts, the president of WASU, expressed the views of many of the students when he remarked that after nearly a hundred years of British rule, West Africa still had problems of illiteracy, poverty and disease. He contrasted the situation in West Africa to that in the Soviet Union which, he argued, showed that illiteracy was not a difficult problem to combat. He concluded that if an Allied victory meant a continuation of British rule, West Africa could not expect a bright future.

'Home from home': discrimination and accommodation

WASU's Africa House was still one of the few hostels open in London to black people, and even the Colonial Office was forced to use it to house munitions workers and others temporarily resident in Britain during the war. In October 1942 Solanke addressed a party of West African technicians who were visiting London, and pointed out that West Africans were not fighting for their own countries. He explained 'nowhere will men work or fight as they might, unless they are free, unless they govern themselves as freely as the British govern themselves'.[55] The issue of why West Africans were contributing to the war effort was especially important at this time, since the attitude of the British public to their colonial allies and the effects of the colour bar were again under the spotlight, as was the treatment of Africans in the colonies. In a war ostensibly fought against the doctrines of racial hatred, the British and Allied governments had to convince the colonies that they held the moral high ground. As colonial powers they already had a difficult task, but this could only be made worse by Government or individual acts of racial prejudice. In 1942 the Colonial Office Public Relations Department was established to provide propaganda for the colonies and wide publicity was given to the Government appointments of the Jamaican Una Marson and Sierra Leonean Ivor Cummings as examples of the absence of the colour bar in Britain. The whole issue of discrimination and the colour bar was discussed in detail in the Colonial Office. Legislation was ruled out, but officials felt that more public education might be the answer and acknowledged that previous government policy both in Britain and the colonies was largely to blame.[56]

WASU continued to campaign against the colour bar in Britain and West Africa. In 1942 it acted on behalf of Olive Johnson, a former member of the Union and Dr M.A. Majekodunmi, formerly a medical student in Dublin, who subsequently became Minister of State in Nigeria's first post-independence government. Olive Johnson had been refused a nursing appointment in her native Sierra Leone because of 'lack of personality and character'. Dr Majekodunmi had been appointed but denied the advertised salary for a post in Nigeria. Both had British qualifications. The Colonial Office denied that any discrimination had taken place, but WASU pursued the two cases, gaining support from Lord Listowel and others, and finally both gained satisfactory appointments. In alliance with the LCP, WASU also involved itself in the case of the black munitions workers who were facing discrimination at the Royal Ordnance Factory at Fazakerley near Liverpool.

At this time WASU was very much a base and 'home from home' for African and Caribbean service personnel, munitions workers, health workers and others as well as African students throughout the British Isles, who used it as a postal address, cultural centre and restaurant. One student wrote to Solanke that he did not realise the full meaning of WASU until he came to Britain and faced the 'feelings of the despondency of social outcasts'. WASU also acted as a contact point for the many West African prisoners of war and servicemen and women stationed all over the world. Solanke personally received letters from captured West African airmen and from the POW Department of the Red Cross. The Union also maintained close links with the BBC, and many of the students participated in wartime broadcasts to West Africa.[57]

Solanke was always concerned to defend the dignity of those West Africans who were contributing to the war effort. In the autumn of 1942, for example, he protested about an article in the journal *Flight* entitled 'RAF in West Africa', which stated: 'It has to be admitted that West Africans are about the laziest people in the world'. Solanke wrote to the journal, which subsequently apologised, and to other publications bitterly attacking such reporting, detailing the sacrifices that were being made and stressing that, as he and other Africans saw it, 'our country is not ours' and yet Africans were still making major contributions for an Allied victory.

Early in 1943 WASU became concerned about the immediate threat of conscription of 'the colonial peoples temporarily resident in Great Britain', which it felt was implied in a speech made by Ernest Bevin, the Minister of Labour and National Service. The Union's resolution on the matter was sent to the Colonial Secretary and the press. The resolution asserted that WASU felt 'a people's government [was] a necessary prerequisite for popular conscription', and that 'in the interests of justice, democracy and freedom', the Government should grant the West African colonies 'internal responsible self-government now, as well as make the Atlantic Charter directly applicable to them', in order to 'make the people fully conscious of what they are fighting for and heighten their morale, while making the conscription both popular and effective'. A few weeks later however the Colonial Office was able to reassure the students that subjects from British colonies including students were still exempt from conscription. Nevertheless WASU continued to use every opportunity to press home its demands for self-government and to stress that West Africa's sacrifices during the war must be rewarded if the war was genuinely being fought for freedom and democracy.[58]

As always the colour bar was a constant reminder of the second-class citizenship enjoyed by Africans both in Britain and throughout the Empire. The discrimination faced by African professionals when seeking employment was just one such reminder, as was the exclusion of students from local dance halls and hotels. Racism was firmly entrenched in British society and necessitated a constant struggle. At the end of 1943 WASU complained, without success, to Agatha Christie and the Colonial Office about the title of the book *Ten Little Niggers*. Indeed throughout that year the problem of the colour bar and discrimination received more and more publicity. The LCP had also demanded action following an infamous incident when Learie Constantine, at that time in the employ of the Ministry of Labour, was barred from a London hotel.[59] A joint LCP/WASU delegation visited the Colonial Office in mid-1943 and proposed the creation of an 'Anglo-Colonial Committee', to include representatives of government, the churches and the media, which might act to deal with the problem of the racism and the colour bar. The Colonial Office disliked the idea, and despite questions in Parliament and demands by Reginald Sorensen MP for changes in the law, no new steps were taken.

One of the major campaigns waged by the Union concerned the film *Men of Two Worlds* and its subject matter, the struggle between the modern and the traditional in an African society. The idea for the film originated in the Colonial Office and was being promoted by the Ministry of Information as propaganda about colonial rule. WASU was only invited to comment on the script when they refused to assist in finding African actresses. The script had however already been approved by both the Colonial Office and the Ministry of Information. For WASU the subject matter of the film and the prominence given to 'Witch-doctors' only encouraged greater prejudice which they resolved to correct, and a resolution calling for the film to be re-written or scrapped was sent to both the Colonial Office and the Ministry of Information. Subsequently Solanke entered into a lengthy correspondence with the film's director and perhaps partly due to WASU's criticisms, some changes were eventually made. For the Colonial Office however, the Union's complaints were entirely unacceptable not least because, as one official put it, they would if accepted have given the film 'an anti-imperialist tinge'.[60]

West African organisations

Because of the important role that the students were able to play during the war years WASU did all it could to unite other African students' organisations throughout the British Isles, and to build unity between these groups and nationalists in West Africa. Students returning to

West Africa were encouraged to remain politically active where possible, and to seek to join organisations such as the Nigerian Union of Students, which in 1939 referred to itself as the 'Local branch of WASU', and by 1942 was officially affiliated to WASU, as was the Sierra Leone Students' Union. It seems that many younger people in West Africa looked as much to the organisations in Britain, especially WASU, as they did to the youth movements in West Africa, for leadership and inspiration.[61]

The Edinburgh Africa Association was one of the organisations in close contact with WASU, principally through its energetic vice-president J.C. de Graft Johnson.[62] In 1941 Solanke had invited the Association to join WASU, and had argued that the times demanded that 'all West African students all over this country should make themselves one in only one effective organisation'; de Graft Johnson favoured such unity but opposition from the large number of students from the Gold Coast, who had their own separate association in Edinburgh and who were wary of the Nigerian dominated WASU, prevented the realisation of Solanke's plans.

WASU member Cobina Kessie had been known to favour the unification of the various organisations as early as 1940, and it seems he made some attempts in this direction through the short-lived Africa League. In 1943 the Sierra Leonean Dr Robert Wellesley Cole proposed a 'West Africa Committee of Great Britain and Ireland' which he thought might even include organisations in West Africa, and which could represent Africans in their contact with the media and publish its own non-political journal. Indeed in the same year Wellesley Cole and Irene Cole formed the Newcastle-based Society for the Cultural Advancement of Africa, which despite its name immediately declared that one of its objects was 'the ventilation of the constitutional and other reforms advocated by the Gold Coast Youth Movement'.[63] Also in 1943, de Graft Johnson urged the establishment of a 'Society for Peoples of African Descent' along the same line as the Dublin based ASAD, to unite all black people in the Britain Isles. However, nothing much seems to have come of these plans, and as the GCSA was generally inactive, WASU continued to act as the main African pressure group in Britain.[64]

The Colonial Office also took an interest in the student organisations outside London. In 1939 Ivor Cummings had attempted to establish an 'Aggrey House' in Edinburgh. During the early years of the war the Victoria League was encouraged to make contact with the students in Edinburgh and the Colonial Office also supported efforts to establish a colonial students' club in the city. Reports that there was 'strong colour prejudice at Edinburgh' led them to intensify their activity, as African students reported that conditions might 'one day embitter the relationship between Black and White', and thus damage the attitudes of future African leaders. As a result of war-time conditions the Colonial Office also established relations with the African and Caribbean members of the Dublin based ASAD. Of the thirty members of this organisation formed in the early 1930s, twenty-six were West Africans. The war cut them off both from Britain and financial support from West Africa and they felt stranded and isolated in Dublin. In 1940 J.A. Wachuku, on behalf of the ASAD, appealed to the Colonial Office for help, with the aim of establishing an 'Africa House' in Dublin, but little government assistance was given.[65]

In early 1943 WASU was visited by the Colonial Secretary, Colonel Oliver Stanley, who was presented with the customary WASU address, to which he promised to reply. The Union again demanded internal self-government, drew attention to the new concept of 'partnership' between colonial subjects and their governors and questioned how it was applied in practice since Africans were still being discriminated against when applying for jobs in West Africa. On this occasion Solanke had consulted with, or at least informed other West African students throughout the country. As a result they asked WASU to incorporate their own questions and concerns in the address. The West African Students' Club at Cambridge sent Solanke a number of political demands to put to the Colonial Secretary and in addition asked for a party of West African journalists to visit Britain at the Government's expense, to report on the war effort. The ASAD in Dublin asked Solanke to put their own resolutions to the Secretary of State, including the demand for more research facilities to investigate traditional African science and culture.

The links between WASU and other organisations continued to grow throughout the war years, and despite the Colonial Office's best efforts, the Union was widely seen as a representative body. Indeed the visits to WASU by leading politicians only served to enhance the Union's status and reputation. It had established relations with organisations in the United States including the African Students' Association, and in Britain had links with a wide range of organisations, such as the African Provident Society, the African News Agency and the Liverpool-based Negro Welfare Centre, the International

Coloured Mutual Aid Association in North Shields, *The Negro Citizen* in Birmingham, and the Coloured Colonial Improvement Association in London. WASU was also in contact with the International Friendship League, Common Wealth, the International Youth Council and many others. In September 1943, *West African Review* spoke of the Union as 'the nearest approach there is to a British West Africa High Commission in London', and stressed, 'WASU is of the people and the people will listen to it. This puts a responsibility on its shoulders'.[66]

WASU and West African nationalism

As well as its links with organisations in Britain, WASU naturally maintained strong contacts with individuals and organisations in West Africa, such as Wallace Johnson's West African Youth League, and workers' and farmers' associations throughout the region, especially those in Nigeria. Visitors or ex-members returning to West Africa were often sent with instructions and messages aimed at increasing the effectiveness of the nationalist movements. As well as its links with student unions, the Union acted as the UK representative of the Nigerian Union of Teachers, at that time the largest union in Nigeria, and the Sierra Leone branch of the NCBWA. Solanke personally corresponded with many of these organisations. He encouraged the Nigerian Union of Students (NUS) to extend its activities to Northern Nigeria and to work with the Nigerian Youth Movement (NYM), and he encouraged the Sierra Leone branch of the NCBWA to resuscitate the other West African branches. Solanke also wrote to H.O. Davies to try to get the NYM to co-operate with the NUS and WASU, and to Nnamdi Azikiwe, Obafemi Awolowo and others to try and establish some unity amongst Nigeria's nationalist politicians. Some ignored WASU's agitation, while the Sultan of Sokoto and other Northern Nigerian rulers completely rejected the 1941 WASU conference resolutions, and voiced their objections to people living overseas making such suggestions, which they considered were made in ignorance by those who knew nothing of local traditions. Awolowo summed up the views of many in West Africa, when in 1943 he wrote to Solanke of his 'unqualified admiration' for WASU, but admitted, 'We at home have neither the unity, nor the will to make heavy sacrifices, both of which are indispensable if our demand for self-government is to be seriously respected by our overlords ... it is going to be a very tough fight in our case to win freedom'.[67]

In August 1943 eight West African newspaper editors, including Azikiwe, visited Britain as the guests of the British Council. The visit had been organised by the Colonial Office and the Ministry of Information with the aim of pacifying the West African intelligentsia, and presenting a favourable picture of Britain and the work being undertaken by West African wartime volunteers. However, the Colonial Office found that they soon ran into a number of problems, including the prejudices of leading hoteliers who refused to accommodate the delegation of 'somewhat primitive people'. Naturally the delegation spent a lot of their free time with WASU and on a number of occasions appeared to echo the Union's political views. Indeed the demand for self-government was almost commonplace amongst West Africans by this time, partly as a consequence of the stand taken by WASU. At a WASU reception for the editors, Bankole Awooner-Renner delivered a powerful speech demanding freedom for West Africa and denouncing indirect rule, and reminded the delegation of the racial discrimination that was still practised in Britain.[68] At the official opening of the visit, one of the editors, T.J.D. Thompson of the *Freetown Daily Mail*, had called for a 'speedier move on towards self-government'. At the end of their visit the editors produced a joint memorandum which called for internal self-government in West Africa for 10 years, 'responsible government' for 5 years and then dominion status. The editors claimed that the memorandum was based on Clause 3 of the Atlantic Charter - the right of self-determination - and quoted British politicians such as Creech Jones, Sorensen and Haden-Guest, as well as Lord Hailey to support their demands. But as Azikiwe later acknowledged, it was the ideas of WASU and in particular the resolution of 1942 which had a significant influence on what he referred to as 'the national consciousness already generating in Nigeria and the Cameroons'.[69]

The second mission to West Africa

At the beginning of 1944 WASU was incorporated into a Limited Company. Its directors included: Lord Listowel, as chairman, Sorensen, Canon H.M. Grace, ex-principal of Achimota College and secretary of the Council of Missionary Societies of Great Britain and Ireland, Solanke, and Robert Wellesley Cole. The main reason for the incorporation was to enable the Union to take legal control of Africa

House, as the dispute with the CWAE had been finally settled. The Union had agreed to pay the outstanding mortgage on the property, and to accept the appointment by the Colonial Secretary of Lord Listowel as one of two trustees.

However, no sooner had the Union extricated itself from one entanglement than it plunged itself into another. The new threat came from the Anglo-African Committee (AAC) of the Missionary Council of the Church of England, better known because of its chairman, as the Dean of Westminster's Committee. For some time the AAC had expressed concern about the welfare of African students in London. It now proposed an African student centre in London under Christian auspices, and made its intentions known to the Advisory Committee on the Welfare of Coloured Peoples in the United Kingdom (ACWUK), the body established in 1942 by the Welfare Department of the Colonial Office, in order to deal with the influx of Caribbean and African workers and service personnel during the war years. Canon Grace, an active member of the AAC, with the assistance of Robert Gardiner, another member of the Committee, had already presented some of the Church's opinions in a small publication entitled *The African Student in England*. Grace and Gardiner had explained: 'It is not quite true to say that if you win the African student you win his people; but it is quite true to say if you don't win the student you will be faced with almost insuperable difficulties'.[70]

Their plan therefore was that Church and State should work together to ensure the co-operation of future African leaders and to counter the effects of the colour bar. They felt that the Church could help, as many students were nominally Christians, and that they might work with and through WASU. The Church was also concerned that it was losing its influence in West Africa, so that courting future leaders was in its own self-interest.

The Colonial Office was initially wary of the overtures from the AAC, which it thought might disrupt its own relationship with the students. This attitude meant that ultimately the AAC dealt directly with WASU and eventually, in 1944, came to an agreement with the students to help raise money for a new hostel. The AAC hoped that they would have the assistance not only of committee member Robert Gardiner, but also other 'steady Christians' within WASU. Negotiations led to a plan for a new centre which might include both a chapel and a chaplain. The AAC would also assist the Union by launching a fund-raising appeal. From WASU's perspective this was seen simply as another revenue source to be tapped. Solanke had also for some time been contemplating launching a second fund-raising trip to West Africa. The decision to undertake such a mission was agreed by the new directors in March 1944, and links with the AAC and their fund-raising in Britain fitted well into these plans, although Sorensen warned Solanke about becoming too dependent on the AAC. WASU hoped that its appeal to raise £50,000 could be realised within six months, but in the event Solanke and his wife spent almost four years in West Africa, during some of the Union's most active and also most difficult years.[71]

There is no doubt that WASU played an important role during the war years. It had a closer and often beneficial relationship with the Colonial Office, and was widely recognised in Britain as representing West African opinion. Its West African Parliamentary Committee was able to question and influence government ministers on a wide variety of topics, and to consolidate the links between West Africans and the future Labour government. It also acted as a training ground for the students, a place where 'Young West Africans - the future leaders of their country - who regularly attend the Committee quietly and systematically learn a good deal . . . to qualify them the better for the future work of good leadership in the development of their country and people'.[72] Perhaps most importantly WASU, through its resolutions and publications acted as a constant reminder to all that the demands for self-government and an end to colonial rule in West Africa must and would intensify as the war came to an end. In 1944, for example, Solanke together with H.O. Davies and Akinola Maja, two of the leaders of the NYM, sent a cablegram to Azikiwe in Nigeria, calling on him and other politicians to gain the support of the Nigerian people and send a declaration to the British government demanding immediate internal self-government and dominion status within fifteen years. Similar demands, following discussions with WASU had already been expressed by Sorensen in Parliament. For the students, what they referred to as 'acquisition of political power by the people' was 'the right key to the solution of all problems in West Africa'.[73]

Notes

1. Such demands were normally made by organisations such as the LAI, led by or connected with the international communist movement. For an

example of radical student demands see J. W. de Graft Johnson, 'After India – What?', *Elders' Review*, April 1930, p49.
2. *West Africa*, 11 February 1939, p158 and 11 March 1939, p292.
3. L. Solanke, 'WASU Xmas and New Year's Address', 26 December 1939, SOL 58/8.
4. Solanke to Ernest Ikoli, 10 November 1941, SOL 57/5.
5. Olusanya, *op.cit.*, pp50-51.
6. For student views see e.g. *Wasu*, 6/2, p63 and p66; H.O. Davies, *West African Review*, December 1937, p24 and W.E. Ofori Atta, *ibid.*, March 1938, p12.
7. Laminah Sankoh had been a founder member of the NCBWA. In 1949 he founded the People's Party in Sierra Leone and later became the vice-president of Milton Margai's Sierra Leone People's Party.
8. WASU to the Under-Secretary of State for the Colonies, 5 October 1939, SOL 58. This was not the first occasion on which Jones had faced discrimination. See. K. Little, *Negroes in Britain*, Kegan Paul, London 1947, p257 and pp263-4.
9. *West Africa*, 28 October 1939, p1452. For a further case of alleged discrimination in the London ARP see the *Daily Mail*, 3 May 1941, p3. For details of other West Africans in the ARP see *LCP Newsletter*, June 1941, pp57-9.
10. In fact Keith admitted that the policies pursued by the Home Office, Colonial Office and Trades Unions had led to 'segregation in Cardiff and Liverpool and to general prejudice against colonial subjects who were regarded as unwanted aliens'. J.L. Keith memo, 11 December 1941, PRO CO 859/80/7. See also *LCP Newsletter*, August 1941.
11. *West Africa*, 11 November 1939, p1506, and *LCP Newsletter, ibid*. Various forms of discrimination continued in the armed services and elsewhere throughout the war, see e.g. M. Sherwood, *Many Struggles: West Indian Workers and Service Personnel in Britain (1939-45)*, Karia Press, London 1985.
12. E.g. *The Nigerian Eastern Mail*, 16 November 1940.
13. Vischer to J.L. Keith, 17 April 1940, PRO CO 859/21/1.
14. See e.g. the *Evening Standard*, 4 May 1940, p9, *West Africa*, 28 August 1940, p868 and the *Daily Worker*, 6 May 1940.
15. J.L. Keith note, 26 June 1940, PRO CO 859/21/1.
16. J.L. Keith memos, 21 May and 27 June 1940 and CO to Ministry of Information, 14 May 1940, *ibid*. At this time the CPGB was totally opposed to the continuation of the war. See S. Howe, *Anti-Colonialism in British Politics – The Left and the End of Empire 1918-1964*, Clarendon Press, Oxford 1993, p119.

17. L. Solanke, 'Moral Issue Closes Club', 6 May 1940, SOL 58.
18. Colonial Secretary to WASU, 24 March 1941, PRO CO 859/43/7.
19. *Wasu*, 8/1, May 1941, p2.
20. The students had been concerned about these issues for some years. See e.g. H.O. Davies, 'West Africa's Greatest Asset – A Contented Peasantry', *West African Review*, October 1935, p46.
21. Nathaniel Akinremi Fadipe, a Nigerian, had been involved with WASU since the mid 1930s. From that time until his untimely death in 1944 he was a prolific writer and propagandist for the Union and one of Solanke's closest co-workers. During the 1940s he was employed by the UAC, following the completion of his doctorate on the Yoruba language at London University. Some of Fadipe's earliest published articles were concerned with South Africa, and in the 1930s he also wrote articles condemning the Italian invasion of Ethiopia. He was for a time closely connected with Aggrey House, but he also worked closely with Padmore, Buckle and Blackman.

    During the 1940s Fadipe collaborated with Solanke drafting various Union memoranda, conference papers and resolutions. In 1940 he drafted WASU's memorandum to the Government on the 'price-fixing' of West African commodities, and his work seems to suggest that he was one of WASU's main theorists, but one who clearly was by no means a radical nor even a Union member. From Fadipe's articles and letters as well as his obituaries it is clear that he exerted something of a moderating influence on the younger and often more radical WASU members.
22. *Wasu*, 7/1, May 1940, pp14-15.
23. *Wasu*, 8/1, May 1941, p2 and PRO CO 852/349/1.
24. *Wasu*, 7/1, May 1940, p9 and p16.
25. 'WASU Address to Lord Lloyd', 29 August 1940, PRO CO 859/21/3. The visit and Address were widely reported in the British press and in West Africa. See e.g. Olusanya, *op.cit.*, p122 note 6.
26. 'WASU Address' *op.cit*. The Union was, for example, openly supported by many of the traditional rulers of the Gold Coast. *WASU*, 8/1, May 1941, p2.
27. 'WASU Address' *op cit*.
28. *West Africa*, 24 February 1940, p164 and Coker to Solanke, 4 February 1940, SOL 15/5.
29. PRO CO 554/125/17.
30. Olusanya, *op.cit.*, p52.
31. *West Africa*, 23 August 1941, p818. The Atlantic Charter's third clause stated that the Allies were fighting to ensure 'the right of all peoples to

choose the form of government under which they will live'. Churchill's subsequent statement only served to intensify anti-colonial sentiment throughout the war, and in Britain led to various demands for a 'charter for colonial people'.

32. Olusanya, *op.cit.*, p52.
33. 'WASU Resolutions of the Conference on West African Problems', August 1941, SOL 58. In particular the conference called for a united federal government in Nigeria, the first time such a demand was made.
34. The demand for a West African university had first been raised by Edward Blyden at the turn of the century and periodically resurfaced as a demand of West African nationalists including the NCBWA. In 1939 the conference of West African Governors had also recommended the establishment of such a university.
35. *West Africa*, 27 September 1941, p935. According to the press reports there were some fifty or sixty participants at the conference.
36. Solanke to O.A. Alakija, 7 October 1941, SOL 6/7.
37. F.J. Pedler minute, 14 October 1941, PRO CO 554/130/7.
38. In 1940 Sorensen declared to the students: 'I elect myself to be one of the speakers in the House of Commons not only of your grievances but also of your aspirations... I want to see the time when West Africans will be able to govern themselves'. *West Africa*, 29 June 1940, p649.
39. WASU maintained close links with the FCB and Rita Hinden in particular, and WASU members were regular speakers at FCB conferences. In 1942 WASU and the Nigerian Civil Servants' Union were both invited to join the FCB, an offer which seems to have been declined.
40. R.D. Pearce, *The Turning Point in Africa: British Colonial Policy, 1938-48*, Frank Cass, London 1982. During the war major political changes, including universal adult suffrage, were already being introduced in Jamaica.
41. Robert Kweku Atta Gardiner became Ghana's Ambassador to the UN and head of Ghana's civil service. In 1941 he was a student at New College, Oxford, and had formerly studied at Achimota College and at Selwyn College, Cambridge, where he had been president of the students' union. He soon became Solanke's confidante and an influential member of WASU, but also worked closely with the Colonial Office, where some officials credited him with 'improvements at WASU'. In December 1941 he wrote to J.L. Keith, 'I think I can get WASU to make a move but would like to know which moves you would consider desirable'. Gardiner to Keith, 9 December 1941, PRO CO 859/43/7.
42. R.K.A. Gardiner, 'WASU New Year's Message', 30 December 1941, SOL 58. Several MPs and members of the Government, Conservative and

Labour, participated in the study group meetings. Olusanya, *op.cit.*, pp65-66.
43. *West African Pilot*, 25 February 1942, p2. See also Olusanya, *op.cit.*, pp63-64.
44. F.O.B. Blaize to Solanke, 1 April 1942, SOL 71/4.
45. Olusanya, *op.cit.*, pp66-68. Members included Labour MPs Creech Jones, Haden-Guest, Ben Riley, David Adams and Rita Hinden of the FCB. See also *Wasu*, 12/1, March 1945, pp21–22.
46. WASU Resolution, 4 April 1942, PRO CO 554/127/33544. This would appear to be the first time such a demand for self-government in West Africa had been made.
47. G. Oddoye to Solanke, 3 January 1943. The West African Students' Club formed in 1942, was suggested by Mrs Olu Solanke and the English sociologist Kenneth Little, to 'act as a medium of co-operation and exchange of views between Africans and Europeans'.
48. A.A. Kyerematen to Gardiner, 25 May 1942, PRO CO 876/56. It is interesting to note that the Colonial Office found it necessary to intercept and read Gardiner's mail.
49. PRO CO 554/127. The exchange of telegrams between WASU and Azikiwe was intercepted by the Nigerian government.
50. F.O.B. Blaize, 'Internal Self-Government Now', *West Africa*, 29 August 1942, p836. One supporter of the Resolution was the Communist MP William Gallaher.
51. F.J. Pedler minute, 16 June 1942, PRO CO 876/56.
52. *Wasu*, 11/1, June 1944.
53. Colonial Office officials noted that WASU's economic demands were very similar to the proposals made by Lord Swinton, the cabinet minister responsible for the West African Colonies.
54. Olusanya, *op.cit.*, p53.
55. *West Africa*, 17 October 1942, p1010.
56. PRO CO 859/80/7.
57. On West African participation in the RAF see R. Lambo, 'Achtung! The Black Prince: West Africans in the RAF, 1939-46', in D. Killingray (ed.) *Africans in Britain*, Frank Cass, London 1994, pp145-63. Some twenty-five WASU members joined the RAF.
58. *West Africa*, 20 February 1943, p144.
59. P. Fryer, *op.cit.*, pp364-67.
60. PRO CO 876/78. WASU was also critical of other Colonial Office inspired films such as *Primitive People* and *An African in London*.
61. The Nigerian Union of Students rapidly became one of the most influen-

tial nationalist organisations in Nigeria. In 1944 it played a leading role in uniting various organisations in the National Council of Nigeria and the Camerouns (NCNC), the main Nigerian nationalist organisation of the early post-war period.

62. J.C. de Graft Johnson was also, in 1948, president of the Gold Coast Students' Union in Britain. Subsequently he had a distinguished academic career and was Ghana's ambassador to the EC.
63. *West Africa*, 27 February 1943, p167. The Association also campaigned against discrimination in employment in West Africa.
64. In 1940 Solanke also made attempts to establish a WASU branch in Bristol.
65. Jaja Wachuku became Minister of Economic Development in Nigeria's first post-independence government in 1960.
66. *West African Review*, September 1943, p9.
67. Awolowo to Solanke, 5 August 1943, SOL 9/10. See also Olusanya, *op.cit.*, pp50-51.
68. See Appendix. Awooner-Renner was co-founder with Wallace Johnson of the militant West African Youth League, from 1942-44 he was a councillor on the Accra Town Council.
69. N. Azikiwe, *The Development of Political Parties in Nigeria*, Office of the Commissioner for the Eastern Region of Nigeria, London 1957.
70. See PRO CO 876/23.
71. Olusanya, *op.cit.*, pp69-74.
72. *Wasu*, 11/1, June 1944, p6.
73. *Ibid.*, p20 and N. Azikiwe, *op.cit.*, pp12-13.

Africanisation and Radicalisation: Cold War Responses 1945–49

The period from the end of the war until the early 1950s was one of the most significant for WASU and West African students in Britain. After the war there were increasingly large numbers of students entering Britain, partly due to the 'Africanisation' of local government and need for trained personnel in West Africa, which added to the strength of the student organisations. A number of students who were already politically active entered Britain from the United States and from West Africa itself, and linked students in Britain even more closely with the growing nationalist movements in West Africa.

Naturally after the sacrifices of the war years and vague government promises, there were also the growing expectations in West Africa and among the student-politicians in Britain, that political changes would be made in the colonies. Those who had joined the forces were particularly determined to end colonial rule. One soldier from the Gold Coast who had fought in Burma wrote, 'We have fought against fascism, the enemy of mankind, so that all people, white or black, civilised or uncivilised, free or in bondage, may have the right to enjoy the privileges and bounties of nature'.[1] Self-government, in some form, was still the goal and it was widely believed that the new Labour government would be sympathetic to colonial aspirations. The students with their close links to Creech Jones and the Fabians must have felt that they were in a position to influence government thinking. However, early post-war pronouncements led many of the students to lose patience with the Government. They became convinced that more radical measures were needed to achieve the end of colonial rule, solutions that only seemed to be offered by communism or a Marxist influenced Pan-Africanism.

Africanisation and Radicalisation

The leftwards shift in the politics of WASU might also have been facilitated by the absence of the Solankes who remained in West Africa on their fund raising mission until 1948. However, this was also a period of splits in the Union's ranks and of growing competition from other organisations. Political divisions in West Africa, especially in Nigeria, readily transferred themselves to Britain and led to the creation of student and other organisations based around distinct nationalities. The idea of West African nationhood, however, also reached its apogee with the formation of the West African National Secretariat (WANS). Also increasingly prominent were student organisations that limited their membership to those from a single colony and which agitated, although often in concert, for political reforms within one colony.

One of the most fundamental changes after 1945 was the increase in the number of West African students, including women, in Britain. J.L. Keith, of the Colonial Office, reported that before the war there were only four hundred colonial students in Britain. By 1945 this figure had risen to over a thousand, about two thirds of whom came from Africa, the vast majority of these were West African, (mostly from Nigeria and the Gold Coast) only sixty five students came from East Africa. Not only were there more West Africans, they also studied at more universities and colleges and were therefore not just to be found at the old established Oxbridge colleges, or at London, Edinburgh and Durham. Many more students were deciding not to study the traditional law or medicine, so there were also many more scientists, engineers and teachers.[2] For the Colonial Office, finding additional accommodation, while trying to contend with the colour bar, became even more important as student numbers grew rapidly. By 1948 there were over 1000 West African students in the country; and the Colonial Office Welfare Department found it necessary to open new student hostels in London, Cambridge, Edinburgh and Newcastle and to appoint liaison officers to deal with the influx. The Colonial Office even considered trying to limit the numbers of West African students who entered Britain, especially because of the usual fears of students becoming contaminated by real and imagined subversive influences.

WASU on the other hand welcomed what it called 'the invasion of the UK by West African students', and in the Union's Annual Report for 1945 claimed that its membership had increased over the previous year from thirty to one hundred, while the larger numbers of students outside London, led to the Union appointing its own liaison officers to maintain communications.³ Solanke's absence did little to diminish the Union's activities nor the personality and political clashes between its members. From 1944-45 the Union campaigned over a range of issues including the case of Phillip Berry, a black ex-seamen who was condemned to death in March 1945 for shooting in self-defence his racist attacker, and who was eventually reprieved by the Home Secretary.⁴ WASU also concerned itself with government controls on the export of West African cocoa; the rehabilitation and resettlement of West African troops after the war; the colour bar; the conditions of black merchant seamen at the Colonial Centre in Cardiff; and the expulsion and conscription into the army of students from Kings College, Lagos, which led the Union to declare 'that in West Africa there is no question of the indigenous people living as British citizens in their own land as the British Administration there is based on the exercise of autocratic and arbitrary powers'.⁵

The Union also maintained its contacts with the other West African student organisations; the ASAD in Dublin, and the various African student clubs formed at Cambridge, Edinburgh, Glasgow, Newcastle and Exeter. *Wasu* had a wide circulation and by March 1945, 3000 copies were being printed, the vast majority for distribution in West Africa.⁶ However, relations within the Union were often tense, especially between the editorial board and the executive committee. Partly this seems to have been due to the personality of Solanke, who before his departure was relieved of the responsibility of editorial work, but when acting secretary-general H.O. Davies replaced him, matters only worsened.⁷

Davies' personality may not have suited him for this difficult post; certainly his political affiliations did not. For a time he clearly bore the brunt of complex political differences which not only led to major splits in WASU, but also affected the entire nationalist movement in Nigeria. In Britain the difficulties began when he received a letter asking for WASU's support from the secretary of the newly formed Cambridge branch of the Ibo Union, which claimed to have been formed to develop education in south eastern Nigeria, not to disintegrate the WASU or any other West African organisation. Davies, with Solanke's backing, opposed the Ibo Union which it was felt was acting as a 'separatist movement' and 'promoting tribalism' within WASU. Eventually the dispute became more acrimonious as the Igbo members of WASU complained bitterly of Davies' personal unsuitability for the post of warden and acting secretary-general, and some accused him of attempting to encourage the formation of a Yoruba Union in Britain and a branch of the Nigerian Youth Movement (NYM) within WASU. Finally in March 1945, a WASU general meeting established a commission of enquiry to investigate the allegations against Davies.[8]

The commission's report gives some idea of the tensions and political differences within WASU at the time. It seems that many of the members, possibly even including Solanke himself, had been considering the need for new organisations. However, the main cause of the problem seems to have been the split in the NYM in Nigeria, which had led to the resignation of many of its Igbo members, who were subsequently united under the leadership of Nnamdi Azikiwe.[9] Davies was criticised by the commission, but the charges against him were never firmly established, although it is clear that the NYM did aim to strengthen its links with WASU and the West African Parliamentary Committee, which it viewed as being 'of the greatest importance to the NYM – nay to all such organisations in West Africa'.[10] Davies, and his wife remained unpopular figures, both for their personalities as well as their politics. As an open enemy of Azikiwe, Davies was clearly unsuited for the job of maintaining unity within WASU, especially at a time when, according to one report, as far as the Igbo students were concerned Azikiwe could do no wrong.[11] Solanke became increasingly alarmed at developments in WASU. He believed that Davies, possibly under the influence of Obafemi Awolowo, who was also in London at this time and who subsequently founded the Yoruba nationalist organisation Egbe Omo Oduduwa, was 'active in turning WASU to Nigerian affairs absolutely', and that therefore the students from the Gold Coast were becoming alienated and leaving WASU.[12] Solanke was subsequently reassured that the whole matter had been overstated, but the dispute with some of the Igbo students continued to rumble on even after Davies and his wife had left.

WASU and Nigeria

The introduction of constitutional proposals in March 1945 by the Governor of Nigeria, Sir Arthur Richards, was a turning point in the history of the colony. The Richards Constitution was bitterly attacked by Nigerian nationalists, not least because it was introduced without any consultation, but also because it appeared to weaken the prospect of self-government, strengthen colonial control and regionalise

Nigerian politics. It was introduced alongside so-called 'obnoxious ordinances' that 'vested mineral rights and publicly purchased lands in the Crown, and gave the government powers to depose and appoint chiefs'.[13] WASU sent its own memorandum to the Colonial Office to protest against the proposed Constitution, while Awolowo wrote a series of protest articles in *West Africa*.[14] In Nigeria the newly formed National Council of Nigeria and the Cameroons (NCNC) and the NYM organised campaigns against the Richards Constitution and the ordinances, while WASU was joined in its protest by the other West African student organisations in Cambridge, Edinburgh, Glasgow, Newcastle and Exeter, as well as by ASAD in Dublin. In a letter to WASU concerning the ordinances, ASAD pointed out what it called the 'gravity and repercussions of these measures to the whole future of the people of Nigeria and the African race', and spoke of the need to combat 'economic slavery'. ASAD had already sent a telegram 'to the people of Nigeria', which was published with Azikiwe's assistance, pledging its solidarity with their protests and offering assistance.[15]

The co-operation between the student organisations in Britain and the nationalists in Nigeria deepened still further during the Nigerian General Strike, which began in June 1945; in some areas it lasted as long as 52 days, and involved as many as 200,000 workers. Railway, port and telecommunication workers all went on strike, and other workers staged sympathy strikes, when the colonial government refused to raise wages and salaries to keep pace with the rising cost of living. The strike naturally assumed a political and anti-colonial character, not least because there was evidence that European employees of the Government had been receiving pay increases denied to most Africans. Moreover, in July, the Government banned Azikiwe's *West African Pilot* and the *Daily Comet*, two of the leading anti-colonial papers, which had supported the strike.[16]

The General Strike occurred at a time of rapid development in the Nigerian trade union movement. By 1945 there were over 90 unions in Nigeria, and the Nigerian Trade Union Congress (NTUC) had been officially recognised in 1942. In February 1945 T.A. Bankole, the President of the NTUC had travelled to London to participate in the World Trade Union Conference. As well as establishing contact with other trade unionists, he and M.A. Tokunboh, the former NTUC secretary-general, kept in close touch with Padmore and the newly formed Pan-African Federation (PAF) and with WASU. While he was in London, Bankole also participated in a West African Parliamentary

Committee meeting at the House of Commons.[17]

On 15 July 1945, the PAF together with WASU, the IASB, Negro Welfare Centre, Negro Association, African Progressive Association, the Colonial Peoples United Council, the Brotherhood of African People and others organised a rally in support of the General Strike at Conway Hall in London. Members and ex-members of WASU took a prominent part. The meeting was chaired by the WASU president R.W. Beoku-Betts, and addressed by Koi Larbi, Dr E.Udo Udoma, and H.O. Davies, as well as by Padmore, Reginald Bridgeman and others.[18] The meeting passed several resolutions, which were sent to the Nigerian government, the Colonial Secretary, MPs, the TUC and the press, condemning the actions of the Government, calling for the lifting of the ban on Azikiwe's newspapers and supporting the demands of the strikers. In addition H.O. Davies gained the support of Sorensen in Parliament and wrote an article for the ILP's the *New Leader* appealing for financial support for the strikers.[19]

The Nigerian General Strike united the West African and Pan-African organisations in Britain much as the Italian invasion of Abyssinia had during the 1930s, and also received significant international support from political and workers' organisations in Jamaica, Trinidad, Barbados and the US. Once again WASU and other West Africans played an important role. H.O. Davies, in spite of his other difficulties, was honorary secretary of the joint PAF-WASU Strike Relief Committee, which also included Koi Larbi, Udo Udoma and Kwame Nkrumah newly arrived from the US. Nkrumah had already become Regional Secretary of the PAF, and in October 1945 was elected vice-president of WASU.

The Manchester Pan-African congress

1945 was a year of international conferences. The World Youth Conference met in Britain, and presented another opportunity for West African youth and student delegations, such as the Sierra Leone Students' Union and the West African Youth League to visit London. WASU, which had already met with the International Youth Council in 1944, now demanded a seat on the executive of the World Youth Council as the 'representative' of 25 million inhabitants in West Africa. The latter instead asked the Union to suggest responsible West African organisations that could provide delegates to the Conference, but agreed that the

Union could suggest one nominee for a co-opted position on the executive. At the subsequent World Youth Council, which was held in Prague in 1945, the Nigerian Max Iyalla represented WASU.[20] The Student Christian Movement and the Edinburgh Africa Association also took advantage of the occasion of the World Youth Conference by organising a British West Africa students' conference, entitled 'Working in Colonial Africa', which was held in Bristol in September 1945.

In June and October of 1945, two Subject Peoples Conferences organised by the PAF, WASU and, amongst others the Ceylon Students' Association, and involving African, Asian, and Caribbean organisations were held in London, to discuss 'the present condition of the subject world'. The conferences included delegates 'from the colonial labour parties and trade unions' and aimed 'At the setting-up of some permanent organisation for the co-ordination of the Colonial struggle'. Speakers at the first conference included H.O. Davis, who was also the secretary of the organising committee and Jomo Kenyatta. The conference issued its own manifesto *The Colonies and Peace* which declared that for people in the colonies the Allied victory would have no meaning 'if it does not lead to their own liberation from the tentacles of imperialism', and which called for world-wide support for the anti-colonial struggles.[21] All of these conferences were significant in that they showed the concern of the students and others from the colonies to examine and find solutions to the problems of the colonial world, and were evidence of a growing Afro-Asian as well as Pan-African unity. However, it is the Manchester Pan-African Congress, organised mainly by the PAF, which has since assumed most historical significance.

The PAF had organised a number of preliminary meetings throughout 1945 and had managed to contact not only the trade union delegates to the World Trade Union Conference in London, but a number of other organisations in West Africa, the US and the Caribbean, as well as uniting the various black organisations in Britain. As a consequence of close links with the PAF, WASU, and Nkrumah in particular, became involved with the preparations for the Manchester Pan-African Congress, which eventually met in October 1945.[22] WASU had originally argued that the Congress should take place in Africa rather than in Europe, and in a letter to W.E.B. Du Bois, the Union suggested 'the Republic of Liberia as perhaps the ideal choice'. However, when this proved to be impossible, the Union gave its support to the proposal to hold the Congress in Manchester, although it still aimed to hold a further Pan-African congress in Liberia in 1947.[23]

In April 1945 WASU joined with the PAF, the IASB, the LCP, and colonial trade union leaders and others to send a *Manifesto on Africa in the Post-War World* to the United Nations Conference in San Francisco. The Manifesto was drafted by Desmond Buckle and signed by R.W. Beoku Betts on behalf of WASU. It called on the UN to intervene to promote economic, political and social advancement in Africa, including full self-government, as well as to end the exploitation of Africa's resources and to eliminate the influence of racism and fascism on the continent. The *Manifesto* shows the unity that existed amongst the African and Caribbean anti-colonial organisations in Britain and the firm links that had been established not only with the nationalist organisations in West Africa but also with organised labour.[24]

Six months later WASU joined the PAF in sending an *Open Letter to the Prime Minister* condemning imperialism and racism and demanding for the colonial peoples 'the immediate right to self-determination.[25] In October WASU sent four official delegates to the Manchester Pan-African Congress, Ako Adjei, F.O.B. Blaize, J. Appiah and F.R. Kankam Boadu, while H.O. Davies attended as the representative of the NYM.[26] ASAD and the African Students Association in Edinburgh sent one delegate each, J.A. Wachuku and J.C. de Graft Johnson respectively. A number of other West African students and ex-students also attended. Many of West Africa's future post-independence leaders were present, including Awolowo, Nkrumah, and I.M. Garba-Jahumpa. Jomo Kenyatta and Hastings Banda also attended, as did W.E.B. Du Bois, Amy Ashwood Garvey, Wallace Johnson and George Padmore.[27]

The proceedings of the Congress show something of both the militancy and confidence of the students. An air of optimism was evident not least because for the first time both intellectuals and workers' representatives were united around common goals. WASU representative F.O.B. Blaize spoke of the problems of black seamen and 'coloured' children in Britain, while de Graft Johnson stressed the need for unity between students and workers. Representatives of workers and farmers in West Africa, such as Wallace Johnson, Ashie Nikoi, (West African Cocoa Farmers' Delegation) and J.S. Annan demanded an end to colonial rule and were supported by Blaize, who called for general strikes and boycotts throughout Africa. In conclusion he stated: 'We have seen the remarkable rise of the Soviet Union. This can be done for the colonies, and we demand that it shall be done. Freedom is our right and we have got to fight until we get it'.[28]

The Congress demanded an end to racial discrimination and the colour bar in Britain, and also passed several resolutions concerning West Africa, which denounced European colonialism and the 'systematic exploitation' of West Africa by 'alien imperialist powers'. One resolution stated: 'the British Government in West Africa is virtually controlled by a merchants' united front, whose main objective is the exploitation of the people', and it condemned the reliance of West Africa's economies on single crops and the control of the markets for these crops by monopoly concerns. The resolution concluded with the declaration 'That complete and absolute Independence for the Peoples of West Africa is the only solution to the existing problems'.[29] The Congress drew up a *Declaration to the Colonial Workers, Farmers and Intellectuals*, drafted by Nkrumah, calling on them to organise and take part in the political struggle for independence. 'Today there is only one road to effective action – the organisation of the masses. And in that organisation the educated Colonials must join'.[30]

The Manchester Pan-African Congress has been seen as 'the zenith of the Pan-African movement'. Nkrumah claimed that it 'provided the outlet for African nationalism and brought about the awakening of African political consciousness. It became in fact, a mass movement of Africa for the Africans'.[31] The Congress clearly demonstrated the political militancy and optimism of the anti-colonial movement in the immediate post-war period, and showed how the unity of Pan-Africanism was now based around the analyses and language of the movement's Marxist wing. Whatever the influence of the conference on the wider Pan-African world, it could not fail to have a profound effect on West African students in Britain. Of particular significance was the role of Nkrumah and the new demands that he articulated which temporarily radicalised West African nationalism. 'We condemn internal self-government within the Empire', he declared, 'We stand for full and unconditional independence'. West Africans were now not just demanding independence, some also recognised that the way to achieve it meant the organisation of the masses of the people and the possible use of force.[32]

The West African National Secretariat (WANS)

WANS came into existence as a direct result of the Manchester Pan-African Congress and was formally founded on 14 December 1945 by

Nkrumah, Wallace Johnson, Bankole Akpata, Nii Odoi Annan, Koi Larbi, Kojo Botsio and Bankole Awooner-Renner.[33] It is quite likely that other WASU members joined WANS, or at least were very closely associated with it. There can be little doubt that the politics espoused by the new organisation summed up the views of many of the students, fervent nationalism tinged with varying degrees of Marxism.[34]

WANS was formed 'following and on the basis of, the suggestion sent by the Gold Coast Aborigines' Rights Protection Society (GCARPS) and the Sierra Leone Section of the WAYL'. Ashie Nikoi of the GCARPS and Wallace Johnson of the WAYL appear to have initiated the idea which was then agreed by others at the December meeting. Nkrumah became secretary-general and Wallace-Johnson the chairman of the new organisation. The original aims of WANS suggest that it saw itself as a co-ordinating and information bureau for the struggle against imperialism. It aimed to work amongst organisations within West Africa to build unity, and 'with a view to realising a West African Front for a United West African National Independence'. It also aimed to work among 'the peoples and working class in particular of the imperialist countries', to educate them about West Africa's problems.[35] WANS also declared that it believed: 'that Imperialism and colonial liberation are two irreconcilable opposites; a compromise between them is impossible. The death of the one is the life of the other'.[36]

The aims of the organisation make it clear that it saw itself very much as the vanguard, not only in the struggle for 'absolute independence for all West Africa', but also in the struggle to unite West Africa as 'one country'. At a time when narrow nationalism was becoming more prevalent in West Africa, WANS' revolutionary optimism may have been misplaced. However, what was new and dynamic about their conception was that West African nationhood was now socialistic and could be seen in terms of a West African 'Soviet Union', which would stretch as far as Kenya and the Sudan in the east and included British, French and Belgian colonies. Subsequently WANS issued an appeal for an 'All West African National Congress', with the aim of planning 'the democratic federation of all West African territories', and 'for the unity and independence of West Africa'. WANS clearly saw this congress as 'the nucleus of the Government of the State of West Africa', but for financial and other reasons the proposed congress was never held.[37]

Nkrumah also instituted 'The Circle', a small, secret revolutionary group which operated amongst the students to promote the idea of a

Union of African Socialist Republics and to train members as leaders who could continue the struggle in West Africa. Presumably, many of the leading members of WANS were members of 'The Circle', which probably also functioned as a vehicle for the transmission of the ideas of the Communist Party of Great Britain (CPGB). WANS members began to work closely with the CPGB and their regional politics seems to be something of a departure from the Pan-Africanism of Padmore and the Manchester Pan-African Congress. However, despite these political differences, Padmore maintained contact with the members of WANS and WASU during this period.[38]

From March 1946 WANS published *The New African*, 'a monthly newspaper devoted to African National Affairs, containing articles of outstanding African leaders', however the paper only appeared in five editions, the last in July 1946. Throughout the five months of its existence *The New African* maintained its coverage of topical events and issues in West Africa, Britain and throughout the African continent, and contained a number of articles reprinted from the *Moscow New Times*. One new departure, in keeping with the WANS' concept of West African unity, was the appearance of articles which dealt with the situation in the French and Belgian colonies and which were written in French. Indeed in 1946, as part of its policy of unity with those in the French colonies, Nkrumah travelled to Paris to hold discussions with the African members of the French National Assembly.[39]

WANS collapsed soon after Nkrumah's departure for the Gold Coast in 1947, but it was extremely active during its short life. In February and March 1946, two public meetings were held and resolutions sent to the newly formed United Nations condemning imperialism and demanding complete independence for the colonies. The WANS resolutions also demanded greater representation for Africans at the UN and called on that body to put an end to the colonial system. WANS also made sure that its views were known through the pages of *West Africa* arguing continually for a united and independent West Africa. Its notion of a united West Africa 'irrespective of artificial territorial divisions' received some criticism from West Africa and also from Canon Grace of the Dean of Westminster's Committee, who publicly condemned WANS' propaganda criticising British colonial rule, and claimed that West Africa was not ready for self-government. Subsequently, Grace and the Conference of British Missionary Societies (CBMS) reached a settlement with WANS, and in 1949 the CBMS declared that they regarded 'with deep sympathy and understanding ... the nationalist movements which aim at freedom and self-determination by constitutional means'.[40]

In some ways WANS was politically just a more radical version of WASU. It clearly grew out of the politics of the Manchester Pan-African Congress, but was also a reflection of the new politics in West Africa, with its emphasis on mass organisation and the demand for complete independence. But its concern with West African unity prior to Pan-African unity or the independence of the 'nation-state' made it something of an anomaly in the immediate post-war period. A united and independent West Africa was seen as the 'lever with which the whole continent would be freed'. WANS members were active in WASU, and they also maintained links with both the anti-colonial forces in Britain and the nationalists in West Africa, as well as with others with common interests in the US and elsewhere. WANS and Nkrumah in particular also paid attention to the black population in Britain. Public meetings were held in Liverpool, Manchester, Cardiff and other areas and a number of articles on racial discrimination appeared in *The New African*.[41]

WASU and WANS held their first joint conference in September 1946 which attracted over two hundred students. Despite the general unity at the conference, which included speakers from Senegal and Dahomey, one member of the WASU, Kwesi Lamptey, questioned whether WANS had the backing of the people of West Africa as he claimed WASU had.[42] However, the conference was enthusiastically reported in *Wasu*, as 'the beginning of a new epoch in West Africa's struggle for freedom and self-determination'. It was certainly significant for the inclusion of two delegates from French West Africa, one of whom, Sourous Apithy, represented Dahomey in the French Assembly; and for the fact that it argued for an anti-imperialist movement with a socialist basis.[43]

The students and the Labour government

The leftwards shift of both WANS and WASU can be most clearly seen in their attitude to the newly elected Labour government. The West African students in Britain had for many years formed a close relationship with members of the Labour Party, such as Sorensen, Hinden, Creech Jones and others, who were seen as the friends of West Africa and therefore much was expected of a post-war Labour government.

The Conservatives on the other hand were seen as the party of colonialism, even more so after Churchill's comments on the Atlantic Charter, and the lack of recognition given to colonial troops after the war.[44]

In June 1945 Harold Laski had written to H.O. Davies telling him, 'If as we hope, the Labour Party is successful in the present General Election, we shall hope to do all in our power to sustain and further the good of West Africa and above all its drive towards democratic freedom'. The students supported the Labour Party during the July 1945 election, and Davies told Laski: 'It is our firm conviction that genuine efforts will now be made to advance West Africa to self-government as quickly as possible in accordance with the colonial policy of the Labour Party'.[45] In fact the colonial policy of the Labour Party contained no such grounds for optimism. In its policy statement of 1943 it had referred to the four West African colonies, amongst others, as 'inhabited by backward peoples or peoples of primitive culture...whose economic and political systems are so backward that they are "not yet able to stand by themselves"'. The statement concluded 'For a considerable time to come these peoples will not be ready for self-government'.[46]

It was clear that the Labour government would pursue the paternalistic policy of 'partnership' with the colonies, so that, as Rita Hinden explained, Commonwealth might gradually evolve from Empire under British tutelage. The great and rapid changes sought by the students were entirely absent from the Labour government's plans. For example, when the delegation representing the farmers of the Gold Coast and Nigeria wanted to meet the new Colonial Secretary, George Hall, to discuss the removal of wartime economic controls, they were not even received by the Colonial Office. Furthermore, Creech Jones, the Under-Secretary of State for the Colonies, made speeches attacking the right of the delegation even to represent the farmers. As the leaders of the delegation included Ashie-Nikoi and Blaize, it was a matter that WANS and WASU could not ignore.

The New African reprinted a letter from Ashie Nikoi to Creech Jones that condemned the attitude and actions of the Government. Ashie Nikoi concluded that 'the Labour Government of Great Britain must redeem their pledges to the Colonial peoples or for ever cease to pose as advocates of the cause of the oppressed peoples'.[47] For WANS the colonial policy of the Government confirmed their view that: 'whether the designers are Socialist or Conservative, so long as the principle of administration is based on the foundation of Imperialism, the trend must be towards the safeguard of the interest of the twin sister of imperialism, which is capitalism'.[48] WASU viewed the actions of George Hall, as 'a set back and an eye opener', and *Wasu* commented that 'Governments may fall and Governments may rise, Colonial policy changeth never'. The students noted that US Imperialism seemed to be a greater champion of colonial independence than 'British Socialism.' The bubble had clearly burst and in 1948 African students heckled Creech Jones when he tried to outline colonial policy at a London meeting.[49]

Even the attempts by the FCB, which was dubbed the 'unofficial mouthpiece' of the Government by WASU, to explain government policy failed to pacify the students. Rita Hinden's book *Colonial Problems*, which was part of these attempts, was savagely attacked in *Wasu*. The FCB took the full force of the student's wrath partly because it was more accessible than the Government, but also because it represented the hypocrisy of a Labour Party given the opportunity to end colonial rule, but failing to live up to the pronouncements made by Attlee during the war years. In April 1946 the FCB held a conference on the 'Relationship between Britain and the Colonial People' to attempt to placate some of the critics. WASU and WANS took part and Nkrumah, who was one of the invited speakers, received enthusiastic support when he again demanded complete independence for West Africa and concluded: 'the masses of the colonial people have nowhere to retreat. They have only one battle-cry: "Advance and destroy Imperialism" '.[50] Incidents such as the impounding in Accra of two hundred copies of Padmore's *How Russia Transformed her Colonial Empire*, or the infamous incident at the Bristol Hotel in Lagos, when Ivor Cummings of the Colonial Office was denied accommodation because he was an African, only seemed to show that under Labour nothing had changed.[51]

The students were equally critical of so-called development schemes which, it was argued, would turn the African colonies 'into a huge granary of empire', and which they alleged were only undertaken because Britain itself had severe economic problems. Colonial Office officials noted that among both West African and West Indian students there was 'considerable mistrust of our Economic policy. They seem to think it is Imperialism and intended solely for the benefit of the UK'. Consequently the Colonial Office Information Department was urged to provide speakers for the student organisations who might explain the policy and be involved in 'counteracting communist propaganda'. This 'communist propaganda' the Colonial Office believed came not only from WANS but also from the PAF, Padmore and 'other able, trained Communists'.[52]

The Labour government certainly had complex post-war problems to solve; the Cold War was intensifying, but it was also a time when Britain was attempting to re-establish itself as a global power. Part of the Labour government's strategy was to rely more heavily on the economic resources of the colonies and to attempt to establish even closer political control. The Government feared political rivalry in Africa from the Soviet Union, and also the economic and political rivalry of the US. The economic development of the colonies was seen as Britain's natural defence, vital strategically as well as economically. Colonial exports could provide dollar earnings and strengthen Britain in its attempts to stand up against both superpowers. Opposition to Britain's plans to strengthen itself economically and politically in the colonies might be seen as part of the Soviet threat, but anti-communism, whatever the reality, was a useful and powerful weapon to be used to label the real threat of anti-colonialism.[53] The students in Britain and the nationalists in West Africa did not think that Britain's problems should be solved at their expense, even though not all West Africans shared in the condemnation of the Labour Party and the FCB, and many WASU members maintained cordial links with Hinden, Sorensen and even Creech Jones. When the latter lost his parliamentary seat in 1950, Solanke wrote to him on behalf 'of thousands (and of probably millions) of other Africans' who highly appreciated 'the benefits' enjoyed by the colonies, apparently as a consequence of the policies of Creech Jones and the Labour government.[54]

The students and the Colonial Office

The students' dissatisfaction with the Labour government naturally contributed to the leftwards shift in their politics and the increasingly prevalent view in official circles that the students had become contaminated by communism, and relations with the Colonial Office generally remained strained. As far as WASU was concerned, Colonial Office policy was to continue to deny them any official recognition so far as political issues were concerned. The Colonial Office refused to meet WASU delegations concerning such issues as the Nigerian General

Strike and the West African Produce Control Board. Relations were also soured through the public row between Solanke and the Governor of Nigeria, Sir Arthur Richards, over the latter's attempt to stop the 'Native Authorities' in Nigeria contributing to WASU's hostel appeal. This was receiving much publicity in Britain, had the support of the Lord Mayor of London and the Archbishop of Canterbury and had received a £1000 donation from the UAC.[55]

At first officials in the Colonial Office were concerned that Richards' attitude, which stemmed from his dislike of WASU's political activities, might have unfortunate consequences. Certainly Solanke, Sorensen, and Hinden questioned the legal right of the colonial government to stop the Native Authorities from contributing to the appeal. Solanke and WASU considered the whole affair an important political issue, especially since Richards was directly answerable to the Labour government. Solanke argued that Richards was not carrying out Labour Party policy and should be removed from office, and reminded Creech Jones, the new Colonial Secretary, that such attitudes only fuelled resentment in West Africa. Even the FCB protested to Creech Jones, stating that it felt 'a certain sense of uneasiness' regarding the whole issue, and that they too were concerned about the political effects in West Africa. Such incidents only served as further proof for the students and those in West Africa that they could place little hope in the Labour government.

In early 1947 WASU held an Extraordinary General Meeting and passed a resolution addressed to the Prime Minister on the 'Termination of British Rule in West Africa and Declaration of Independence of the African Peoples as Sovereign Nations'. The resolution condemned the inactivity of the Labour government on the question of self-determination and declared: 'the time has come when the question of national independence of the African peoples and their complete break from the imperialist domination of Great Britain must be decided once and for all in the interests of world peace'.[56] WASU demanded that the British government 'relinquish the unjust claim' and 'terminate immediately their imperialist domination' over the West African colonies. It also demanded that the peoples of West Africa immediately empower a political organisation 'to form a Provisional National Government in each country', a further development of the concept of West African independence.

The resolution, drawn up or strongly influenced by WANS members, was widely supported in the West African press and provided further evidence to substantiate the concerns of the Colonial Office and others about WASU's politics. According to J.L. Keith, WASU was 'falling into chaos' during Solanke's absence in West Africa, and WANS members were now taking over the Union and using it for their own purposes.[57] This view was further substantiated by the actions of Solanke himself, who wrote to Richards and Creech Jones to distance himself from the resolution. Solanke even argued that Richards should assist the WASU appeal so that he could return to Britain and keep the students in check.

In the summer of 1947 a delegation of the NCNC, including Azikiwe and the union leader M.A.O. Imoudu visited Britain to meet with the Colonial Secretary, Creech Jones. The delegation submitted a memorandum to the Colonial Office complaining about government legislation, the 'obnoxious ordinances' and demanding changes in the Richards Constitution. WASU organised a public meeting in support of the delegation, co-operated with Padmore and others in organising a second meeting, and with WANS organised a demonstration to Trafalgar Square to protest against the Richards Constitution. The demands of the delegation were largely ignored by Creech Jones, who instructed its members to return to Nigeria. This provided the students with yet another example of what many viewed as the hypocrisy of the Labour Party, and confirmed their view that the politics of independence must be based in West Africa, not in London; that 'the day of such delegations and deputations is long past'. The organisations in Britain might support the anti-colonial struggles, but despite their growing militancy the main battleground would be in the West African colonies themselves.

The Dean of Westminster's Committee

Colonial Office fears about WASU's activities were shared by the members of the Dean of Westminster's Committee, who despite their joint fund-raising, had not had the easiest relationship with the students. Their British appeal for funds on WASU's behalf had been handicapped by Solanke's determination to ensure that the Dean's Committee or its nominees did not take control of WASU. But while in West Africa, Solanke tried to use members of the Committee to keep a check on the political activities of the students. Since this was already their intention, Solanke found no difficulty in enlisting the support of

Canon Grace and other church representatives. Indeed the political activities of the students encouraged the Dean's Committee in its efforts, especially as rumours were rife that 'WASU is completely in the hands of the Marxists and now exists chiefly to get hold of young West Africans coming to this country and convert them to Marxism'. Some clergymen wanted to know why Christians were being asked to support such an organisation. Grace argued that WASU was 'no further left than the Oxford Union was before the war', but as this was of little consolation, he added that the 'Bolshies in their number' were well known to the police and everybody else and that if, as he hoped, the students might be influenced by a future white chaplain who could 'sweeten' their political debates, then this would amount to 'a very important strategic position' for the Committee. He also thought that a more luxurious hostel would assist in moderating WASU's politics.

Rather than attempt to get rid of Solanke and ban politics from the Union, as some were suggesting, Grace still saw Solanke and his wife as an important rallying point for the students. He argued that the Committee must be able to 'handle this kind of difficult bloke or we shall lose our colonial empire. If once you get them in your pocket you can do anything with them'. Grace was however concerned to do all he could to limit Solanke's mission to just fund-raising and as far as possible to steer him away from political controversy.[58]

The Accra riots and the Cold War

Whatever the attempts to reach an accommodation with the students in Britain, West African events always intervened and pushed the resolution of the colonial question to the fore. Perhaps the most significant political event of these years was the shooting of ex-servicemen in Accra in February 1948. In that month the Ex-Servicemen's Union in the Gold Coast held a demonstration in Accra, at the end of which they intended to present a petition to the Governor in protest at economic and social insecurity. However, the demonstration was stopped by the police, who fired on the crowd, killing two and wounding several others. Rioting and looting broke out in several other towns, resulting in a further 26 people being killed and over 200 wounded. The colonial authorities lost control of the situation and a state of emergency was declared throughout the country. Six leading members of the United Gold Coast Convention, the main anti-colonial organisation in the country, who were thought to be implicated in the disturbances were arrested. Amongst those arrested were former WASU members J.B. Danquah, Nkrumah, Ako Adjei, William Ofori Atta and E.O. Lamptey. Subsequently the British government appointed the Watson Commission of Inquiry to investigate the disturbances.

During the days immediately following the shooting, WASU sent telegrams of protest to the Prime Minister, the Colonial Secretary, the UN and several British politicians, as well as to other organisations and individuals throughout the world. In March 1948 WASU together with the Gold Coast Students' Union and WANS, met officials of the Colonial Office and subsequently held a press conference to condemn the shootings. They organised a mass rally at Trafalgar Square followed by the presentation of a 'condemnatory resolution' to the Prime Minister at Downing Street. Two further protest meetings were held and a fund started for the 'dead, wounded, and dependants of victims' of the Gold Coast shootings.[59]

The events in the Gold Coast obviously angered the students and stirred even more militant calls for self-government both in Britain and West Africa. To many it seemed incredible that as J.E. Appiah, the WASU vice-president said: 'the ex-soldiers of the late war, those who fought against Fascism in Europe, in Burma and elsewhere... they are fired upon by the troops. These men who were called upon to save the liberty of others now find that it is denied to them'.[60] WASU later gave evidence to the Watson Commission and cited economic, social, and educational as well as political causes for the disturbances, in particular highlighting social segregation and job discrimination. The submission also mentioned the discrimination faced by West African troops during the war and the lack of resettlement programmes and employment after it, as well as the general economic and political grievances in the colony, which included the treatment of the West African farmers' delegation to Britain in 1945. The Union also condemned the 'arbitrary denial of legal rights to the leaders of the Gold Coast Convention', and the suppression of the rights of the press.[61]

The feelings of the students are perhaps best summed up by the Executive Committee of the West African Students' Club at Oxford, which also sent a resolution of protest to the Colonial Secretary. It stated:

> We the West African students at Oxford view with grave concern the recent shooting of our unarmed countrymen on the Gold Coast. We deplore the sending of troops from outside against these people, when

they were demonstrating against the failure of the Gold Coast Government to meet their grievances. We condemn wholeheartedly the attitude of the Under-Secretary of State for the Colonies, who said he was almost certain that there must be Communist incitement. We feel that he was prejudicing the issue, and that does not speak well of a Minister of the British Government. He was shifting the responsibility on the Communists, and giving the impression that Africans are incapable of asking for their rights without incitement from outside. We sincerely hope that a public inquiry will be set up. It must be realised that the Gold Coast Government is involved in the case, and it is imperative that only parties not concerned with it should be made judges. We need not emphasise that such situations are bound to shake our faith in the sincerity of the British Government when they say that imperialism has been thrown overboard.[62]

The disturbances broke out at a time when the Cold War was at its height, but the Government's initial view, which also appeared in some press reports, that the disturbances in the Gold Coast were part of a communist conspiracy, was later shown to be without foundation. However, communism and especially Marxist ideology were playing an increasingly important role in the politics of many of the students in Britain, and to some extent this influence was spreading to West Africa. Between 1946 and 1948 many of the most prominent members of WASU were also members of WANS, so that, as was noted in the Colonial Office, 'It is sometimes difficult to appreciate exactly where WASU activities end and the WANS begin'. Bankole Akpata, Kojo Botsio, Bankole Awooner-Renner and Nii Odoi Annan belonged to both organisations, and it is likely that others, including J.E.Appiah and E.K. Dadzie did too.

A number of people, including Solanke himself, began to express concern at the level of alleged communist influence amongst the students. Even one of the founders of WASU, Dr Bankole-Bright felt it necessary to warn the students against what he referred to as 'European Communism', and said that no support should be given to Africans who professed it. Colonial Office reports contain numerous signs of alarm at what was referred to as 'the addiction of so many of the young West African intelligentsia to form Communist associations in the UK and the printing of Communist articles in the West African native press'.[63]

In 1948 the Colonial Office was able to gather some information concerning the influence of communism amongst the students from the

Watson Commission, but even before the Gold Coast disturbances it had established an informal group to investigate 'the Political Significance of Colonial Students in the UK'. The first meeting of this group, chaired by Sir Charles Jeffries, the Deputy Under-Secretary of State, was held in January 1948, and included amongst its membership both Rita Hinden and Kenneth Little. During 1947 the Colonial Office produced a report detailing official concerns about the politics of students and intellectuals, which it claimed had upset Colonial Office 'calculations and disturbed the even tenor of political developments among the slow moving masses'. Officials recognised that 'the whole political future of the African colonies is bound up with these few men' and as in the past sought ways to 'counter if possible the extremist political propaganda and atmosphere to which students are subjected in this country'. One suggestion was that of 'the incorporation of this class in a realistic way in the social, political and economic scheme', by, for example, the recruitment of intellectuals into local government in West Africa. The other main concern was the necessity for the Colonial Office and others to provide the political education 'of this class for their high calling as leaders and eventually rulers of their people'. The informal group and the Welfare and Information departments of the Colonial Office continued to discuss what could be done to combat communist influence, and, as in the past, sought to encourage social relations between Africans and the ruling class in Britain, and to develop more fully the use of anti-communist propaganda.[64]

Kenneth Little and other members of the informal group had argued that one way of increasing co-operation with the students was official opposition to the colour bar. The Colonial Office acknowledged that 'the existence of colour prejudice in the UK greatly increases anti-British feeling amongst Colonial students and enhances the attraction of Communism as a political creed which repudiates the colour bar'.[65] Some tentative moves to address the issue of the colour bar were undertaken, but the Lord Chancellor and Attorney General were opposed to any anti-racist legislation. Moreover, as J.L. Keith pointed out, the African situation was a 'more important cause of trouble over here than lack of social and other amenities'. He continued: 'In my opinion what drives African students into undesirable political fields is what has happened and is happening in Africa ... African colonial government is not "democratic" until it is there will be political feelings and agitation among the students of a kind which plays into the hands of Communists and other propagandists'.[66] Keith believed that while the students were in Britain they would become even more aware of the lack of democracy in the colonies, especially when they were in contact with 'reputable bodies' which were sometimes critical of colonial policy such as the FCB. The students would oppose everything imposed in the colonies, and initiatives from the Colonial Office would continue to be viewed with great suspicion. The FCB voiced its own concerns about the students, noting that 'while the Labour Party does nothing to meet and greet these people, the Communist Party does everything', including 'expressing a readiness to take up any grievances or problems'. In response to these criticisms, the Labour Party appointed a 'Commonwealth Officer' with the task of contacting colonial students, and attempting to gain their trust and support for Labour Party colonial policies.[67]

West Africans and the CPGB

In the immediate post-war period many West African students and some workers became much more closely involved with the CPGB. Desmond Buckle, the former student from the Gold Coast who had joined the CPGB in the late 1930s, had become a member of the party's Colonial and African Committees, and was in contact with WASU and other students. WASU also established links with the new international youth and student organisations, which were viewed by the British government as communist-front organisations. WASU was affiliated to the International Union Students (IUS) and had its own representative, Bankole Akpata, on the executive of the World Federation of Democratic Youth (WFDY).

In April 1944 a large WASU delegation attended the CPGB's Colonial Information Bureau conference in London. In March 1945, WASU sent five delegates to the Party's Colonial Conference, and it seems that after the war the CPGB took a much greater interest in the students in general and WASU in particular, as it recognised the growing importance of the African colonies. From 1947, the Party's Africa Committee published the monthly *Africa Newsletter*, which was widely read not just in Britain but also throughout West Africa. According to Colonial Office reports, since 1945 the CPGB had:

> Organised special study classes on the basic principles of Communism for West Africans in the UK; the Party's West Africa Committee has

invited sympathisers to attend its meetings, copies of the Committee's Africa Newsletter, circulated in the UK find their way to West Africa; finally the Committee has assisted and encouraged the activities of the WASU in the UK and has maintained personal contact with the WANS.[68]

It is now clear that WANS members such as Nkrumah, Akpata, Botsio, Annan and Awooner-Renner were closely connected with the CPGB's Africa Committee, regarded themselves as communists, and were viewed as such by the Colonial Office and the operatives of MI5. The latter viewed Bankole Akpata, who joined the CPGB in 1948, as the 'principal link between the Communist Party and the West African communists in the UK', and WANS as 'composed almost exclusively of Communists'. Awooner-Renner's *West African Soviet Union* and his letter to Stalin asking for land in the USSR for the poor and exploited in West Africa, make clear his sympathies for communism.[69]

But two important points need to be borne in mind here. First that the students supported and gravitated towards those who were most consistently anti-colonial; to many at this time the communist movement seemed to fit the bill. Communism and the Soviet Union had tremendous international prestige during this period, as is clear from the files of the British Cabinet itself. In these circumstances it would have been strange if students and those in the West African colonies had not been influenced by or supportive of communism. Ayo Rosiji, later Nigeria's Minister of Health, claimed that he joined the CPGB, the FCB and the Labour Party, while studying law in Britain. Even H.O. Davies had attended a course of Marxist classes in Nigeria run by a member of the CPGB, who had been stationed there during the war. When he was in Britain after the war Davies kept in touch with the CPGB, and according to a Communist Party report 'hopes were placed on him as a developing Marxist'. But such hopes were evidently misplaced and the report concluded that his 'character as a Yoruba separatist and splitter of the national movement is now so well known that it requires no further comment'.[70] Some other WASU members had also come into contact with Marxism in West Africa. In 1945, CPGB supporter Amanke Okafor had formed the Marxist Talakawa Party in Lagos, which claimed to be a political party of the working people of Nigeria, and which aimed to achieve a free independent and a Socialist Nigeria. The development of various Marxist groups in West Africa, especially in Lagos was clearly significant as many of the leading members of these groups eventually came to London as students. However, as in the case of H.O. Davies not all were committed communists, and many subsequently fell foul of the CPGB.

WANS certainly provided the most organised means for the spread of Marxism amongst the students and was important in that it gave the ideology a particularly West African form. As for WASU, it also continued to maintain its contacts with the CPGB, which in 1948 had decided to intensify 'the drive to develop cadres among African students in Britain'. At the WASU's annual conference in July 1948 the students were addressed by leading CPGB member Emile Burns, who had already organised regular classes on Marxism for some forty West African students in London. A few weeks before, the executive of the Communist Party had passed a resolution on West Africa calling for 'full democratic self-government'; the abolition of all discriminatory legislation; financial assistance from the British government for industrialisation and welfare; the withdrawal of British armed forces and police; and what it called the 'ending of the British dictatorship in Africa'.[71] It is not clear how many West Africans actually joined the CPGB at this time. MI5 only knew of about twelve students who might be labelled as communists. Certainly many were close supporters and during 1948 the CPGB organised a special meeting for its Nigerian contacts, addressed by Rajani Palme Dutt and held a conference, which many West Africans attended, 'On the Crisis of British Imperialism'.[72]

Student politics

In addition to its communist links and those with organisations like the PAF, WASU also maintained contact with Fenner Brockway, the ILP and the British Centre For Colonial Freedom, formerly the British Centre Against Imperialism. In June 1948, WASU participated in the First International Conference of the Peoples of Europe-Asia-Africa Against Imperialism (COPAI), which was held in Paris. Also in attendance was the newly formed Nigeria Union of Great Britain and Ireland, represented at the conference by its president, J.O. Ajibola and honorary secretary, T.O. Ojiako. Both organisations were represented on the COPAI International Committee, and participated in the British section of the COPAI in London.[73] WASU also had contact with organisations as varied as the Young Liberals International

Committee (London), the All-India Muslim League (London), the Women's Co-operative Guild, the Student Labour Federation, the Racial Relations Group and WASU members were active in several other organisations, including the declining LCP. The Union also maintained its contacts with organisations in the US, such as the New York based Council on African Affairs.

During the immediate post-war period a number of new student-based West African organisations were established in Britain. The West African Society, founded by R.B. Wellesley Cole in July 1947 and based in Newcastle and London, was established mainly as a cultural organisation and produced a journal *Africana*, which stressed the importance of intellectual and cultural issues in the developing national consciousness in West Africa.[74] According to *West Africa*, the organisation was to be 'West Africa's premier Learned Society of the future'. Within a year of its founding the Society claimed membership in the hundreds, mainly students in Britain, but was also supported in West Africa, especially in Sierra Leone. The student members of its executive and editorial board included K.A.B. Jones-Quartey, Davidson Nicol, and O.K. Ibare-Akinsan.[75]

Some other new organisations reflected the growing divisions in West Africa, especially in Nigeria. By 1948 two rival organisations, the Yoruba Federal Union, formed by WASU member Kola Balogun, and the Egbe Omo Oduduwa, were each vying for members.[76] The two organisations reflected political loyalties in Nigeria; Balogun was a close supporter of Azikiwe and the NCNC, while the Egbe Omo Oduduwa, of which Ayo Ogunsheye was the London secretary, not only fostered Yoruba nationalism, but also formed the basis for the emergence of the rival Action Group led by Awolowo. These organisations and their differences later led to disputes among Nigerian students in London, including those who were close supporters of the CPGB.

In addition to the Yoruba organisations, there was also the Nigeria Union, the GCSA which had re-emerged in 1946 as the Gold Coast Students Union, and the Sierra Leone Students' Group, which had been formed by law student and WASU member H. Maurice-Jones in 1948. In Manchester there was an African Students' Union and an Ibo Union formed in 1946.[77] Other new organisations included the African Friendship Society in Newcastle and the British African Cultural Society in London. One of the most important new organisations was the West African Women's Association. Formed in 1946, it was the first

African women's organisation to be established in Britain.

These new organisations weakened WASU, which whatever its politics, was now less able to claim that it represented the majority of the fourteen hundred West African students in Britain. Its membership was small and the poor attendance at its annual conferences was adversely commented on in the press. The Sierra Leone students independently sent their own resolutions to the Colonial Office, while the Nigeria Union could claim to represent many of the Nigerians in Britain. After Solanke's return from West Africa and as a result of the appeal, WASU was able to purchase a new and more luxurious hostel at Chelsea Embankment in London, which was officially opened by Creech Jones in November 1949. But it soon found itself in debt and disrupted by disputes between Solanke, the WASU executive and board of directors and the Dean of Westminster's Committee.[78] Solanke was concerned about the non-appearance of *Wasu*, the demise of the Parliamentary Committee, the money spent on travel to international events, such as the 1947 International Youth Festival in Prague, and those WANS members on the WASU executive, whom he considered to be communists. While the executive, which included Botsio, Akpata, Appiah and Annan, accused him of squandering money during the mission in West Africa and with being autocratic. Both the Board and the Dean of Westminster's Committee were now much less supportive of Solanke, and it was decided that he would cease to hold the position of secretary-general of WASU, a position he had held since the founding of the Union in 1925. With the opening of the new hostel and the appointment of K.A.B. Jones-Quartey as warden, Solanke's role and influence were to be increasingly marginalised. He remained warden of Africa House, and for several years continued his campaign to save the Union from what he saw as the threat of communism, but his influence became minimal and he took little part in WASU's 'silver jubilee' celebrations in 1950.

Notes

1. *West African Review*, January 1946, p30.
2. J.L. Keith, 'African Students in Great Britain', *African Affairs*, 45/1, April 1946, pp65-72.
3. See *WASU Annual Report 1944-45*, SOL 18/8.
4. The defence campaign for Philip Berry seems to have been organised by

the Committee for the Defence of People of African Descent under the auspices of the African Progressive Association. Little is known of the two organisations, but the officers of the Committee were West Africans K.O. Larbi (chairman), F.O.B. Blaize (secretary) and B.O. Alakija (treasurer). Larbi was one of the barristers involved in Berry's defence. See Blaize to the Secretary, West African Parliamentary Committee, 22 March 1945. SOL 57/4.

5. On the Kings College incident see G.O. Olusanya, *The Second World War and Politics in Nigeria 1939-1953*, Evans Bros. Ltd., London 1973, pp66-68, and *Wasu Annual Report, op.cit.*
6. See *Report of the Editorial Board 1943-45*, SOL 18/6. The circulation figures show that most copies were sold in West Africa: 1500 in Nigeria and 760 in the Gold Coast, compared with 300 in Britain. The circulation subsequently declined but reports show that in 1947 the Union attempted to issue a fortnightly newsletter to replace *Wasu* and in order to keep in touch more regularly with members. See *Wasu Newsletter*, 13 February 1947, SOL 19/5.
7. H.O. Davies was already something of a veteran politician when he came to Britain to study law in 1944. He was the founder and manager of one of Nigeria's main newspapers the *Daily Service* and one of the founders of the NYM. He later became legal advisor to the Egbe Omo Oduduwa and one of Nigeria's first QCs. From 1964-66 he was Minister of State for Industry in Nigeria's post-independence government.
8. G. Olusanya, *The West African Students' Union, op.cit.*, pp76-82.
9. *Ibid.* pp76-82.
10. *Wasu*, XII/I, March 1945, pp6-8.
11. Fola Ejiwunmi to Solanke, 12 July 1945, SOL 22.
12. Obafemi Awolowo (1909-1987) was already a leading member of the NYM and one of the founders of the Nigerian TUC by the time he came to study law in Britain in 1944. He was the most prominent of Yoruba politicians in Nigeria, and founder of the separatist Egbe Omo Oduduwa and Action Group. He served as Leader of Government Business and premier of the Western Region of Nigeria before independence and leader of the opposition in the immediate post-independence period.
13. M. Crowder, *The Story of Nigeria*, Faber & Faber London 1966, p275.
14. *West Africa*, 26 May 1945, p480. *West African Review*, June 1945, pp103-9, and p113 A series of articles by Awolowo appeared in *West Africa* from 1 December 1945.
15. J.A.Wachuku to WASU, 17 April 1945, SOL 57/2.
16. W. Ananaba, *The Trade Union Movement in Nigeria*, Ethiope Pub. Corp.,

Benin 1969, pp44-58.
17. The PAF had been formed in 1944 on the initiative of the International African Service Bureau (IASB) as a Pan-African united front movement. It included most of the black organisations in Britain including the Glasgow African Union and the ASAD, but excluding both WASU and the LCP. The PAF also included representatives from two West African organisations: the West African Youth League (Sierra Leone section) and the Friends of African Freedom Society (Gold Coast). See H. Adi and M. Sherwood, *The 1945 Manchester Pan-African Congress Revisited*, New Beacon Books, London 1995, p13.
18. 'Report on the Nigerian Strike' (PAF n.d.) SOL 58/2. Meetings were also held in Manchester, Liverpool and elsewhere. See also the WASU Executive's *The General Strike in Nigeria*, 9 July 1945, FCB Papers MSS Brit. Emp. S365 70/1. E. Udo Udoma, formally a medical student in Dublin, was at that time the chair of the *Wasu* editorial board.
19. *The New Leader*, 28 July 1945. In total WASU and the PAF raised about £225. The letters of H.O. Davies to the Colonial Secretary show that during the strike and in other matters he was acting on behalf of various workers' and farmers' organisations in West Africa. See PRO CO 554/143/35544.
20. *West African Review*, February 1946, p153.
21. Adi and Sherwood, *op.cit.*, pp19-21.
22. The previous four Pan-African Congresses had largely been organised from the US by W.E.B. Du Bois and the National Association for the Advancement of Colored People (NAACP).
23. For the background to the Manchester Pan-African Congress see Adi and Sherwood, *op.cit.*, pp11-32, and for the WASU letter p73.
24. *Labour Monthly*, January/December 1945, pp154-56.
25. Adi and Sherwood, *op.cit.*, pp23-4.
26. In his *Reminiscences* F.R. Kankam Boadu includes Bankole Awooner-Renner, Michael Peterside and Nkrumah in a WASU delegation of seven, *ibid.*, p34.
27. *Ibid.*, pp125-61.
28. *Ibid.*, p82. The West African delegates to the Congress also sent a telegram to the Colonial Secretary, outlining twelve demands including the repeal of the Richards Constitution and the removal of Richards as Governor of Nigeria.
29. *Ibid.*, p103.
30. *Ibid.*, p56. Wallace Johnson made a not dissimilar point: African students in Britain should not go to their homes in Africa assuming a role of super-

iority, but should co-operate with the workers movement for the advantage of all coloured peoples. *West Africa*, 3 November 1945, p1061.

31. Quoted in Langley, *op.cit.*, pp355-56.
32. Quoted in Adi and Sherwood, *op.cit.*, p4.
33. Bankole Akpata was a WASU member and Study Group leader, in 1946 he was a student at the LSE. Kojo Botsio, a future cabinet minister in Ghana, was in 1946 the acting warden of WASU and was appointed treasurer of WANS. Awooner-Renner was another WASU member, at this time studying for the Bar in London, he was the first president of WANS, and when Wallace-Johnson returned to West Africa he became chairman. Nii Odoi Annan was a law student in Edinburgh, but subsequently joined WASU as well as WANS.
34. For a fuller account of WANS see M. Sherwood, *Kwame Nkrumah; the years abroad 1935-47*, Freedom Publications, Legon 1996 pp125-59.
35. *Aims and Objectives of the WANS*, WANS, London n.d., p8. The GCARPS sought affiliation to WANS in 1946.
36. *The New African*, 1/1 March 1946.
37. *West African Soviet Union* was the title of B. Awooner-Renner's 1946 WANS publication. On the proposed WANS congress see M. Sherwood *op.cit.*, pp147-50. The proposed conference was warmly welcomed in *Wasu* and clearly seen as following in the footsteps of Casely-Hayford and the NCBWA. *Wasu*, XII/5, Summer 1948 pp23-5.
38. It appears that Akpata and Annan were members of the Circle, but Awooner-Renner not necessarily so. See M. Sherwood *op.cit.*, pp125-26 and pp160-63.
39. See e.g. *The New African*, 1/1, March 1946 and L. Senghor's 'Pour une Renaissance Africaine', *ibid*. Senghor was listed as the WANS's 'Paris Correspondent'. See also Sherwood, *op.cit.*, p130.
40. *Ibid*, pp140-41.
41. *Ibid*.
42. Kwesi Lamptey also served as president of the Gold Coast Students' Union and in 1949 was elected chairman of the London branch of the Congress of Peoples Against Imperialism. On his return to the Gold Coast he initially became acting vice-chair of Nkrumah's Convention Peoples Party (CPP), but resigned from the CPP in 1951.
43. *West Africa*, 14 September 1946, p845, *Wasu* XII/3 Summer 1947, p13, and see Sherwood *op.cit.*, p130-31. The WASU remained in contact with student and other West African organisations in France.
44. See G.K. Amachree's 'Why Colonial Students Supported Labour at the Last Election - A Summary of West African Student Opinions', *Wasu*

XII/2, March 1946, p19.
45. Laski to WASU secretary-general, 27 June 1945, *ibid.*, pp31-32.
46. *The Colonies: The Labour Party's Post-War Policy for the African and Pacific Colonies*, Transport House London 1943, p2.
47. *The New African*, April 1946, p16, see also Ashie-Nikoi to the Colonial Secretary, *ibid.*, May 1946, p24.
48. *Ibid.*, March 1946, p7.
49. *Wasu* XII/2, March 1946, pp3-4. WASU's dissatisfaction with the Labour Party may help to explain why the West African Parliamentary Committee temporarily stopped functioning. See also *ibid.*, p6 and *West African Review*, July 1948, p770.
50. *Domination or Co-operation?* FCB pamphlet, 1946, p5 and M. Sherwood, *op.cit.*, pp132-35.
51. On the Bristol Hotel incident see J.E. Flint, 'Scandal at the Bristol Hotel: Some Thoughts on Racial Discrimination in Britain and West Africa and its Relationship to the Planning of Decolonisation, 1937-47', *Journal of Imperial and Commonwealth History*, XII/I, October 1983, pp74-93. On the Accra incident see M. Sherwood *op.cit.*, p140.
52. See PRO CO 537/2574/1120/30/2.
53. On government concerns about communism see the report of the Labour Cabinet in 1948 in PRO CAB 130/137. It was reported that 'the achievements of the Soviet Government in certain directions were remarkable and compare very favourably with British achievements in the colonial territories'.
54. Solanke to Creech Jones, 3 March 1950, Mss. Brit. Emp. s.332, 18/6. Other West Africans and WASU members who continued their involvement with the FCB included: F.A. Ogunsheye, trade union official, secretary of the Egbe Omo Oduduwa and at that time a student of economics at the LSE; de Graft Johnson and Lamptey of the Gold Coast Students Union and Max Iyalla, a WASU study group leader, who had previously been the president of the Fabian Society of Nigeria.
55. *West Africa*, 15 June 1946, p541. By 1948 the appeal had raised £8000 in Britain and over £5000 in West Africa.
56. Olusanya, *op.cit.*, pp89-91.
57. J.L. Keith memo, 7 May 1947, PRO CO 554/143/35544.
58. Grace to Ms M. Wyon, 10 January 1947, and Grace to L. Hartford (Shell, Nigeria), 19 January 1948, Conference of British Missionary Society Papers (CBMS) A/G 27 Box 261.
59. *Wasu* XII/5, Summer 1948, p39.
60. *Report of the First Conference of the Peoples of Europe-Asia-Africa Against*

Imperialism(Paris), 18-21 June 1948.
61. PRO CO 554/143/33544/48.
62. *West Africa*, 20 March 1948, p271.
63. PRO CO 537/2638/14322/2.
64. PRO CO 537/2573/11020/30 and CO 537/2573/11020/30/1.
65. PRO CO 537/5138/96801.
66. PRO CO 537/2573/11020/30/1.
67. D. Goldsworthy, *Colonial Issues in British Politics 1945-61*, OUP, Oxford 1971, pp146-47.
68. PRO CO 537/5263/14298 pt.3.
69. PRO CO 537/4312/14322/5.
70. Ruhemann Papers, Box 1, Communist Party Archives.
71. *World News and Views*, 7 August 1948, p330.
72. H. Adi, 'West Africans and the Communist Party in the 1950s' in G. Andrews, N. Fishman and K. Morgan (eds.) *Opening the Books - Essays on the Social and Cultural History of the British Communist Party*, Pluto, London 1995, p180.
73. *Congress of the Peoples of Europe, Asia and Africa*, COPAI, Paris 1948. J. Appiah, *The Autobiography of an African Patriot*, Praegar, New York, 1990, pp173-77.
74. *Africana*, December 1948, p2.
75. Jones-Quartey from the Gold Coast and Ibare-Akinsan from Nigeria were at this time law students. Davidson Nicol from Sierra Leone was a medical student.
76. Kola Balogun was studying law at the time and was chair of the editorial board of *Wasu*. He one of the founders of the radical Zikist Movement in Nigeria, a leading member of the NCNC and subsequently Nigerian High Commissioner to Ghana.
77. E.B. Ndem, 'Negro Immigrants in Manchester - An analysis of social relations within and between the various coloured groups and of their relations to the white community'. M.A. Thesis, London 1953, pp98-101.
78. The WASU appeal had raised some £17,000, including the £5000 raised by the Solankes in West Africa and a donation of £5000 from the Nigerian Government. WASU also received grants totalling £3000 p.a. from the governments of the Gold Coast and Sierra Leone. By 1950 however, these funds were insufficient to pay a large mortgage and run two hostels.

The 1950s: Communism and Nationalism

In 1949 when Creech Jones, the Secretary of State for the Colonies, officially opened the new WASU hostel, he asked the students 'to believe, whatever their suspicions had been in the past, that Britain was not pursuing a policy of exploitation of the West African territories'. In fact many WASU members and other West Africans were to retain their suspicions during the 1950s, in spite of the rapid strides made towards self-government and political independence in West Africa. By the mid-1950s WASU and the other student organisations were forced to reconsider their separate identities and to reorganise themselves in a new federal WASU, and by the time of Solanke's death in 1958 the status and role of the WASU had completely changed. Decolonisation in West Africa meant that the new West African governments gradually began to take direct responsibility for their students in Britain. However, the opinions and political activities of the students remained significant as this process meant that African affairs assumed a greater importance in British political life.

Despite the massive increase in their numbers, or perhaps because of it, West African students still faced the colour bar, exacerbated by the growth of racism in the wake of post-war immigration from the Caribbean and other Commonwealth countries.[1] As a result, finding accommodation and employment were major problems and many students were becoming destitute. Even the political changes in West Africa did not seem to benefit the students, who, in any case, were often as critical of the new African governments and politicians as they had been in the past of colonial rule and the Colonial Office.

Communism in WASU

The 'threat of communism' remained a popular topic in the press in the early 1950s. In March 1950 Lord Milverton (formerly Sir Arthur

Richards) claimed that WASU was 'a communist medium for the contact of communists with West Africans when they come to this country' and he suggested that an inquiry into the Union's activities should take place. Okoi Arikpo and A.M. Akinloye as president and honorary secretary, respectively, of WASU, issued a press statement in reply, stating that the Union was not affiliated to any political organisation, but that the students were encouraged to take an interest 'in all current world problems'. The statement added: 'Our stand, repeatedly expressed in all our public activities is that of nationalists who desire complete independence for the West African territories at the earliest possible date. This desire, in our opinion, does not require the bait of any foreign political ideology to spur us to our declared goal'.[2]

Reginald Sorensen also wrote to Lord Milverton on behalf of the WASU Board, refuting his allegations that the Union was a communist front. He pointed out that WASU was mainly a welfare organisation, although individual members might hold differing political views. But Milverton remained unconvinced. At least one voice in the Colonial Office seemed to agree with Sorensen; J.L. Keith reported that WASU had definitely improved since it had moved to Chelsea Embankment and sidelined Solanke. According to Keith 'WASU is very politically minded and takes an active interest in Colonial Affairs. But very largely thanks to Mr Sorensen's guidance, activities in this direction are far less unreasonable than they have been in the past ... WASU serves a very useful purpose'.[3]

Solanke however, clearly saw things differently and perhaps in an attempt to regain his lost influence continued his anti-communist campaign inside and outside WASU. He was very concerned about what he saw as young, inexperienced students handling the Union's affairs in an 'unsatisfactory manner', as well as his own loss of power. He could now claim that all problems were the result of 'communistic influence'. According to Solanke, it was because he refused to join in with their subversive activities that the young students were again spreading rumours about his extravagance during the mission to West Africa. His great hope was that Sorensen would help him to overcome the influence of communism in WASU.

According to Solanke, J.E. Appiah and Adenekan Ademola, in 1950 the WASU president and honorary secretary, and Ade Thomas, were the main communist ringleaders, who had the support of a large number of WASU members.[4] Solanke tried unsuccessfully to defeat them at the annual election in 1951 by establishing his own 'anti-communist party', but he was defeated amidst complaints of vote-rigging and accusations that those elected showed more interest in international meetings in Prague, Korea and Warsaw than they did in West African affairs.

Financial problems added to WASU's other difficulties, and by the end of 1951 the hostels had debts of over £3000 per year, despite substantial Colonial Office support. Although the Union already received annual grants from three of the West African governments, the Colonial Office and some supporters of the new Conservative government agreed to argue the case for further funds. There was concern that if the WASU hostels were forced to close, not only would officials be widely criticised for failing to meet the accommodation needs of the students, but also that their hope of attempting to counter communism by catering for these needs, would lie in tatters. They hoped that eventually they might persuade the Nigerian or other West African governments to intervene directly, and provide their own accommodation to deal with the ever-increasing numbers of students. These problems led to discussions within the Union and the Board of WASU Ltd. about the closure of one or both of the hostels. Despite Solanke's vigorous opposition, at the end of December 1952 the decision was taken to close down the older WASU hostel in Camden. Solanke and his supporters decided to carry on and in January 1953 formed themselves into a body called WASU Un-incorporated, in order to maintain the status of Africa House. Solanke attempted to raise funds and did what he could to persuade his friends to break off relations with WASU at Chelsea Embankment. He had hoped that the politicians in Nigeria, many of whom were former WASU members, would support Africa House, but in spite of some promises he was to be disappointed.[5] This in itself must have been very disheartening for Solanke who had devoted his life to WASU and the struggle for West African and especially Nigerian independence. He used his own money to maintain the hostel in Camden, just as he had done in the past, but now found himself in severe financial difficulties, with few supporters.

The formal split between Solanke in Camden and WASU at Chelsea Embankment marked the end of his involvement with the Union. Henceforth he devoted himself to his family and the running of the hostel in Camden. His departure clearly marked the end of an era, when his brand of nationalist politics had been influential not only in West Africa but also in the anti-colonial struggle in Britain. With the emergence of the Nkrumah government in the Gold Coast, the regional governments in Nigeria and constitutional changes in Sierra Leone and the Gambia in the early 1950s, a new type of nationalist politics also emerged, and as has been noted, the struggle in West Africa took greater precedence over any agitation in Britain. The new West African governments also began to take more responsibility for their students in Britain, so that by the mid-1950s WASU's role as a provider of a 'home from home' was no longer so vital. Solanke's relative lack of activity in the next few years was also occasioned by growing illness, the cancer that was eventually to lead to his death in 1958.

The Hans Crescent strike

The Colonial Office had been monitoring the developments in WASU, just as it also kept abreast of the emergence of the other West African organisations, such as the Nigeria Union (NU) and the Gold Coast Union (GCU). When a WASU deputation had visited the Colonial Secretary in May 1950 to plead for financial assistance, officials had shown some sympathy, and the Colonial Secretary privately admitted that: 'There is no doubt that the Union is playing a very important role in fostering the well-being of the students and in providing centres in London with a special African atmosphere'.[6]

The Colonial Office was concerned that the increasing number of West Africans in Britain (by 1952 over 1000 in London alone) should be adequately accommodated so as to avoid the problems associated with the colour bar and disaffected students. The two WASU hostels catered for at least some of these needs, so it was in the interest of the Colonial Office to try to maintain them, at least until they could find an alternative.

From 1950 the British Council, financed by £450,000 from the Colonial Development and Welfare Fund, was responsible for the accommodation and welfare of colonial students. It administered three hostels in London as well as properties in Edinburgh and Newcastle and in October 1950 a new hostel opened at Hans Crescent, Knightsbridge. However, the following year it was announced that only a third of the students resident at Hans Crescent would be able to remain for a further academic year. The remainder would have to make way for new overseas students expected the following autumn. The existing students, including a large number of West Africans, objected to the decision, even though they had been assured that the British

Council would assist in rehousing them. They complained bitterly about the need for more hostels and the difficulty of securing alternative accommodation. In June 1951, the students attempted to petition the Colonial Secretary and to enlist the support of Nkrumah and Botsio, respectively the 'Leader of Government Business' and the new Minister of Education and Social Welfare in the Gold Coast. The Colonial Office made the mistake of adopting a heavy-handed approach to the dispute and the students responded by threatening to write to the press and over forty of them, including fourteen from West Africa (predominately Nigerians), participated in a stay-in strike, led by amongst others M.A. Aderemi, president of the Hans Crescent students' house committee.[7] The students demanded that the Secretary of State give a written undertaking that additional accommodation would be provided.

The Colonial Office believed that isolating colonial students in their own accommodation would increase the chances that they might fall prey to subversive influences. Officials wished to integrate African and Caribbean students into university halls or private family lodgings and in this way hoped to counter any anti-British sentiments. The Hans Crescent strike did little to allay existing Colonial Office fears, as it became clear that many of the leading protesters had communist affiliations. The Colonial Office's position was all the more problematic because alternative accommodation, especially in London, was in short supply and insufficient to cope with the increasingly large numbers of students. In these circumstances the Colonial Office was keen to play down the whole affair and in particular to avoid the creation of possible student martyrs.

The West Indian Students' Union (WISU), the NU, the GCU, the recently formed Sierra Leone Students' Union (SLSU), and the Malay Society of Great Britain, who all had members at Hans Crescent, formed a Colonial Students' Council which demanded a meeting with the Colonial Secretary. Aderemi, on behalf of the students' house committee, wrote to the British Council demanding increased hostel accommodation for colonial students. He also called for the widest publicity for the students' grievances, explaining the problems created by the colour bar and arguing that the British Council and the students should join forces and appeal to the Colonial Office for increased funding. As part of the campaign a Nigerian student wrote provocatively to Aneurin Bevan, who had recently resigned from the Cabinet, explaining:

> The disadvantage our colour places on us militates against our studies, destroying the essential faith some of us have in socialism, and increasing our bitterness towards the white man ... Are we to go back to landladies who regard us as lower than 'vermin'? We fear to go to them for there is no certainty of tenure. Our stay in flats is dependent on the mood of whoever the landlady is, a thing as uncertain as the celebrated English weather.[8]

That there were also important political issues involved was made clear in a letter from the house committee to the Colonial Secretary, complaining that more support was given in Parliament to legislation concerning pets than to the legislation against the colour bar proposed by Reginald Sorensen.[9]

> When a Labour Government came to power in Britain, Colonial students rejoiced that the days of colonialism were over, and waited expectantly for the often stated policy of Mr Creech Jones to be fulfilled. We have been repeatedly disappointed, and it is scarcely surprising if in the midst of our disillusionment we feel only bitterness and disgust towards those who raised our hopes so high. If it is the desire of the Government to establish good relations with colonial peoples and a basis for co-operation in the future this can only be done by ensuring that their representatives in this country receive equitable treatment, if on the other hand they wish to build a heritage of distrust and even hate between our two people then they could not do anything more calculated to achieve this result than to continue the present policy with regard to colonial students in this country. We hope that the time will come when a British Government will tackle the colonial problem and make it possible for coloured students to live friendly (sic) with the British people. Till then Sir, we have no other alternative than to work for more hostels.[10]

Further evidence that a concerted and widespread campaign was developing on the eve of the General Election arrived at the Colonial Office in the form of a confidential telegram from the Gold Coast Governor who asked for more information about the dispute as, he explained, 'a press campaign of a most unhappy kind appears to be beginning'. Making use of the fact that he was a prince, Aderemi wrote to several MPs, and provoked numerous parliamentary questions. He and another Nigerian law student Uche Omo, the assistant secretary of the NU, emerged as two of the main leaders of the dispute and the students' 'Action Committee'.[11] They both featured prominently in the many press reports of the dispute and were also the main movers behind a NU resolution which supported the 'stay put' and called on the Nigerian government to provide its own student hostel. During the campaign letters of protest were also sent to the Colonial Office by the LCP, the Caribbean Labour Congress and Janet Jagan of the Peoples' Progressive Party in British Guiana.

The Consultative Committee on the welfare of colonial students

The Colonial Office was soon able to bring the dispute to an end. First officials met the students and promised that extra hostel accommodation would be made available and that they would look into the problem of the so-called 'colour-tax', that it was alleged was levied by certain landladies, as well as other examples of discrimination.[12] Finally it was announced that the Colonial Secretary would establish a consultative committee with student representatives, to establish better relations between them and the Colonial Office and so avoid future confrontation. Naturally both sides claimed a moral victory. The students believed that they had wrung valuable concessions from the Colonial Secretary and this seems to have been the opinion of most of the press. The Colonial Office took the view that a few timely concessions had led to a gradual winding down of the dispute. J.L. Keith was certainly relieved that the Gold Coast students had not featured prominently in the dispute and suggested that this was as a result of their meetings with Botsio and Nkrumah. The Colonial Office remained very cautious about its relations with the new Gold Coast ministers and wished in particular to avoid entanglements with Gold Coast students which might lead to serious conflict with Nkrumah. The new Consultative Committee on the Welfare of Colonial Students in the UK first met in November 1951, and was chaired by Lord Munster, the Parliamentary Under-Secretary of State for the Colonies. MPs in attendance included Sorensen as well as representatives of the Colonial Office, British Council, London University and the National Union of Students. Colonial students from the West Indies, Malaya and East Africa were represented, along with those from West Africa. The West African organisations represented included the GCU, the NU, the SLSU, as well as WASU.

The Colonial Office, having formally recognised WASU and other West African student organisations as representatives of the large number of West African students in Britain, now found itself in the difficult position of having to recognise the officers of these organisations, often the most politically active and hostile to its aims. J.L. Keith, for example, was reluctant to have on the committee the newly elected WASU president Joe Appiah, whom he described as 'a disaffected "communistic" person', who expressed 'violent and anti-British sentiments'. Indeed he hoped to avoid both Appiah and Ade Ademola, the honorary secretary of WASU, whom one official described as 'a communist', but also 'an able young man and son of a very good judge'. There was also concern about M.A. Oyewole, president of the NU, who was referred to as 'a man who is well known to have Communistic tendencies and expresses himself rather freely against the Nigerian Government'. But Oyewole's position meant that he too joined the committee where officials hoped he might be kept 'on the right lines'.[13]

The consultative committee continued to meet regularly throughout the early 1950s, although by 1955 Colonial Office officials were complaining that student representatives seldom attended meetings. From 1954 the West African governments established their own student units in Britain and these gradually took over responsibility for student welfare. Apart from a few vociferous early complaints from the student representatives, the worst fears of the Colonial Office were not realised. Oyewole, Ademola and Appiah took part in the work of the committee, which served very much as a safety valve, just as the Colonial Secretary had intended.

Racism and the colour bar

Of all the problems facing the students the colour bar and racism created the most practical difficulties, had a major effect on the students and those concerned with their welfare, and were often mentioned in the meetings of the consultative committee. Such problems ranged from the colour bar in accommodation, discrimination at the labour exchanges and in employment, to police inactivity regarding racist murders. Racism was no doubt also partly responsible for the large number of West African students who suffered nervous breakdowns while they were studying in Britain. The case of Seretse Khama, exiled by the Labour government from Bechuanaland because of his marriage to an Englishwoman, highlighted the issue of racism still further and caused consternation not only in the ranks of the Labour Party but also in the Colonial Office. Many West African students took part in the Seretse Khama Fighting Committee based at the WASU hostel at Chelsea Embankment and joined the protest rally in Trafalgar Square organised by the Africa League.[14] In a letter of protest to the Prime Minister, the West African Students' Club at Oxford condemned the Government's action, which it pointed out could not 'inspire the confidence of Colonial Peoples in Great Britain or help them to see any more clearly the essential difference between the methods of democracy and those of totalitarianism'.[15]

The late 1940s and early 1950s witnessed an increase in physical racist attacks and even murders of black people in Britain. In July 1949 some forty to fifty African workers resident at a common lodging house in Deptford, south London, were subjected to a colour bar in local 'coffee stalls, cafes and public houses, as well as by some local employees'. Apparently organised gangs from outside the area had threatened stallholders and others with violence if they served Africans. The gangs then launched an attack on the lodging house. In the ensuing fight large numbers of police arrived and 14 Africans, mostly Nigerian workers, were arrested. Incidents such as this often provoked enormous press coverage, and the intervention of those British organisations committed to fighting against racism. On this occasion the NCCL represented all the arrested men, and most were acquitted or received nominal fines.[16]

The press continued to report the many cases of discrimination throughout the country, ranging from black mothers barred from buying children's clothes and hairdressers refusing to cut black children's hair, to problems of accommodation and employment. Many Africans and other black people were barred from public houses and hotels. In 1953, in the so-called Baynes St Riot, a gang attacked Nigerians living in north London, while two years later, similar attacks were reported in east London.[17] In some parts of the country African students and workers organised their own opposition to racism and the colour bar. In Manchester in 1951 for example, the Africa League with a membership of some two hundred students and workers had sent a letter of protest to the Colonial Secretary demanding 'the appointment of a committee to study the general conditions of Colonial workers all over Britain and to make recommendations'. They also demanded social and educational centres for colonial workers in Cardiff, Hull, Liverpool, Birmingham and Manchester.[18] In Birmingham the League of Africans and People of African Descent organised protest meetings against the colour bar.[19]

WASU viewed the problem of discrimination as a consequence of Africans' colonial status and this led to it challenging not only continued colonial rule but also the whole notion of democracy in Britain. A *Wasu News Service* editorial in September 1953 explained that student difficulties were inextricably linked with colonialism, and, 'to obviate these difficulties and to enlarge his rights the desideratum of national freedom cannot be over stressed'. The article concluded that the student 'will win his rights if he wins the freedom of his country from its degrading colonial status'. Earlier that year WASU had joined with other colonial and British student organisations in a Colonial and Dominion Students' Conference held in London. The conference had discussed the problems of racism and resolved to 'launch a country-wide campaign on the question of the colour bar' and 'to campaign for more hostels at lower costs'.[20]

The Colonial Office was concerned about the situation resulting from the colour bar, but largely powerless to change it. Press reports stressed that the colour bar was playing into the hands of communists who, it was said, at least treated colonial subjects as equal citizens. Numerous newspaper articles, letters and parliamentary questions forced the Colonial Office to take up individual cases and to attempt to put pressure on government departments such as the Board of Trade and organisations such as the British Travel and Holidays Association. The mood of the times is summed up by a *Daily Herald* headline that proclaimed 'Colour Bar – to pretend it doesn't exist in Britain is hypocrisy'.[21]

The influence of communism

The onset of the Cold War intensified official concern about communist influence on the students. The insurrection in Malaya and the so-called Mau Mau rebellion in Kenya heightened fears of real and imagined communist conspiracies throughout the early 1950s. Colonial policy in West Africa was therefore designed to lead to eventual self-government within the Commonwealth, but the whole process of the

Africanisation of civil service and other posts in the colonies was designed to create the basis for neo-colonialism and to act as a defence against the threat of communism

The policy of Africanisation meant an increase in the number of West Africans studying and training in Britain and in the political significance of the students. As the pace of decolonisation quickened, so the Colonial Office intensified its social and political training of future African politicians and administrators and tried, through the Consultative Committee to monitor and influence student activity. Funding student unions and associations, providing good accommodation, and developing stronger personal links with individual students, were all strategies aimed at containing communism. In West Africa, the banning of communist literature, restrictions on travel to Eastern European countries, and the eventual bans against the employment of communists in the civil service in the mid-1950s, served a similar aim.

The Attlee government had recognised the need to counter communist influence amongst the students, and discussions about the solutions to this problem took place at the highest level, the Colonial Office, the Commonwealth Relations Office and the Foreign Office, and also amongst the Joint Chiefs of Staff and in the Cabinet itself. In August 1950 the Foreign Office produced a report entitled *A Survey of Communism in Africa*.[22] The report conceded that communist influence existed amongst students, mainly due to the activities of the CPGB, but it was confident that few students retained these ideas when they returned to West Africa. Of special concern were the activities of the IUS based in Prague, and the scholarships awarded to West African students by bodies, such as the Central Union of Czechoslovak Students, which from 1949 awarded seventy scholarships a year to colonial students. One of the first West Africans to study in Prague was Bankole Akpata, who in 1949, with the assistance of the CPGB, joined the High School of Political and Economic Sciences in Prague. A number of other West Africans also studied in Prague, and the early 1950s had established a West African Students' Committee at Charles University. By 1952 there were also eleven Nigerians who had been awarded scholarships to study in East Germany.[23]

The CPGB's International Affairs Department included not only an Africa committee but also a West Africa sub-committee. Over 150 Nigerians joined the Party in London, where they were initially placed in their own 'Robeson branches'. The CPGB also maintained strong links with WASU, and with the Africa League, the GCU, the NU and the Gambia League. It is also clear that although it was mainly students who became communists, the CPGB also had some success with West African workers.[24] Affiliations were also maintained with the West African nationalist and labour organisations and with the members of various Marxist groups in Nigeria, some of whom such as Ade Ademola, Ayo Ogunsheye, and M.A. Aderemi, were students in London. Despite the presence of Desmond Buckle and its links with the members of WANS, the CPGB appears to have had most success with Nigerians and fewer supporters from the Gold Coast and the other West African colonies.

The CPGB was hopeful that through its links with West African and especially Nigerian students in Britain, it might assist the development of a communist movement in West Africa. However, the students' interest in Marxism did not mean that they became disciplined revolutionaries, and they often also showed an interest, as Ogunsheye seems to have done, in interpretations of Marxism not favoured by the CPGB, such as 'Titoism'. Other West African CPGB members formed their own West African Youth and Student Organisation, subsequently the African Workers' and Students' Association, claiming that they had no confidence in Ade Thomas and those placed in leadership positions by the CPGB.[25]

The CPGB and its Africa Committee were themselves somewhat confused about the situation in Nigeria and the various strands of the nationalist movement. They sought to understand the 'national question' in Nigeria and to discover the basis for a Marxist leadership that might form a Nigerian communist party. Nigerian students who were members of the CPGB were also involved in the internal party disagreements over the relative merits of the NCNC and Action Group, and were often on different sides, and these political differences also emerged in the ranks of the student organisations such as WASU. Therefore although the CPGB had some influence on the students, divisions both in Nigeria and in Britain, as well as the political immaturity and background of many of the students, limited the effects of this influence on the struggle for independence.

In West Africa the struggle for independence increasingly became a series of negotiations between the nationalist organisations and the British government. As the colonies moved towards self-government and career prospects opened up, many returning 'communist' students became as 'bourgeois in Lagos' as they had been 'proletarian in

London'. A confidential CPGB report on the situation in Nigeria in 1953, noted with obvious disappointment that Ogunsheye was 'very anti-Soviet, and very pro-Action Group', and that he 'no longer represents the revolutionary movement'. While Amanke Okafor 'was still studying the situation at home', and was not politically active. The report concluded that 'our Nigerian comrades do return to our Fatherland and that is all we hear of them'.[26]

The communist movement in West Africa was also severely hampered by legal restrictions and the banning of anti-imperialist and communist literature and activities. WASU protested when in 1953 the Nigerian government banned the World Peace Council's *The Road to Peace*. More severe steps were taken in the Gold Coast, when the Convention People's Party suspended some of its leading members because they had attended the Vienna meeting of the World Federation of Trade Unions, held earlier that year. In February 1954, the CPP government banned communists from entering the civil service in the Gold Coast, and in October similar measures were taken in Nigeria, after a further ban on communist literature.

West Africa perceptively commented that the bans in Nigeria were 'a warning to Nigerian students overseas'. Some students clearly welcomed such a ban, and hoped that it might lead to the decline of communist influence in WASU and elsewhere. One of the most enthusiastic supporters of the bans was George Padmore who, in an article entitled 'Communist Activities In The Colonies Exposed', wrote disapprovingly of the British Communist Party: 'recruiting and training communists from among disgruntled and frustrated Colonial students - some of whom have failed to pass their final legal examinations for which they blame the Colonial Office'. According to Padmore's account, several Nigerian communists had left Britain 'with instructions to infiltrate into the Action Group' and the other political parties in Nigeria. There they were to work under the instruction of Bankole Akpata, who returned to Nigeria in 1954. Padmore reported that 'British Communists have not been as successful in indoctrinating Gold Coast students as they have been among Nigerians', and that 'Sierra Leone and Gambian students, as well as Moslim (*sic*) students from Northern Nigeria are said to be violently opposed to the Red doctrine'. Padmore's strongly anti-communist article argued that communist conspiracies aimed to incite violence in the Gold Coast and to discredit Nkrumah and accused West Africans of 'flirting with Communists and doing their dirty work of sabotaging their own country's struggle for freedom'.[27]

Student reactions to the bans are difficult to ascertain. H.S. Sowemimo, the secretary of WASU explained that he was opposed to 'Communist infiltration into West African affairs', and welcomed the ban. However, there was no WASU disaffiliation from the IUS, and Ade Thomas, a leading member of WASU was prepared to speak openly at the second conference of the Communist and Workers Parties within the British Commonwealth and Empire held in London in 1954. He welcomed the 'growing interest in Marxism among the most active and younger elements in Nigeria', and explained: 'There can be no real advance in Nigeria's fight for national liberation until all the genuine Marxist elements come together into a united party which can fulfil the role of Marxism and working-class leadership within the broadest national front, and so advance the struggle in Nigeria against imperialism and its reactionary puppets'.[28]

West Africans and the international student movement

One of the main concerns of the Colonial Office was the contact between the students and organisations such as the IUS and the WFDY. WASU had been in contact with the IUS since its founding in 1946. By the early 1950s the IUS had over 5 million members from 71 countries and an International Student Relief (ISR) organisation which assisted students who faced economic, social and political disadvantages. From 1947 the IUS published a monthly bulletin on the 'life and struggles' of colonial students, and had established 'A Bureau of Students Fighting against Colonialism', which campaigned 'actively with students in colonial, semi-colonial and dependent countries in their fight for freedom and national independence'. Together with the WFDY the IUS had even declared 21 February the 'Day of Solidarity with Youth and Students Fighting against Colonialism.[29]

The anti-colonialism, anti-racism and internationalism of the IUS and ISR clearly impressed many WASU members. *News Service* explained:

> As colonials we realise that we cannot and must not isolate ourselves from the struggle of our peoples for independence. For it is when this is achieved that we can enjoy fully the fruits of education and use it for the building of a better society for our peoples. We realise too that our struggle is a part of the universal one for a better world and as such we must

co-operate with all those who are engaged in this battle fully realising that it is a joint struggle that can rid the world of its present day conflicts. In the IUS we have found a sincere friend for indeed its slogan 'Unite for Peace, National Independence and Democratic Education' is a genuine guide in the struggle against racism and Colonialism.[30]

However, the Colonial Office viewed the IUS and its affiliates as 'little more than the student section of the Cominform'. Officials were particularly concerned that at a time when the British government feared global Soviet and communist expansion, and was actually fighting against communists in Malaya, students were openly embracing such an organisation and in some cases journeying beyond the 'Iron Curtain' to cities such as Prague, which one official described as 'the enemy's main indoctrination centre'.[31] Student visits to Eastern Europe most regularly took the form of attendance at the World Festival of Youth, organised by the IUS and the WFDY, or at the annual IUS congresses, and the ISR provided aid and scholarships for those students who wished to study in Eastern Europe, and even free medical care. The first World Festival of Youth took place in Prague in 1947, and again in Budapest and Berlin over the next four years. At the Budapest Festival in 1949, Bankole Akpata represented the Youth Congress of Nigeria and the Cameroons. In 1951 over seventy West Africans from Britain attended the Festival, organised by their own West African Youth Festival Preparatory Committee. It was following their visit to the Berlin Festival that many West Africans joined the CPGB.[32]

The Colonial Office remained uncertain about how it should counter this growing student contact with Eastern Europe. Attempts were made to make travel difficult, especially directly from West Africa, and those who did travel were closely monitored by the security services. Whatever the restrictions, many West Africans managed to reach Eastern Europe during these years, where they always received an extremely warm welcome, and were liable to comment on the lack of racism or the colour bar in these countries, as well as the opportunities for students and life in general. Those who chose to study in Eastern Europe sent back glowing accounts of their experiences. In March 1953, for example, *News Service* contained a report on 'The Peoples' Democracies of Central and Eastern Europe', explaining that West African students in Czechoslovakia and East Germany had been given scholarships by the IUS, that they also received allowances, lived in better conditions and that the standard of education was higher than in Britain. Unlike in Britain, the students were housed with 'native students', in order to learn the language and culture of the particular country. They also mentioned:

> the deep sympathy of the people of these countries for the struggles of the African people for self-determination and human rights. The presence of West Africans in their countries is a practical expression of this sympathy; it also helps to increase and strengthen the friendship and understanding between our peoples.[33]

The reader was thus forced to agree with the conclusion that 'there are real peoples' governments in these countries'.[34]

Clearly links with the IUS, and Eastern Europe made some impression on the students. Even the name of the *Wasu News Service* seems to have been borrowed from the publication of the IUS, and the students were prepared to defend their affiliation with the organisation. However, since the international student movement also found itself a victim of the Cold War, supporters of the IUS in WASU quickly found that it was at loggerheads with the National Union of Students in Britain (NUSB). It was only in February 1952, after a long struggle, that WASU was officially recognised by the NUSB and permitted to send an observer to its council meetings 'to speak on matters concerning West African students', This WASU agreed to do, stating that it would use 'every opportunity to carry further the fight for improved conditions for our students here and at home and to bring more into the proceedings of Council the struggle of our people for independence'. However, in spite of this recognition, WASU was openly critical of the NUSB for its failure to take a stand on major international issues such as peace and disarmament, and because it failed to discuss colonial problems and the anti-colonial struggles for independence. According to WASU, the NUSB did not wage 'active campaigns ... in defence of those colonial and semi-dependent peoples whose students are oppressed and victimised constantly'.[35]

One of WASU's main concerns was that after the IUS congress in Prague in 1950, twenty-one national student unions, including the NUSB, met in Stockholm to voice their dissatisfaction with the IUS and the alleged domination of its activities by communist and pro-communist students' unions. This group reached agreement on the Students' Mutual Assistance Programme (SMAP) 'to strengthen their co-operation especially with student organisations in colonial territories', planned a 'good-will' delegation to visit East and West Africa, and asked for the West African students' support. WASU was suspicious of the motives behind the SMAP, especially since they claimed that no African, Asian, or Latin American representatives had been consulted; moreover the NUSB had never before shown any great interest in the affairs of colonial students, and it had not supported the 1951 strike at Hans Crescent.[36]

After WASU and other colonial student unions had refused to co-operate with the scheme, the NUSB refused it official recognition, and sought to establish relations with other West African student groups in Britain. These attempts were unsuccessful and this probably led to the subsequent recognition of WASU, which claimed that eighty per cent of West Africa's students were students in Britain, therefore any international co-operation should start in Britain, and start with their participation. It totally opposed attempts by the NUSB and others to establish independent contact with student unions at Fourah Bay, Achimota and Ibadan in West Africa, and argued that if absolutely necessary there should be a joint NUSB-WASU delegation to West Africa.[37]

At the IUS Council meeting in Warsaw in 1951, WASU representative James Vaughan delivered a report on the conditions of West African students in West Africa and Britain which suggested 'the sending of a Commission by the IUS to West Africa to investigate conditions of education there', and 'the organisation by the IUS of a student or cultural exchange in West Africa'. The anti-colonialism of the IUS clearly suited the purposes of WASU better than the vague aims of the NUSB. At the same time the communist members of the Union, such as Vaughan, were opposed to the attempts of the NUSB and others to split the IUS.[38]

In 1952, after a further meeting of anti-IUS student unions in Edinburgh, the NUSB formally disaffiliated from the IUS, and in an article in *News Service*, the president of the NUSB openly attacked the IUS as a communist front. Such actions were condemned by WASU executive, which also opposed further attempts by the NUSB to encourage other West African student organisations to join a new international student organisation based in Copenhagen. The split in the international student movement left WASU firmly in the IUS camp and it openly declared, 'We believe warmly in world student solidarity and we detest attempts to create a breakaway group from the IUS in whose ranks there is genuine comradeship for all students'. Defending itself against the accusation that it was unduly under the influence of certain 'political trends', the Union explained:

> If our members seek to see the building of a new and better life in the Peoples' Democracies; if they love to learn from the Chinese students the role they played in getting rid of a hated regime and how they are building the new China; if we maintain our sanity in discussing the Soviet Union, well realising that the Soviets have no soft spots for Dr Malan and anyway do not share in the exploitation of our territories.... it is not because of 'political trends' but for our passionate belief in truth and sincerity.[39]

WASU's links with the IUS continued throughout the early 1950s, and provide one of the best examples of the political influence of the international communist and anti-imperialist movement on West African students. This influence was particularly noticeable in the style and content of the *News Service* as well as in various resolutions passed by the Union. Solanke had attempted to encourage the younger students to relaunch *Wasu* (it ceased publication in the summer of 1949). When *News Service* appeared in the summer of 1952 Solanke attempted to get his supporters to stop selling it. Indeed he openly stated his opposition to the affiliation of the Union to outside bodies, and its policy of collecting money for ISR. The Colonial Office shared Solanke's concern about WASU's new publication, as many of its issues were seen as 'extremely hostile to H.M. Government's policy in the Colonies', and because it 'generally follows the line of communist publications, such as the *Daily Worker* in this country'.[40]

WASU *News Service* and student politics

News Service, like its forerunner, contained articles concerned with WASU affairs and with events and struggles in West Africa and throughout the African continent, but it also carried reports on the activities and policies of the IUS, and reports of student struggles from around the world.[41] A clear Marxist and internationalist perspective was always evident in articles on Vietnam, Korea, and Malaya, where the Union had opposed the sending of African troops, and in a letter to the Colonial Secretary had reaffirmed its solidarity 'with the Malayan people fighting for their freedom'.[42] The political affiliations of WASU were most clearly evident on the occasion of the death of Joseph Stalin in 1953.

News Service devoted its editorial to Stalin's obituary, declaring that Stalin's youth had provided 'shining examples to all youth'. On the Soviet Union it stated 'It is idle to pretend to ignore this force or to deny that the stepping-up of colonial struggles for freedom is unrelated to the well-known achievements of the Soviet people'. The explanation for these achievements, it explained: 'naturally lead us into those theories associated with the names of Marx, Engels, Lenin and Stalin', and it added, 'it is true that for an appreciation of what is happening in the world today ignorance of the writings and teachings of Marxism-Leninism is a positive disadvantage'. The editorial concluded by asserting: 'if in the second half of the 20th century colonial countries achieve their freedom and fundamental human rights, history cannot fail to record in this the tremendous influence of Stalin'.[43]

A feature of the new journal was the occasional 'themed' issue; in December 1952 a 'Special Kenya Edition' of *News Service* appeared, necessitated by 'the trend of events in Kenya'. The State of Emergency introduced in Kenya in October 1952 in response to the 'Mau Mau' uprising, not only led to the proscription of anti-colonial political organisations, but also the imprisonment of their leaders, including Jomo Kenyatta. The students, as might be expected, were entirely opposed to the actions of the Kenya government and the European settlers. Kenyatta and some other East Africans had been close to WASU during their student days in Britain, and the Union declared that it would, 'seek to stop the attacks on the Kenya Africans and demand the release of their leaders'.[44] WASU was joined in its protest by the representatives of the GCU, NU, SLSU, West Indian Students Union, LCP and Zanzibar Students' Movement, who formed their own 'Kenya Committee' and organised a boycott of Colonial Office functions, the first of which was a Christmas dance, hosted by the Colonial Office's Student Liaison Officers. The NU president, M.A. Oyewole, issued a statement condemning the Government's actions in Kenya, and asking if further proof were needed 'to convince ourselves that under the British flag racial discrimination is established, practised and encouraged'. Was this, he asked 'Britain's idea of Partnership?'[45]

In WASU too, the students viewed the Government's actions as proof that the days of imperialism had not passed, and that the notion of 'partnership' was an attempt at deception. Those who failed to speak out on the Kenya situation, such as the NUSB, were considered agents of imperialism. The students enthusiastically supported the Kenya Committee led by CPGB members, and acted to defend Kenyatta, along with his legal representatives D.N. Pritt, and former WASU members H.O. Davies, Kola Balogun and Cobina Kessie. A WASU delegation, led by the president V. O. Ibeneme participated in the 'Hands off Kenya Day', organised by the Kenya Committee in December 1953, which included a lobby of Parliament to protest at '12 months of British Terrorism'.[46] Much to the concern of the Colonial Office, *News Service* continued to focus on Kenya throughout the early 1950s, and arrangements were made for representatives of the Colonial Office's Information Department to give talks to the students at Hans Crescent to 'correct' their impressions of Kenya. Similar concern was expressed over WASU's opposition to the proposed Central African Federation, a policy which was strengthened, after the students had been addressed by Joshua Nkomo, then president of the Southern Rhodesian African National Congress.[47]

Another concern for WASU was the Government's reaction to the election of the People's Progressive Party (PPP) in British Guiana. Once again the students saw government action as entirely undemocratic, but providing rich lessons for those struggling for self-government in West Africa. A *News Service* editorial claimed that, 'we expect that a full appraisal of the situation in British Guiana must spur us on to a fiercer struggle for national independence'.[48] The Union sent a resolution to the Colonial Secretary, while *News Service* contained a message of support to the PPP and a chronicle of the events that had led to the suspension of the constitution in British Guiana. *News Service* was especially concerned about the Colonial Secretary's statement that 'Her Majesty's Government shall not allow the organisation of a communist state within the British Commonwealth'. In defence of such communist states the students explained that:

> Oppressed colonials have been subjected to a continuous blast of propaganda against the Soviet Union and the Peoples' Democracies, and have been told lurid stories of slave camps and whatnot in the Soviet Union. Yet it cannot be said that the Soviet Union is totalitarian. Perhaps, with all its immense cost, the Russian Revolution is the greatest and the most beneficent event in modern history since the French Revolution and that it has opened more awareness of creative fulfilment to more people than even its remarkable predecessor.[49]

News Service argued that the countries of Eastern Europe and China had done much to break down 'barriers of colour and wealth' and that if the Government was opposed to totalitarianism in the Commonwealth, then how could it justify its actions in Malaya and Kenya and its support for the regime in South Africa.

Decolonisation in West Africa

Events in Malaya, Kenya, South Africa and British Guiana led many West African students in Britain to adopt a more critical attitude to the process of decolonisation, which was taking place in West Africa itself. Even in the Gold Coast, where from 1951 Kwame Nkrumah headed the new CPP government, some saw 'a need to struggle more energetically for freedom'. WASU declared that, 'since we are a student organisation not tied to any political party, we reserve our rights to criticise any West African organisation'. The students tried to exert some influence over events in West Africa through *News Service*, and especially during visits to the hostel by Nkrumah, Botsio, Okoi Arikpo and other West African ministers, many of whom were former WASU members.

WASU members were especially critical of what were seen as CPP compromises over constitutional changes in the Gold Coast, and *News Service* warned the CPP that it could not afford to deviate from the policies 'which built its reputation and followership', and explained that 'nothing will be satisfactory for us which does not have room for an eventual federation of all the West African states'. The students tried to be constructively critical, and were strongly supportive and indignant when Nkrumah was not invited to the 1952 Commonwealth Prime Minister's Conference. On other occasions, however, neither Nkrumah's former membership of WASU nor his prestige could save him from criticism. Many WASU members clearly took exception to Padmore's *The Gold Coast Revolution*, first published in 1953. *News Service* claimed that Padmore's friendship with Nkrumah had blinded him to the reality of the situation in the Gold Coast, and criticised his 'religious veneration' of Nkrumah. Much of the criticism was of a political nature, clearly stemming from Padmore's rejection of communist orthodoxy. Other articles in *News Service* show that WASU was growing concerned about reports of corruption and lack of freedom of expression in the Gold Coast, as well as the fact that Nkrumah's CPP appeared to be working in close partnership with the British government.

WASU focused much of its attention on events in Nigeria and was critical of the 1951 Macpherson Constitution, which established regional governments with limited powers, claiming it had been used 'to set region against region' and so delayed self-government. Proposals by the new Conservative Colonial Secretary to increase regional autonomy in the country were condemned by the students who sent an immediate cablegram of warning to the political leaders in Nigeria. The latter seem to have taken little heed of this cablegram, nor of a memorandum drafted by the Union for the constitutional conference held in London in the summer of 1953. However, WASU remained adamant that 'Nothing but a Unitary Government can bind Nigeria into a homogenous and a powerful country'. It was critical of all those nationalist politicians who had gone 'all out to strengthen the regions at the expense of the centre', and in particular of the actions of the Colonial Secretary, whose 'dastardly policies in Kenya, British Guiana and Central Africa have recalled to mind the worst aspects of Hitler's policy in Europe'.[50]

West African organisations in Britain

WASU's influence on the anti-colonial movement in Nigeria was somewhat limited, especially as decolonisation gathered pace. Clearly there was close contact with ex-WASU members and ministers like Arikpo and NCNC politicians such as Kola Balogun, but the students remained critical of all the major nationalist parties. Many of WASU's Nigerian members also belonged to the NU that claimed to have a membership of over two thousand workers and students. By 1955 it had become a truly national organisation, its executive members drawn from Hull, Birmingham, Newcastle and Dundee as well as London and Dublin. The aims of the NU included: 'the fostering of a spirit of Nigerian citizenship and general dissemination of a Nigeria-wide outlook among its members and other Nigerians', and 'the encouragement of social cultural and other useful contacts and understanding among the various ethnic groups in Nigeria'.[51] It was opposed to a disunited Nigeria and held a number of public meetings and residential 'schools' on this issue. Visiting Nigerian politicians tended to speak at meetings hosted by the NU rather than at WASU meetings as in former years, and the NU became significant enough to warrant political attacks from Awolowo's Action Group (AG) in Nigeria.

THE 1950S: COMMUNISM AND NATIONALISM

The NU had at first aroused the suspicions of the Colonial Office because it included amongst its leading officers suspected 'fellow travellers' such as M.A. Oyewole, M.A. Aderemi and Uche Omo. However, after the Union's elections in January 1953, the Colonial Office noted that Omo and Aderemi were not re-elected, while E.E. Obahiagbon, a student at the LSE, replaced Oyewole as the new president. The Colonial Office was of the opinion that Obahiagbon's views were 'pretty Marxist, but tinged (or adulterated) with titoism', but officials were convinced that he was not a communist. One official claimed that Obahiagbon's politics were 'thought to be a mixture of those of Marx, Tito and Mr Bevan'.[52]

Obahiagbon had protested at the appearance of a CPGB speaker at the Union's 1952 Summer School, and seemed, to the Colonial Office, to be a more reasonable customer than the 'ardent nationalist' Oyewole. Officials believed that the NU was under new direction and that its views were now 'surprisingly good and responsible'. Obahiagbon's presidential address in 1953, *A Preface to Policy*, still claimed that there was 'common ground between the colonial peoples and the communist world', and that nationalists should 'work with communists in our common opposition to "classical imperialism" '. But he was also critical of the formulations of Palme Dutt concerning the nationalist movement in Nigeria.[53] For the Colonial Office, this approach to communism seems to have been more important than Obahiagbon's more severe criticisms of both the Macpherson Constitution and the Labour Party. The Colonial Office was even more impressed by the NU's statement to the Governor of Nigeria and the leaders of Nigerian political parties in July 1953, which called on the politicians to stay in Nigeria and resolve their differences, and on the Governor of Nigeria to help them do so. It concluded that it was now important to co-operate with the NU and to help finance some of its activities, such as the summer schools and the 'useful work' undertaken by the Union's branch in Dublin.

Sir Charles Jeffries, Deputy Under-Secretary of State at the Colonial Office reassured the Governor of Nigeria, Sir John Macpherson, that the NU posed no major threat, and explained that it was better to cooperate with such organisations than to drive them underground into 'the laps of communists'. Colonial Office officials attended the NU Summer School held in Hastings in September 1953, and shared some of the cost. They noted the low attendance, some twenty participants, and were relieved to find that Idris Cox, who was representing the

CPGB, 'made no attempt to proselytise'. The following summer the NU hosted a reception for Macpherson, to honour his appointment as Governor-General of Nigeria. Macpherson promised to establish a more permanent liaison between the NU, the Colonial Office and the new Nigeria Office in London, a move welcomed by Oyewole, subsequently re-elected as NU president, who stressed that such links were necessary to guide the energies of the students.[54]

The NU was also closely involved with the FCB, its general-secretary Lawrence Fabunmi, another student at LSE declaring, 'we consider the Fabian Society as one of our friends in Britain'. FCB members attended the NU conferences, as did representatives of the Union of Democratic Control (UDC), the Africa Bureau, the COPAI, the CPGB and the major political parties. In 1954 the NU conference was also addressed by an attaché from the Egyptian embassy.

A number of other Nigerian organisations were also active in Britain during this time. Most seem to have been London based, such as the branches of the AG and NCNC, which met at the old WASU hostel in Camden. There was also a Nigerian Students' Union formed in Halifax in 1955, and a Nigerian led Pan-African Society in Belfast. Yoruba students might be members of such organisations as the Egbe Omo Ijebu and Egbe Omo Egba based at Hans Crescent, Itsekiri students formed a branch of the Warri National Union, there was a Calabar Union, while students from northern Nigeria formed their own Northern Nigeria Association of Great Britain and Ireland.

There is little doubt that politicians in Nigeria looked upon these organisations and especially the AG and NCNC as recruiting and nurturing grounds for their members. I. Dafe, a CPGB member was the vice-president of the NCNC in London, while O.A. Bamishe, the first chairman of the AG in London and for a time a CPGB member, returned to Nigeria to head the AG in Ibadan, Nigeria. The ethnic and national divisions so obvious in Nigerian politics were reflected in the emergence of so many organisations in Britain at this time.

Many Gold Coast students were members of the GCU, which evolved out of the GCSU, and which, because of its generally more moderate membership, was initially seen by the Colonial Office as a 'reputable body'. Although the GCU also had criticisms to make of the Gold Coast government, and for a time was led by former WANS member E.K. Dadzie, it seems to have enjoyed extremely good relations with the Colonial Office. By 1953 it claimed to have 600 members throughout the UK, and proposed to establish its own 'provisional centres' in Dublin, Newcastle and Edinburgh, but little is known of its activities. It organised meetings and conferences, was in contact with the Paris-based Togoland Students' Union, campaigned for a 'Gold Coast House' or embassy in London, and looked after the funeral arrangements for those of its compatriots who needed such assistance. The Union also produced a quarterly newsletter, and in 1956 announced plans to produce a bi-monthly magazine called *The Citizen*.[55]

The Gambia and Sierra Leone students also had their own student unions. The Gambia Students' Union (GSU) was formed in April 1953 by H.L. George, a member of WASU executive, who was the GSUs first chairman. It seems probable that the GSU was established with the help of WASU as part of their reorganisation plans. These plans favoured a federal WASU, which incorporated all the individual West African unions. At a time when there was a debate over whether the independence of the Gambia was viable, or if it should join with French Senegal, WASU maintained that an independent Gambia could survive within an eventual West African federation.[56] The Sierra Leone Students' Union (SLSU) emerged in 1950 from the Sierra Leone Study Group formed a few years earlier. The SLSU was a member of the British Council's Consultative Committee of Colonial Student Unions in 1950, and was initially led by Ben Davies, Maurice Jones and Wadi Williams. It took part in the Colonial Students' Council established by the students during the Hans Crescent strike, and in 1953 produced its own publication, *The Sierra Leone Student*.

By the late 1950s there was a significant increase in the numbers of student and other organisations, including a West African Students' Committee in Leicester, a Colonial and Young Dominions Association at Bristol University and an Afro-Asian Students' Association in Cardiff. The more significant organisations not only maintained links with each other and with organisations in West Africa, but also with many other anti-colonial organisations in Britain. Even before the famous Bandung Conference, nineteen African and Asian student organisations in Britain, including WASU, held an Afro-Asian Students' Conference in London in 1955 and a second conference the following year. The students were also in contact with such organisations as the UDC, the Movement for Colonial Freedom (MCF), and the FCB. Those closest to the UDC, which began a new lease of life during the 1950s, included Ayo Ogunsheye, A. Amponsah of the Africa League and Ade Ademola, who all spoke at the UDC's 'Crisis in Africa' conference in 1950. Ademola was the joint editor, with Basil

Davidson the UDC's general secretary, of *The New West Africa*, a collection of articles on political developments in the region. Thomas Hodgkin's involvement with WASU members dates from early 1947, and both he and Basil Davidson spoke at the 1952 NU conference. WASU attended the founding conference of the MCF in 1954, as did a number of the Nigerian organisation based in Britain. WASU, the NU and various individual West Africans were active within the MCF's West African sub-committee, which for a time was led by George Padmore.[57]

West African women in Britain

One of the most important developments in student affairs during the 1950s was the growing concern with women's issues and organisations.[58] Much of this concern was due to the fact that between 1947 and 1950 the number of West African women studying in Britain multiplied fourfold. Official estimates put their number at over eight hundred in 1953, nearly half originating from Nigeria. At the same time there was also a growth of women's organisations throughout West Africa and particularly in Nigeria, where the Federation of All Nigerian Women's Organisations was formed in 1953. The vast majority of women students were in Britain to train as nurses, but a minority embarked upon studies in law, medicine and other fields. The British Council established special hostels for women students, while from the late 1940s, the Welfare Department of the Colonial Office and a West African women's liaison officer had the responsibility of looking after their general welfare.

WASU became particularly concerned about the position of women in Nigeria following the arrest and trial of Mrs Funmi Ransome-Kuti and forty-one other women for 'unlawful assembly', following police attempts to halt a rally organised by the Nigerian Women's Union (NWU) at Abeokuta in July 1952. WASU executive wrote a letter of support to Mrs Ransome-Kuti and the NWU in order 'to express our gratitude and admiration for the fight which you and Nigerian women are conducting against British rule and for social and political rights for our women'.[59]

In the autumn of 1953, WASU elected its first woman vice-president, Mrs Fola Ighodalo, a student of economics at the LSE. At the same time, Fola Ighodalo became president of the first Nigerian women's organisation in Britain, the Nigerian Women's League (NWL), which was formed to educate women for 'good citizenship and feminine leadership in future', and declared itself to be a non-political organisation. The NWL issued an appeal that stated:

> We believe that the women of Nigeria are capable of following in the courageous footsteps of the many brave women of other lands who have in the past fought against prejudice and overcame overwhelming obstacles in achieving great victories in the field of human endeavour.... Ours is the cause of Nigerian womanhood and we ask you to help us shoulder the precious burden by joining us in our newly formed league. We are at present quite a small band but our hopes are high because our faith in our fellow women is strong.[60]

The NWL seems to have occupied itself with social functions and dances, but it did organise an 'Easter School' in 1954 entitled 'Our changing society and us'. Other regular events included debates on topical issues, often organised jointly with the NU. At their first AGM Fola Ighodalo reported that membership had grown from an initial twelve to around seventy, that it had been a very good first year and, 'A real test of what Nigerian women can do in a foreign land'. She stated that the NWL wanted 'to learn to live with people here as equal human beings, to make our influence felt in all aspects of social, economic and political life in our community'.[61] There seems to be little more information about the NWL, but many of its members were student nurses. It was closely linked to the NU and some women were clearly members of both organisations.

In August 1956 the NU provoked some comment in the Nigerian press, but little controversy in Britain, when it elected a medical student, Ms A. Adenubi, as its first woman vice-president. But the following year WASU's latest publication the *West African Student* could still complain about the 'apathy of the West African woman', and expressed the view that 'our society has not been able to produce women of our mothers' calibre'.[62]

The reorganisation of WASU

In 1952 WASU began considering plans for its reorganisation. The need for such a move seems to have been prompted by the desire of the

Union to become more representative of all the West African students in Britain especially in the light of the existence of other organisations such as the NU and the GCU. The constant need to appeal to the West African governments for funding meant that the separate territorial organisations had to co-ordinate their efforts. In its relations with the Colonial Office and its Consultative Committee, and other bodies such as the NUSB, the Union had to be seen to present coherently student concerns. Essentially WASU proposed to form a federation with the other territorial organisations, making their presidents vice-presidents of the Union in a new executive body. Plans for a federal organisation were also evidence of the difficulty of establishing West African unity in the face of political developments and realities in West Africa, and student rivalries in Britain.

Many had felt the need for changes to the Union. A letter to *West Africa* in July 1954 claimed that WASU no longer stood 'for the ideals it chose on its formation' and was simply, 'a version of the Nigerian Union with a taint of other colonial dyes'. The letter complained that because of the formation of the other territorial organisations, WASU had become less important, and it had 'simply degenerated into an instrument for leftish political propaganda'. (*sic*) The Union's political affiliations were also criticised, and the writer claimed:

> WASU's leadership is passing to people who, it seems would be prepared to take orders from Moscow. The External Relations Secretary, the Finance Secretary, the Social Secretary, President, General Secretary and the former editor have all taken sponsored trips to Iron Curtain countries. One official once wrote a letter of commendation to the *Daily Worker*. This caucus took exception to flags being hung from the WASU hostel during the coronation.[63]

Subsequently a WASU president claimed that federation of the Union was attempted to overcome 'the continued domination of an autocratic and unrepresentative Nigerian majority riddled with contending cliques', which 'had dominated all elections by manipulating a flood of votes from henchmen who took no other interest in the union'.[64]

WASU's reorganisation plans were complicated by the negotiations with the West African governments for funding, the dire financial position of the hostel at Chelsea Embankment, and the fact that by 1954, as a step towards 'greater degrees of self-government', the Colonial Office was handing over responsibility for student affairs to London representatives of the West African governments, having convinced them a year earlier to contribute some £3000 for the running of the new hostel at Chelsea Embankment.[65]

One possible outcome of the new arrangements was that provision would be made for separate hostels for students from different West African territories. Such a proposal was made by Okoi Arikpo, the Nigerian minister responsible for student affairs, when he visited WASU in 1952. However, the students told him that they opposed any moves that would weaken West African unity and allow the Colonial Office 'to drive a wedge between us'. The reorganising WASU and the other West African organisations continued their appeals for finance to the West African governments, but by the summer of 1954 the finances of the WASU hostel had reached crisis point. The response of the Board was to propose that the hostel be sold, debts paid and that the Union secure the purchase of cheaper accommodation. Eventually in 1956, after other financial difficulties and the sale of the hostel at Chelsea Embankment, the students moved to a new hostel at Warrington Crescent. WASU's appeals to the West African governments for finance were more successful after the reorganisation of the Union had been completed at its congress in January 1956. According to *West Africa*, on that occasion 'a resolution was passed disassociating WASU from any political body whatsoever'. At the congress Dr William Lutterodt, a Gold Coast doctor who had returned to Britain for a post-graduate medical course, was elected deputy president. Lutterodt then toured West Africa as the representative of the Union and urged the West African governments to find the £13,000 needed to secure the new premises.[66]

News Service claimed that the successful appeal for funds was due to 'constitutional advancement in our countries and the replacement of "white officials" by our West African personnel'. However, the Nigerian High Commissioner in London had argued against Lutterodt's mission and stipulated that the Nigerian government would only finance the hostel if certain conditions were met, including the prohibition of 'all Communist activities by the Union'. He also demanded that 'the students must be in a minority' on WASU's board, as they were only temporarily resident in Britain, and that the Nigerian government wanted its own representative on the Board. Unfortunately for the Nigerian government, its presence on WASU's board and its finance for the hostel only gave some say in how the hostel was administered. It was unable to force any major political changes on the Union.

At WASU's Second Congress in March 1957, following a four hour debate and a close vote, the Union decided to continue its membership of the IUS and a Chinese delegate from the IUS was welcomed to the congress. There was also a warm welcome for a representative of the Paris-based Fédération d'Étudiants l'Afrique Noire en France (FEANF), who also spoke in support of the IUS. Some years before in 1951, WASU and other West African organisations had attended the Paris conference of the Rassemblement Democratique Africain (RDA) and had in turn been visited by an RDA delegation.[67] Ever since the days of WANS the students in Britain had maintained regular contact with their counterparts in France. WASU viewed its relationship with the FEANF as a 'necessary condition' for the attainment of what was referred to as 'a homogenous West African unit which may or may not assume a unitary form'.

But clearly not all the students welcomed continued affiliation to the IUS, many still fearing that they would 'continue to be called Communists', and would fall foul of their governments. Others were more hostile to the new West African governments and especially towards their officials in Britain, and wished to stress WASU's independence. They felt strongly that the West African commissioners and the new student units were still firmly under the control of the Colonial Office, and that they were intent on creating divisions among the students. Even though subsequently, three Nigerian government commissioners became directors of WASU Ltd and were able to exert some influence over the running of the hostel, WASU continued its historic tradition of seeking to control the Union's premises, arguing that the money had been donated to them and not to WASU Ltd.

Reorganisation failed to solve the organisational problems facing WASU and in particular the 'scandal of the quarrels' between Nigerian and Ghanaian students. Other disputes included the alleged theft of gifts for the Union and other 'misconduct' by members of the executive at the 6th World Festival of Youth and Students, held in Moscow in the summer of 1957, and at previous festivals. As a result the NU had threatened to break away if the culprits were not dealt with. At the third WASU congress in 1958 there was also a strong demand to break with the IUS and a proposal to establish stronger relations with the rival International Students' Conference. There was also said to be a 'deep fear of Communist domination over WASU', and the Union's president claimed that 'No other subject has caused us the same extremity of unceasing embarrassment, as well as the loss of influence with fellow West Africans whom we seek most to influence'.[68] At the congress the WASU president proposed that the Union continue to 'tolerate all Communists ... and resist the pressure to expel them simply for being Communists', but in the future wrongdoers might be expelled for 'promoting efforts to subject WASU to any external body over which WASU has no constitutional control'. He hoped that this rule 'should go far to discourage the belief that WASU is dominated by undesirable influences'.[69] The president believed that communist influence within the Union had declined, especially after reorganisation in 1955. Of course those students who were sympathetic to communism cannot have failed to have been affected by changes in the international communist movement occasioned by the death of Stalin, Krushchev's 'secret speech', the Soviet Union's invasion of Hungary and political differences within the CPGB. However, at the end of 1958 Reginald Sorensen was still complaining that WASU 'is not now the representative body it once was, being dominated by a small number of students with very leftish leanings'.[70]

From 1954-1957 *WASU News Service* only appeared annually and from 1956 was decidedly less stridently political than in previous years. Nevertheless it maintained a strong interest in international affairs and was written from an anti-imperialist perspective. In February 1957 it appeared in a new and more professionally produced format and continued for the next two months. It was renamed *The West African Student* in May of that year, but only seems to have lasted for one further edition. To judge from these publications the essential concerns of the students did not change significantly.

Self-government in West Africa

The independence of the new West African state of Ghana was declared in March 1957, and WASU devoted the whole of the March 1957 edition of *News Service* to this momentous event. Naturally *News Service* was full of congratulations to Nkrumah and the whole of Ghana, although it remained cautious about the country's future, but felt able to comment that 'Kwame has remained true and faithful to his – original mandate – power has not lulled him into sneering at the masses'. Nothing could stifle the celebrations organised by West African and especially Ghanaian students throughout Britain. The students urged an independent Ghana to remain neutral in international affairs. They also congratulated themselves that the nationalist movement in Ghana revealed 'the strong connections of WASU'.

WASU maintained its connections with the nationalist movement in Nigeria, and was in contact with the delegates to the 1957 Constitutional Conference held in London. Some of the delegates recognised the contributions that the students might continue to make in the struggle towards independence. Events in West Africa however, were generally outside of the influence of the students. Many remained idealistic and still called for the 'Pan-West Africanism' which had been a goal of the Union since its formation in the 1920s. Many more discarded the mantle of radicalism and communism to return home and secure a lucrative career in government or their chosen professions, as the other West African colonies moved towards independence in the early 1960s. The student and other West African organisations in Britain remained, as did the perennial problem of racism.[71] But the WASU lost its former influence and significance as it became part of the wider pan-African Committee of African Organisations formed in March 1958, and as the students and their well-wishers, such as Sorensen and Listowel, fought over the ownership of the two remaining hostels.[72] In the case of the hostel at South Villas in Camden, the legal dispute continues to this day.

Notes

1. In 1952 official figures show over two thousand West African students out of a total number of just over five thousand colonial students. By 1955 the numbers of West African students had almost doubled.
2. *West Africa*, 27 May 1950, p465.
3. J.L. Keith memo, 4 April 1950, PRO CO 876/193/11034/25.
4. Joe Appiah (1918-1990) came to study law in London in 1943. He was a founder member of WANS and a future political opponent of Nkrumah, but from 1950-54 acted as official representative of Nkrumah and the Convention Peoples' Party in Britain. Ademola was the son of Solanke's old friend Sir Adetokunbo Ademola, later the Chief Justice of Nigeria. Adenekan Ademola was himself subsequently a judge in Nigeria's Appeal Court.
5. G. Olusanya, *op.cit.*, p93-97.

The 1950s: Communism and Nationalism

6. Colonial Secretary to West African Governors, 2 August 1950, PRO CO 876/193/11034/25.
7. Prince M.A Aderemi, a twenty-four year old law student was the son of one of Nigeria's most important traditional rulers, the Oni of Ife and honorary secretary of the NU.
8. A. Bevan to J. Griffiths, 28 May 1951, PRO CO 876/194/11034/37. The letter was addressed to Bevan as 'a champion of Socialism'.
9. In November 1950 Reginald Sorensen, supported by eleven other MPs, presented a private members' Bill against racial discrimination. The Bill got no further than a first reading in Parliament.
10. Hans Crescent House Committee (signed by M.A. Aderemi, U. Omo and A.T. Warner) to the Colonial Secretary, 11 June 1951, PRO CO 876/194/11034/37.
11. Uche Omo, a twenty-three year old law student was at the time a CPGB member. Called to the Bar in 1952 he subsequently became a judge in the Nigerian Federal Appeal Court.
12. On the 'colour tax' see e.g. A.T. Carey, *Colonial Students – A Study of the Social Adaptation of Colonial Students in London*, Secker & Warburg, London 1956, pp68-71 and 154-56.
13. PRO CO 537/6702.
14. WASU member Nii Odoi Annan was joint secretary of the Seretse Khama Fighting Committee. The Africa League, 'a nationalist organisation which fights for the freedom of Africa', was founded in 1950 with a membership of both workers and students, 'to work for the creation of a United States of African Socialist Republics on a federal basis'. The Africa League seems to have been founded in Manchester and grew out of the activities of the African Students' Union formed in that city in 1946, which amongst other activities, organised protest meetings following the 1948 Gold Coast riots and after the shooting of Nigerian miners by colonial police in 1949.
15. FCB Papers, 91/3.
16. *Civil Liberty*, 10/3, February-March 1950, p1.
17. *New Statesman*, 9 October 1954 and *Evening News*, 1 May 1956.
18. E.B. Ndem, *op.cit.*, pp97-100 and 150-56.
19. *Birmingham Post*, 22 January 1951.
20. *Wasu News Service (NS)*, 2/2, September 1953, pp1-3 and *NS*, 1/8, March 1953, p12. *Wasu News Service* was intended as a monthly publication. It was launched in August 1952 following the demise of *Wasu* that had not been published since 1949.
21. *Daily Herald*, 8 May 1951.
22. PRO CO 537/5263/14298.

23. H. Adi, 'West Africans and the Communist Party in the 1950s', *op.cit.*, p179.
24. See e.g. *Africa Newsletter*, 3/11, November 1950, p12.
25. Ademola Thomas, a student at Brixton School of Building became both a leading WASU member and one of the most prominent West African members of the CPGB. Subsequently a wealthy businessman, he became Nigeria's Minister of State for Finance in 1979.
26. 'Confidential Report', 27 May 1953, Ruhemann Papers, box 2.
27. *The Beacon*, 4 June 1955.
28. *Report of the Second Conference of the Communist and Workers' Parties within the sphere of British imperialism*, CPGB, London 1954, p95, see Appendix.
29. *NS*, 1/4, November 1952, pp9-10.
30. *Ibid.*, p12.
31. PRO CO 876/153/11024/13.
32. Interview with Kay Beauchamp, 4 April 1988.
33. *NS*, 1/8, March 1953, pp6-7.
34. *Ibid*.
35. *NS*, 1/2, September 1952, pp11-13.
36. *NS*, 1/3, October 1952, pp9 and 21.
37. *Ibid.*, pp21-24.
38. Report of IUS Council, Warsaw 1951, Sorensen Papers (SOR) 168. The two other members of the WASU delegation were CPGB members Uche Omo and Ade Thomas.
39. *NS*, 1/3, October 1952, p3.
40. J.L. Keith memo, 14 January 1953, PRO CO 1028/13.
41. The first editor of *News Service* was J.O.B. Omotosho. Initially a law student he joined the CPGB and was a member of the editorial board of *Africa Newsletter*, and subsequently president of WASU.
42. WASU to the Colonial Secretary, 2 August 1951, PRO CO 876/157.
43. *NS*, 1/9, April 1953, pp1-3.
44. *NS*, 1/5, December 1952, pp2-3.
45. *Ibid.*, p7.
46. *NS*, 2/5 December 1953, p4.
47. WASU to the Colonial Secretary, 22 April 1952, PRO CO 1028/13.
48. *NS*, 2/4, November 1953, pp1-3.
49. *NS*, 2/5, December 1953, p7.
50. *NS*, 2/7, February 1954, pp1-3.
51. Address of N. Azikiwe to NU, 14 October 1955, FCB Papers, 85/2.
52. Sir C. Jeffries to Sir J. Macpherson, 13 July 1953, PRO CO 1028/14.

53. *A Preface to Policy* can be found in the Appendix.
54. In 1956 the NU produced its own journal the *Niger Beacon*.
55. PRO CO 876/151 and 876/152.
56. *NS*, 1/10, May 1953, p4 and 1/3, October 1952, p2, and *West African Review*, October 1956, p935.
57. For more details concerning the UDC and MCF see S. Howe, *Anticolonialism in British Politics – the Left and the End of Empire 1918-1964*, Oxford University Press, Oxford 1993, pp191-96 and 231-81.
58. See e.g. P. Davies, 'West African Women's View of Britain', *West African Review*, June 1953, and A. Wilson, 'West African Women –An Appeal', *NS*, 1/4, November 1952, p16.
59. *Ibid.*, p2.
60. *West Africa*, 16 January 1954, p46.
61. *West Africa*, 25 September 1954, p9-10.
62. *West African Student*, June 1957, p3.
63. *West Africa*, 31 July 1954, p706.
64. 'Presidential Address to the Third WASU Congress', SOR 174.
65. PRO CO 1028/13.
66. *West Africa*, 28 July 1956, pp533-34. It was estimated that in 1956 there were some four thousand West African students in Britain.
67. The FEANF, formed in Paris in 1950, was a federation of fourteen separate organisations of students from the French West African colonies. Amongst its early leaders was the future Senegalese historian Cheikh Anta Diop. The FEANF had been in contact with WASU since 1955. The RDA was formed in 1946 to co-ordinate African anti-colonial activities throughout French West Africa, and maintained strong links with the French communist party. See *NS*, 1/1, n.d. p2.
68. 'Presidential Address to the Third WASU Congress', *op.cit.*
69. *Ibid*.
70. 'Report of Meeting of Commissioners', 19 December 1958, SOR 174.
71. On the persistence of racism and the colour bar see G.K. Animashawun, 'African Students in Britain', *Race*, 5, 1963,pp38-48.
72. K. Armah, *Africa's Golden Road*, Heinemann, London 1965, pp6-14.

Conclusion

West African students and their organisations, such as WASU, played a significant part in the struggle for self-government in West Africa. These organisations also fulfilled a vital welfare role as support networks and refuges, providing a 'home from home' for West Africans in Britain. They were a means of coping with the many problems, especially the racism, which the students faced. The organisations also gave the students a voice, enabling them to agitate or petition for change whether in Britain or West Africa. While conditions in Britain and membership of the organisations provided a training ground of political education, wider knowledge and experience was important for the personal as well as the political development of many of West Africa's leading personalities.

WASU, the most enduring of the organisations, both on its own and jointly with others, created a political milieu in which West African nationalism and various brands of Pan-Africanism could mix with everything from Fabian Socialism to Marxism-Leninism. As the century wore on the most political students certainly grew more radical both in their language and in their demands. Their organisations acted as pressure groups in Britain and West Africa, continually demanding and pressing for changes, where others would not, or could not act, radicalised it seems by their sojourn in Britain. It is true that in some cases this radicalism appeared merely as a passing phase of student life, as Obafemi Awolowo observed in 1939:

> Whilst they are there, they are compelled to endure the stings of 'colour bar'; they appear as the most patriotic and practical men alive. By their words they win the hearts of those of us at home. But as soon as they set their feet again on African soil they are changed men. They are no longer the men who advocated this or that which they now set themselves to condemn. Their ambition is to try by all means to secure changes by which they will be able to lead their less fortunate bretheren by the noses, and in most cases, to fatten themselves at their expense.[1]

Conclusion

But whilst they were in Britain many students clearly shared a common political agenda. Whatever the language used, most of them would unite against the colour bar, and in opposition to colonial rule. As George Padmore explained W.E. Du Bois:

> Living under alien rule, their first manifestation of political consciousness naturally assumes the form of national liberation, self-determination, self-government – call it what you may. They want to be able to rule their own country, free from the fetters of alien domination. On this all are agreed, from even the most conservative to the most radical elements. There might be differences as to the rate at which improvement is made towards the goal and regarding the political form which the objective should take. For example, Left-wing elements among Colonials emphasise self-determination to the point of secession from the British Empire, while the most conservative elements although endorsing our claim for self-determination, clarify it in terms of Dominion status within the British Empire. This does not mean that there are no individual Negroes who subscribe to political philosophies, whether they be Socialism, Communism, Anarchism, etc. But these are more in the nature of personal idiosyncrasies than practical policies. In brief, even those who call themselves Communists are nationalist. That is to say, they realise that their countries must first be nationally free before they can practice their Communism.[2]

In some senses therefore there is a consistency about West African student politics throughout the century. All students suffered very similar problems in Britain, and all suffered as colonial subjects. As long as these problems persisted, changes of government generally made little difference as far as the students were concerned. Their politics was therefore profoundly influenced by their experiences and conditions in Britain, as well as the impact of colonialism in West Africa, and their activities and thinking made an important contribution to political life throughout the West African colonies and indeed throughout the African diaspora, as well as in the heart of the British Empire.

Notes

1. *West African Review*, January 1939, p17.
2. I. Geiss. *op.cit.* pp395–6.

Appendix

Mr Bandele Omoniyi and the Prime Minister

3 Bruntfield Place, Edinburgh
16 June 1906

Sir, – I am duly in receipt of your letter of the 14th instant I sincerely hope the subject will receive your early attention.

I shall also seize the opportunity to express my convictions of what is expected of every well regulated community – It is to secure to all its members, so far as possible, the opportunity of developing their various natural gifts and powers, so far as they can without detriment to the well being of the society as a whole; I believe that it is expected of a well regulated community that the law should be the same for all, both in protecting and in punishing; all citizens being equal in the eye of the law, which undoubtedly is the case in the colonies, but the reason why all the citizens are not equally admissible to all dignities and public places and employments, according to their capacities without other distinctions than that of their virtues and talents, is what I fail to see when all the citizens are equal in the eyes of the law.

The truths that all men are created equal, that they are endowed by the creator with certain unalienable Rights and that amongst these are Life, Liberty and the pursuit of Happiness have been upheld by great statesmen and why these truths have not been upheld by the officials who are at the head of the colonial affairs remains a puzzle. The equality of mankind is asserted to be a self-evident truth which exists independently of any human law and to speak in the dictum of Hobbes, 'that which may perhaps make such incredible is but a vain conceit of one's wisdom which almost all men think they have in a greater degree than the vulgar, that is than all men but themselves and a few others, whom by fame or by concurring with themselves they approve.'

In the life of man we very commonly distinguish three main forms three main forms in which his natural powers can be exercised; thought, speech, action, these three main forms are three distinguishing spheres in which freedom many be claimed.

Freedom of thought which everyone has, cannot be restricted by any one even under oppression and amid bigotry and to think of what may not be uttered becomes a torture which eats the soul, and the intellect that is shut up in its own dark chambers tends to pine away and perish without getting the fresh air of controversy and the sunshine of human sympathy.

In the Crown Colonies the freedom of utterance which naturally follows the freedom of thought is the privilege of a few and it is a privilege dependent on the somewhat uncertain caprice of those in power, for the government having been entrusted to 'an oligarchy of imperialists with almost absolute power – their acts being subject only to revision by a few subordinate officials at the Colonial Office, who very probably have not the slightest notion of the needs or conditions of the places they are supposed to govern from Downing Street. Under this pernicious (crown colony) system patronage is extended by the local authorities to the seemingly influential in each colony' and these people hold their posts so long as they will assist to keep down the masses and even when they decry a system to be too bad, as it will not tend to ensure the happiness of the governed, they are not listened to or the Government passes any bill it chooses irrespective of their protests. I ask in all earnestness and in the name of common humanity that it should be the aim of this government to secure the greatest happiness of the greatest number in our colonies.

I have the honour, Sir,
to be Your Obedient Servant
BANDELE OMONIYI

Source: *Lagos Standard*, 15 August 1906

Open letter to the Negroes of the world
Especially to those in West Africa and America
A Comprehensive Survey of African Conditions,
African Lands now Menaced

Education the Prime Need
American Education the Best for The African – Tuskegees Wanted in Nigeria, Gold Coast and The Gambia

My dear beloved Countrymen,
There is no doubt now that the problem of the future of our race is a

matter of very great concern the world over among the races other than the Negroes; and it is now absolutely incumbent upon both the Negroes of the Motherland Africa and those abroad in America to establish means of closer unity and co-operation with a view to assisting in the right solution of their future.

It may be related that our past History has been a history of physical slavery – from the time of the Phoenicians who bequeathed us to the Carthaginians, then to the Romans and right down to the European Powers. That our present is a history of denial of social equality from which both we on this side of the Hemisphere and our brethren on that side suffer equally and that our future, if we sit down with arms folded and our destiny left entirely in the hands of others to be moulded for us, may ultimately result in mental and intellectual bondage i.e. to become slaves educationally, industrially, economically and commercially – These are facts that cannot be denied.

American Brethren Abroad
In America our brethren are rapidly emancipating themselves educationally, industrially and commercially but they have got several other difficulties, which, unless surmounted, can never allow them to become an independent nation. So far, at present, there is nothing to guarantee any possible solution to those difficulties by themselves alone remaining in that country.

Homeland of all Negroes
Turning to ourselves here in the Motherland Africa our case is a most complex one. In the first place the independence of any purely Negro state has been practically out of existence everywhere in Africa by one means or other, fair or foul, the most recent of which is that of the Egba Country, the proper Homeland of the majority of Negroes in America and elsewhere.

Land Difficulties and British Rapaciousness
Then comes the question of lands, which is a sine qua non concern in the matter of the independence of any nation.

In this matter we have cause to thank the British Government that has, all along since the question first arose in the House of Commons in 1842, been keeping to the good policy of preserving our ownership rights in the lands. But are we to be content with this? Have we no cause to fear that this policy may be departed from either expressly or implicably? (sic) Is there no British Imperial legislation, the all powerful, to

Appendix

take away these rights someday if it pleases? Is the ownership not even departing us by degrees and strategically or otherwise? Well let us see whether we can get any thing to be inferred usefully as answer to this from the following data; namely,

1. The whole of the Belgian Congo lands have since 1884 been seized by that great British Capitalist Lord Leverhulme under the name of 'Concession'
2. Despite the fact that the Negroes in east and South Africa exceed the white in the ratio of four to one yet they are driven to crowd in some small corner of the tremendous country under the name of 'Native Reserves', where under the operation of the various Colour Bar Laws they are to remain, as it were, the *Coloni adscripti glebae* to the rest of their own lands now entirely seized by the white minority.
3. Leaving South, East and Central Africa we proceed to West Africa, and there we find that Gambia is a Colony. Sierra Leone too is for the large part of it a Colony, and although Gold Coast is in large measure a Protectorate, yet a large process of concession of land to gold-grabbers, the foreigners, etc., is going on so that only Nigeria seems at present to be almost totally free from the same temptation, owing perhaps, in a large measure, to the undoubted efforts of that great souled defender of native rights, Mr Herbert Macaulay of Lagos.

The Problem

... Leaving the question of lands, we proceed to that of education. There is no question as to the wonderful progress our brethren are making in this line, but what about us here? This is a real problem, in West Africa especially, in Nigeria the mighty home of the American and West Indian Negroes. Hitherto the control and management of our education has been in the hands of the missionaries and the British Government and we forget that the missionaries and the British Government each went to West Africa originally for quite different purposes. The British Government went to give us, as alleged, law and order, the missionaries, to dose us with elements of spiritualism and knock out those of nationalism and the capitalist to take as much as he can from the soil.

We sit down with arms folded, and as a race of beggars, dependants and incapables, we are expecting these three distinct bodies to supply us with our wants – to educate us, feed us and clothe us and do everything for us, without turning a moment our minds to the fact that these good people have got millions of children dwelling in the slums of their country whom they themselves are not yet able to supply adequately with these wants. Is it not an unnatural, unreasonable and a most absurd thing to expect 'A' to sharpen a knife and hand it over to his neighbour and adversary 'B' for the purpose of cutting his (A's) throat? This is exactly our position and attitude in the matter in West Africa. This is what we are asking the whiteman to do.

We expect the European to educate us in all points as best as he should educate his own child and we even expect him to leave his own children uneducated and to come and educate ours first...

Education Wanted-Needed
In plain language, my dear countrymen, I must tell you that our hope in the right solution of our current problem lies among our brethren in America. All authorities including the British Government have agreed that American education is the best for us. We need to unite and co-operate with our brethren in America in the promotion of the education of the teeming millions of our illiterates in West Africa, especially in Nigeria – that land of sunshine, excellent soil, rich in underdeveloped resources and flowing with 'milk and honey' – the commercial target of the British Capitalists.

Tuskegees Wanted
The British missionaries have done well enough for us... last year or so they spent about $5 per head over education in Nigeria. We need now to take up for ourselves first and then cry to our brethren in America for help financially or otherwise. Although we have sold them to the American slavery yet fortunately and providentially history repeats itself, and they have now become our Josephs, and like Joseph of old they are going to forget the past and so supply us our educational exigencies. We want 'Tuskegees' in Nigeria, Gold Coast, Sierra Leone and Gambia and all over Africa. We want our chiefs and the children of our kings and chiefs to become scientists, engineers and such like professions. We want Negro poets, historians, satirists, shipbuilders, philosophers, anthropologists, agriculturalists, manufacturers of all kinds, inventors of machines of all kinds, bankers and such like in West Africa, and it is sure as sunrise that we can secure these things sooner than ever if only we try to secure the co-operation of our brethren in America.

Nigerian Progress Union
This is the platform upon which the Nigerian Progress Union stands. It is an organisation for the purpose of raising a large sum of money with a view to educating the masses of the Nigerian peoples as well as to send-

ing African youths to America and other countries for higher education. I therefore most respectfully and earnestly appeal first to all our kings, chiefs and the 'Ogbonis' of West Africa, especially Nigeria, to extend to this Union their warmest support, to the end that a National Education Fund of not less than 1m may be raised by West Africa alone within five years from date.

The UNIA

Before I close this my already lengthy letter, I wish to draw the attention of our brethren in America once more to the denial by Lord Leverhulme of the existence of any organising ability in the Negro.

It is a matter of serious concern over there at present as regards the UNIA organisation. It is important for the assistants and successors of Mr Marcus Garvey to note that their organisation has not failed at all but that it has achieved much among us here in the fact that it has aroused in us in a material way our race consciousness, although we may disagree with some of the methods of that great Negro organiser; and we hope his successors may correct those methods or points in which he might have erred. We on this side, at present, need no programme other than the education of our masses first and in this alone we earnestly request their warm support, morally and financially.

Thanking you for your patience,
I am, my dear beloved Countrymen,
Yours Patriotically

LADIPO SOLANKE
10 March 1925

Source: *The Spokesman*, June 1925

The Truth about Aggrey House

Government Plan for Control of African Students.
March, 1934

This month will witness the opening in London of a hostel for African students and students of African descent under the name of 'Aggrey House'.

The British Government which has absolute control over the lives of these peoples in their native lands, has deemed it fit to seek a plan whereby it might exercise the same control over those studying in England; and it has not hesitated to couple with its infamous scheme the name of Dr. Aggrey whom Africans hold in great esteem.

The idea of building a hostel for African students, especially West Africans, in London, was not actuated by motives of philanthropy or generosity but was the outcome of the difficulties experienced at the hands of Indian and Egyptian students of the past decade over whose thoughts and actions in this country the Government had little control and who on returning home battled against the oppression of the Imperial Government.

It was in 1927 that the idea first took shape. The West African Students' Union had thought, in view of the difficulties of West African students in obtaining decent accommodation in this country that it would be desirable to fit up a hostel or residential club for their use. The Colonial Office seized this opportunity to make an offer of co-operation in the establishment of this hostel.

A representative of the Colonial Office approached the Union on the matter and emphasised that the control of such an institution should be in the hands of the students; this was in accord with the intentions of the West African Students' Union. Various meetings were held at which this representative was present and subsequently a memorandum was framed detailing the respective terms of control, finance and management. The main provisions of the Memorandum were briefly these: -

That both the warden and the secretary of such a hostel be Africans; that the Board of Management should consist of representatives of British Universities, the Colonial Office and other British Institutions, and that such officers and Board of Management be elected by the students themselves; that the initial funds be collected by the W.A.S.U. and be later supplemented by funds from the Colonial Government; that no laws or regulations should enforce any African student to make use of such an institution.

It was surprising that the representative of the Colonial Office did not object to the terms of this Memorandum; and the W.A.S.U. resolved to carry out the duties devolving on it under the Memorandum and set about collecting funds towards the initial cost. A representative of W.A.S.U. Mr. Solanke, was delegated to West Africa to collect the necessary funds. So enthusiastic was the Colonial Office about this scheme that its representative promised Mr. Solanke any help which might facilitate the collection of the fund.

Our representative sailed in October, 1929, and immediately on his arrival in West Africa had his campaign backed by official opinion. The following extract from a speech delivered by Sir Ransford Slater, then Governor of Gold Coast before the Liverpool Chamber of Commerce on the 25th October, 1930, is indicative of what was the official mind at that time:-

> It has been long recognised, I think, by thoughtful people that it is desirable that they (African Students in London) should have a club or hostel of their own, not a club or hostel under Government or Missionary auspices, but run by themselves. I have followed with interest a mission which has been undertaken during the last year or two by Mr. L. Solanke, in West Africa to solicit subscriptions for an institution of that kind. I applaud him for doing so, and I am glad to see from the reports in the African Press that he has achieved a certain amount of success.

But it was not long after that events started to take a contrary turn. The Governor of Nigeria, the late Sir Graeme Thomson, who among other West African officials, had contributed to the funds, retired; and Sir Donald Cameron replaced him. Sir Donald was approached for subscription but Mr. Solanke was surprised to receive a reply stating that Sir Donald would be pleased to contribute if the scheme met with the approval of the other Colonial Governments. This attitude viewed in relation to the preceding could only be explained by instructions which Sir Donald Cameron might have received in London prior to his taking office.

The necessity for these instructions was obvious. The reception given to the W.A.S.U. representative and the consequent arousing of National consciousness among the younger elements in West Africa perturbed the various Governments. They had not reckoned with the reaction to the sufferings and oppression meted out to the people in the past and out of which the students were seeking to extricate them. It was just natural that the indignity to which West African students were subjected in this country would serve to remind West Africans at home of their oppression.

At this stage the Colonial Office concluded that the West African Students' Union could not be used in its scheme to bring African students in London under its control. It thereupon set out to pursue its original scheme with the aid of a certain Mr. Koens, a European cocoa planter, who had failed to amass wealth out of the labours of the West African peasants. Mr. Koens set up a club in London preparatory to the establishment of the proposed hostel and speedily proceeded to canvass the members of the Union with a view to their repudiating the mandate given to the W.A.S.U. delegate. He failed, however, to attract the students to his scheme. Thereupon, he went to the Gold Coast to appeal for funds for the establishment of his hostel. The W.A.S.U. in London promptly issued a statement to the Press disclaiming all knowledge of Mr. Koens and his hostel scheme and thereby prevented Mr. Koens from carrying out his original intention of later soliciting funds in Nigeria. This failure to get the backing of the students and to raise funds in West Africa coupled with the subsequent adoption of the W.A.S.U. scheme, in the hope of a remunerative office in W.A.S.U. by Mr. Koens rendered him further useless to the Colonial Office; and it promptly threw him over.

It was, perhaps, thought that the intention of the British Government could better be carried out through a coloured man.

The League of Coloured Peoples was started in 1931 with a certain Dr. Moody, a West Indian coloured physician as its first President. His concern for the good of West African students was so great that he spared no efforts to induce them to join. Those who did were promptly found places on the Executive Committee. Then came the bombshell; the President proposed the setting up of a hostel. The members were rightly apprehensive. The League had been in existence only a few months, possessed only a few shillings, and here it was embarking on a scheme which on the most conservative estimate would cost hundreds of pounds a year besides initial outlay.

Replying to questions put to him at one meeting, the President made out that he personally would be responsible for financing the scheme. The members were, however, sceptical; they had had various experiences of the machinations of the Colonial Office and were not slow in sensing the real situation.

Dr. Moody, thereupon procured a house, No. 47, Doughty Street; named it 'Aggrey House', and persuaded the League to resolve to use it as its headquarters. What generosity! Dr. Moody was indeed becoming the greatest benefactor of coloured peoples.

The revelation was, however, soon to come. In an obscure missionary magazine, Dr. Moody, in appealing for funds for Aggrey House, disclosed the hand of the British Government in the affair. Thereupon the majority of West Africans withdrew their support from the League.

The W.A.S.U. delegate had now returned, and the Union, with the funds collected had set up a hostel free from Governmental control and run by the students themselves. But the British Government was not to be beaten; it openly resumed the responsibility of Aggrey House and issued a list of its Committee of Management – a list which should have gratified the heart of Dr. Moody, for on it this gentleman's name is prominent. But he should not rest secure. He represents no one there, not even his 'coloured' peoples, and when he is no longer needed, he will suffer the same fate as that of former tools of British Imperialism.

This year will see the opening of that hostel. Elaborate plans have been made to coerce West African students into patronising it, and the Government will not hesitate to resort to legislation in West Africa, compelling students in London to be segregated therein. Thus we see that what the British Government has been attempting to do by subterfuge it now seeks to do openly and without scruples.

It will take due precautions that it keeps under control and watches closely the actions of every West African student in England; will see that no West African possesses any opinion contrary to the prolonged existence of capitalist oppression in the Colonies and will utilise the taxes extorted from West Africans to keep their youth in perpetual subjection.

> We appeal to every lover of freedom to help us check this scheme of Imperialism which would strangle the very thoughts of its subjects and control their every action and opinion.
>
> We appeal to all Africans, students or otherwise, to wash their hands of this scheme, in whatever innocent guise it might be represented – a scheme which would destroy their individuality and nullify their souls. We beg them to work unceasingly for the independence of their thoughts and actions which is a necessary preliminary to the greater independence.

Source: *The Truth About Aggrey House*, WASU, London 1934

Speech delivered in London by Councillor Bankole Awoonor-Renner at the reception given by the West African Students' Union of Great Britain and Ireland to the West African Press Delegation to the United Kingdom on August 25, 1943.

My Comrades and Friends,

One of the important things the present war has done, is that it has converted both Mr. Winston Churchill and all rational peoples of the world, especially the people of West Africa to revolutionary.(sic) For we all are demanding a *New World Order*. We all earnestly need a change for the better. West Africa can no longer stand any form of selfish exploitation, be it British, German, French, Italian, American or African. The time has arrived when we Africans must take the responsibility of shaping the affairs of our own country. We believe in the principle and stand by the Atlantic Charter with all its implications and complications even though the British Prime Minister may disagree with us on this point, we believe he is wrong, because nobody dare challenge now, the right of everybody to live comfortably in this world of plenty.

We demand the right to take our rightful place at the Peace Conference table, when the time comes to determine the peace which we are so eagerly awaiting. You cannot free Europe while Africa is enslaved economically, or otherwise. Poland must be free, so too, must West Africa – nay all Africa. We have played and are still playing a conspicuous part in this war of liberation by our contribution in man power, money and raw materials. We too have given our 'blood, tears and sweat' so that man may be free from insecurity and want. It has been echoed in some quarters that South Africa of General Smuts is demanding a 'pound of flesh' from West Africa and other parts of Africa for the part she has played in this war. We condemn any such move which will result in the handing over in any shape or form, or bartering of our country to South Africa, or any other imperialist power. White South Africans have not fought in this war any more than we Black West Africans have fought in it. If these foreign elements now settled in South Africa, I say foreign because the whites of South Africa, it does not matter how long they stay there, will always remain foreign to us Africans, desire to take West Africa as reward for the part they have played in this war, then we have the right too, to claim South Africa.

I am sure my friends that you all will agree, that our claim as hundred per cent Africans and in the majority, is certainly greater than that of any other person who may have artificial claim to that great and benevolent continent. General Smuts and his group must hands off West Africa.(sic) According to certain laws in Australia and other Dominions in the Empire, Africans are not allowed to settle or temporarily make honest living in these places. We claim the right to live in any part of the empire. We demand too, the immediate unification and self-government for All West-Africa. Mistakes may be made from the beginning. And who has never made mistakes? And is it not

Appendix

by correcting one's mistakes that he succeeds? (sic) It is no use telling us to wait until we get on our feet. We have heard this 'loose talk' in the official circles so much so, that, it has now lost its political value. We are already on our feet.

Since my return to this country some four months ago, I have travelled throughout a wide area of the United Kingdom, the more I travel, and I see the great cities, the big buildings, the beautiful parks, the paved streets, the vast industrial centres, the rich upper class, the semi-rich middle class and the poor working class, the more I am convinced of the debt the British people owe to West Africa and to Africa in general for that matter. We Africans must congratulate ourselves that by transferring raw materials from our country for many centuries past, have contributed largely to the prosperity of the 'mother country'.(sic) It is with happy feelings that we also are carrying the White Man's Burden.

To our English friends it is but fitting to remind ourselves, that as you have carried our burden, so too, we are carrying yours. In our contact with Europe we have learnt a great deal from her. And she too, has gained and is gaining handsomely from us.

Now to you my countrymen of the Press Delegation, you have come, you have seen but unlike Caesar you have not conquered, because there is an untold suffering of racial discrimination levelled against us here – we who you are leaving behind. Without mentioning the abuses that are being meted out to us at home. Do not permit the environments of the Hyde Park Hotel to sway your decisions and observations. These insults upon our race and the complexion of our skin, which is fundamentally economic, can only be stopped by an enactment of law. There is no other way. Our great and gallant ally, the Union of Soviet Socialists Republics has already set the worthy example. It should be followed. We know you will do your duty. You must make it quite clear to the British people that we resent bitterly these form of abuses which are daily thrust upon us as a people. We demand absolute equality, if we must live together in this Empire. We demand freedom for the African farmer, his right to sell his produce to any one, either nation or company, who gives him better price. We demand freedom for the African worker without any interference of his rights from any quarter. We demand equality in the Colonial Services. We condemn any form of trade monopoly in our country. We demand West Africa for the masses and governed by the masses. We look forward to the guiding hands of the Soviet Republics and sincere and unselfish United

Nations. In West Africa today obnoxious and oppressive laws are being passed under the guise of war measures. We are not tried by jury in the court of 'Justice' in some parts of West Africa e.g. the Gold Coast.

The indirect rule system is definitely another instrument of oppression with its motive to keep apart the uneducated father from his educated son and the educated daughter from her uneducated mother. In short, its main aim is to create division between the illiterate and literate masses of West Africa, and thereby give stimulus to greater exploitation of the people. While we are contemplating a New World Order it is essential that these evil systems must go. These intolerable conditions the British people must know and it is your duty to let them know.

The question has often been asked by persons interested and disinterested as to 'whether West Africa would like to break away from the Empire'. I would like to answer this question here today. Whether we would like to break away from the Empire or not, depends upon the Policy of the British Government and indeed, to the attitude of the British people in the United Kingdom towards our national aspiration. We see things are happening in the East and other parts of the world. We too, yearn for something progressive, and when I say progressive I do not mean simply something in the shape of the recent parliamentary debate on the so-called Colonial policy. Nay, that debate was to us in West Africa an attempt to divert our attention from our political responsibility. We demand fundamental change not mere patchwork reforms. And we do hope that with the aid of you, who appointed yourselves as our Trustees, but now as partners, this most needed change will be realised. And without you, it will be notwithstanding, for no nation or people can forestall the supreme march of history.

In conclusion, we are indeed thankful to the British Council for having made it possible for our friends to visit this country. We thank you, members of the Press Delegation for the honour you have accorded to WASU in responding to the request of the Union and gracing this occasion. And I must particularly thank our British friends for their presence here this evening. We entertain no hatred for anyone. It is the system which is oppressive and which we must always oppose even with our blood. It is only by telling you what is burning in our innermost hearts, that we may come to understand one another and together create a bright tomorrow.

Source: Solanke Papers

APPENDIX

A preface to policy

The Presidential Address to the Nigeria Union
of Great Britain and Ireland
8 February 1953
By E.E. Obahiagbon

At this first general meeting of the year, we want to try to define broad principles which ought to guide our union activities. This will not be easy for obvious reasons. We are a collection of men and women of different political faiths and allegiances. The four main political parties in Britain are represented amongst us – not excluding the Tory party ! And, what is much more important, some of us are members of one or other of the National Council of Nigeria and the Cameroons (N.C.N.C.), Action Group, Egbe Omo Oduduwa and the Ibo State Union.

Some people hold that because our union is thus composed it should not be, as it is often put, 'political'. To be 'political' is, they say, to court offending some sections of it. Others hold that we must take a positive stand in all matters concerning Nigeria, that not to have a policy of action is to drift, and that we ought to decide even now which of the Nigerian political parties to support.

There is a third point of view which should, in the present state of Nigerian politics, be more acceptable than these two, and I put it before you for consideration. It is that we cannot stand aside from the great controversies of our day, in Nigeria or elsewhere. But although we are obliged to involve ourselves especially in the nationalist struggle at home, we must not, and need not, get involved in the inconsequential wranglings which pass for politics in Nigeria.

Laboratory of Ideas

It is within our power to raise the tone of Nigerian politics. After all, it has been brought to this low pass mostly by the efforts of our friends who have returned home before us. By 1956, it is doubtful that up to ten of those at this meeting will still be in Britain, and it makes a tremendous difference whether, as we drift back home in twos and threes, we take with us a saner attitude to things or plan to seek personal fortune under the patronage of one or other of the clamant prejudices.

Accordingly, while this union will continue to uphold the right of its members to associate with any political party of their choice, either here or in Nigeria, one of its ambitions should be to become a laboratory wherein we examine the convictions and prejudices brought into it by adherents of outside faiths and heresies. Let us provide a platform on which the supporters of the N.C.N.C., Action Group, Northern Peoples' Congress, Northern Elements' Progressive Union (N.E.P.U.), Egbe Omo Oduduwa and Ibo State Union may meet to settle their differences or, failing this, fight it out. I have no doubt that the stable element in this union will overwhelm the partisans that may be in it.

No system of ideas binds this union together. We are dedicated, simply, to the creation of a free, strong and united Nigeria. This, immediately, should be our one standard of judgement. Regionalisation, Yoruba communalism, Ibo irredentism, industrialisation, marketing boards. These, among many others, should be considered in terms of our goal. So that our first question always will be: What contribution does this individual or this institution make to our struggle for a free, strong and united Nigeria? We must come out boldly and clearly with our findings and if we are honest enough in our thinking and in our professions we should agree enough to speak with one voice on a good many issues. The over-riding rule in this war of ideas is that all decisions are accepted in good faith, if, on a specific issue, we find for the Communists as against the Social Democrats, for the Action Group as against the N.C.N.C., we shall not be labelled Communists for doing the one, nor Action Groupers for doing the other.

For the most part, we shall be studying ideas and current problems. The Study Group Organiser will occasionally arrange for someone in or outside the union to read a study paper and there will be internal and joint debates. We hope we can find a suitable place for our second summer school in the middle of the year. If speakers are forthcoming, we may even have a two-day school in London at Easter to discuss Regionalisation in Nigeria. For the next few weeks our time in the study groups will be taken up with discussing constitutional forms – federalism, unitary government and so forth. This will prepare our minds for a better grasp of what will be discussed at Easter.

In inviting speakers to our union we must ensure that we provide audiences only for men and women with facts and arguments to put forward, and not to purveyors of incantations and organised opinions. For it is well to remember that it sometimes makes a difference whether it is a Communist, Socialist or Conservative who addresses us. If you read *Daily Worker*, *New Statesman and Nation*, and *Daily Mail*, you will see what I am trying to say. Happily, there are some who are students or scholars before party men, and while this union may not refuse a speaker because of his or her party it should invite only those who are not likely to place party views before scholarship, unless we especially want to hear party views.

Internal Organisation

You will see that the union is committed to an extensive programme. All this requires money. We are trying to improve on our financial organisation. Membership cards and subscription stamps have been printed. Instead of an enrolment fee of 2/6d. and a block annual subscription of 5/- we now have a monthly subscription of 1/-, or a compounded annual subscription of 10/-. The new system brings in a little more money, but, in many respects, it also eases the problem of collecting and accounting.

If members will pay their dues regularly, with the proceeds from dances and other engagements, we should have enough money to run fairly well. The Treasurer will appoint about a dozen members who are well placed to meet other Nigerians to hold stamps for sale. Those others who want to earn enough money to buy ten cigarettes and a box of matches will find the Treasurer prepared to sell them twelve stamps for ten shillings, cash down! I invite all who can afford the outlay to enter into this trade, which promises to be brisk.

We are providing by amendment to our constitution for election of a Welfare Officer whose main duty will be to welcome Nigerians to Britain. He will introduce the Nigeria Union to new arrivals and help them in other ways within this union's power. He will for the present confine himself to London, but it should be possible, after our internal re-organisation, to extend the service to Liverpool and Dublin. His other duty will be to keep a list of homes and lodgings willing to take in coloured tenants. This is a big responsibility for the union, but with the good sense of all concerned, it will be nobly discharged. Not more can be said of the new office at this stage.

The problem of our union re-organisation is still with us. This was partially discussed at the last summer school in Oxford. The problem, succinctly, is how to associate Nigerians outside London with decisions we take in their name. It is agreed by all that the present position is highly unsatisfactory. The executive will shortly address itself to the problem but we want to see that the search for a more perfect constitution is matched by recognition of the need for a speedy and workable system. It is the provincial branches which will be asked to make the greater sacrifice in this matter. An executive with its officers spread over the length and breadth of these islands is perfect only on paper. In practice it can achieve very little. London is said to contain over two-thirds of the Nigerian population in Britain. If London is a branch, it ought, therefore, in my view, to be one with a difference. May I at this stage appeal for the co-operation of all branches of the union.

External Relations
We shall be ready always to work with any outside organisation in the pursuit of common specific objectives. One example of this association was the recent boycott of the Colonial Office dance, in protest against the Kenya infamies. Let me seize this opportunity to commend the co-operation of the great mass of Nigerians in this singularly successful gesture. Only about a score of Nigerians presumed to think this union misguided in the step it took. They are entitled to their point of view, but I hope those who do not think like them will always prevail.

Your executive, together with the executives of the West African Students' Union (W.A.S.U.), the Gold Coast Students Union, the Sierra Leone Students' Union, is at present discussing certain proposals for reorganisation of W.A.S.U. This discussion is nearing its final stage, but, as I understand it, whatever the four organisations decide together will be considered by present W.A.S.U. alone and accepted as its new constitution, with or without amendments. Your executive cannot be said to have committed this union so far to anything. At some future date we shall be informed of the new W.A.S.U. constitution, and only then can we decide whether or not to be a union-member of that body. The trend of discussions at present suggests that the new W.A.S.U. will be a union of organisations only, or of individuals as well as organisations.

One of the aims of W.A.S.U., it is suggested, will be to work for a federated West Africa. If this is not merely the expression of a pious hope but the statement of an ideal to which all our present thoughts and actions are to be directed, this union must now begin to ask itself whether it can to its formidable internal problem of forging a Nigerian unity add the more formidable and, as it were, external problem of forging a West African unity. Can a union like ours at the same time serve two integral ideas? The answer may be Yes, but if it is No, we ought to say now, before it is too late, that while we are not opposed to the eventual federation of all the West African territories, we feel that W.A.S.U. might best define its aims and purposes for the present as no more specific than to build a closer association among the West African peoples. This union is affiliated to the British National Union of Students and is co-founder of the Co-ordinating Council of Colonial Students' Unions. We shall continue to work with these bodies. We hope before long to establish a link with the student-body in Ibadan University College.

Communists and Nigeria
I do not think our attitude to British political parties requires special definition. Some comments are however, not out of place here about the Communist and Labour parties, the two parties often identified with the struggle of the colonial peoples. There is a common ground between the colonial peoples and the communist world. The former are opposed to imperialism which, for them, is represented in the West. The communists, for reasons of their own are opposed to the Western world. It is, therefore, not accidental that on many issues the colonial nationalist holds the same views with communists.

But the common ground we occupy is being gradually narrowed down by what I would refer to briefly as the tendency of communists to over-simplify in a good many of their interpretations of social forces. I am here concerned with their attitude to Nigerian problems. The Nigerian political scene, with all its nuances, is yet susceptible of the Marxian interpretation. It is a dubious saving of effort to invent facts in order to conclude on a point to which one would still be led by careful regard to the existing facts.

To write, as Mr. Palme Dutt wrote in *For a Lasting Peace, for a People's Democracy*, official organ of the Cominform, of January 9th, that the people of Nigeria 'are beginning to realise that one of the main conditions for victory is the unity of the working class, the alliance of the working class and the peasantry, and the welding of the working class, the peasantry, petty bourgeoisie, and the national bourgeoisie into a united front, under the leadership of the working class' – to write like this is like trying to solve a mathematical problem with the wrong formula.

There is no working class in Nigeria with the consciousness and convictions of which Mr. Dutt writes. The workers' unions are, at best, groups of apathetic wage-earners spasmodically whipped into frenzy, now, by unbearable poverty and, then, by leaders who are themselves under the beck and call of one or other of leaders of the bourgeoisie. At worst they are a treasure-house from which working-class social-climbers and déclassé, middle-class elements feather their nests. The peasantry, far from wanting to ally themselves to the working-class, are under the undisputed control of the bourgeoisie and the 'natural rulers'. As for the leaders of the bourgeoisie, they are 'rivals in the badness of (their) case'.

It may be true, as Mr. Palme Dutt also writes, that 'all the objective conditions exist for the development of . . . a united front'. But, unhappily, the dominant subjective factors in the historic situation are not the type to utilise these objective conditions for the achievement of a united front. For instance, there were objective conditions for a communist revolution in Germany after the first world war, but did not Hitler convert them to the creation of National Socialism? The truth, simply, is that, in Nigeria, all the factors which under the inspiration of wiser and less selfish leaders would produce a united nationalist movement are at present being pressed into the building of class, religious, tribal and regional vested interests. It is a sorry picture, down to its very detail, but only by striving to know the situation as it really is can we at all begin to hope to be able to change it.

I make these comments, fully conscious of the opposition of communists to colonial rule and of their readiness always to spotlight its abuses. No sensible colonial nationalist can be an out and out anti-communist and we, for our part, ought to be prepared, in spite of the many sharp turns noticeable in their global strategy, to work with communists in our common opposition to 'classical' imperialism. But this co-operation must be based on mutual trust and respect if it is to be fruitful.

British Labour Party

Of the Labour party I would not bother to say much if the present tour of West Africa by an official delegation of the party did not serve to illustrate the hollowness, which we all by now know too well, of the party's claim to differ fundamentally, as far as the issue of coloured freedom is concerned, from the Tory party. We want to remember that the Macpherson Constitution was inspired under Labour rule, and Mr. James Griffiths, the Colonial Secretary then, has recently treated us to that obscure reasoning by which he commended that document to the Nigerian people in 1951.

Appendix

In the *Daily Service* of January 12, he was reported to have said at a press conference in Lagos that 'only a federal government could help to preserve the unity of Nigeria. The late Labour government held this view, for the question of Nigerian unity was uppermost in their minds. ... Democracy thrived well in federal countries. Canada had a federal government, the U.S.A. had, and so did Australia. The United Kingdom, it was true, had a unitary government but he could say that far back in the 19th century the Welsh (his own people) had been demanding their own self-government outside the unitary government'.(sic)

Assuming that the *Daily Service* report is correct, we read here the words not merely of a professed socialist but of one reputed to be the most respected leader in the Labour party. The first questions that should occur to one are: How does one keep a thing whole by breaking it into bits? How, indeed, has Nigeria been more than before united in 1953 by giving to the regions in 1951 greater powers than even Lord Milverton allowed them in 1946?

Mr. Griffiths tells us that democracy thrives well in federal countries, but do the opponents of intensive regionalisation fear that it might result in dictatorship? And this man knows, or ought to know, that the case, today, against the type of federalism we are building in Nigeria rests mainly on the obstacles it puts in the way of creating a Welfare state, of evening out the inequalities of wealth and opportunities by planned use of national resources in men and material, with the opportunities it gives for petty and unhealthy rival loyalties.

And then this clear case of intellectual dishonesty: Mr. Griffiths reminds us that the Welsh, his own people, have been demanding Home Rule from as far back as the 19th century, but he will not go on to tell us why neither his party nor the Tory party has so far supported this Welsh demand when out of office, much less grant it when in office; and why he is not himself a leader of the Welsh Home-Rulers rather than of the Welsh miners and the Labour party.

It is by this sort of tactics that our rulers confuse and divide us. An ex-Colonial Secretary tells us that we are best united in division. A Tory Colonial Secretary praises the Western Nigeria's Local Government Law. I do not suggest that the fact of this praise denies the many good parts of the bill but, apparently, some of our leaders do not suspect that if the enemy you claim to fight has a word of praise for your methods it is most probably because they are such as will leave you weak and helpless against him.

Our Friends in Britain

But we must not be led by men like Mr Griffiths to think that all Labourites are mischief-makers. Some are more sincere than even the best we can today point to as leaders in our struggle. I hope we shall have many occasions to welcome to this union such of them as have identified themselves in the past with the struggles of the colonial peoples, especially those of them who constitute the ferment in such organisations as the Union of Democratic Control and the Congress of Peoples against Imperialism. We ought also to watch that wing of the Labour party commonly referred to as Bevanites. True, the Bevanite call for help for the under-developed countries smacks of the United States' 'Point Four', but it is amongst this group and the two organisations I have mentioned that we are likely any day to find men and women ready to stand in relation to us in our struggle as, in the days of India's subjection, Laski, Cripps, Brailsford, Sorenson and Brockway, and the rest of that circle, so admirably stood in relation to her.

Laski and others were, however, able to help the cause of Indian freedom because not only was the Indian nationalist movement strongly based in India, led, as it was, by men whose viceregal (sic) jailers, compared to them today, are but little men; it was worthily represented in Britain by organisations and individuals such as the India League and Mr. Krishna Menon. Progressive circles in this country are relatively silent on Nigeria because they are at a loss to unravel the tangled skein of Nigerian politics. Those of us who might be in a position to help them are ourselves blissfully enmeshed in it. Let the Nigeria Union arise to remedy this.

Composite Leadership

May I end on a more general note. We are all students of one subject or another. It is incumbent on us, as such, that when we express opinions on any matter we show as much of common-sense and reflection as we are expected to show in answering questions in an examination paper. No one person, anywhere in the world, is sufficiently endowed to be able to express a respectable opinion on every question, but we can ensure that in discussing the many tremendous issues which confront us either as a people or individually we do not merely sing the chorus of the market-place.

Often we would need the help, if not the guidance, of the results of other people's thinking and discoveries. For the more we read, the nearer it is borne home to us that in all social relationships – in politics especially – there are few contemporary problems which have not equally puzzled men and women of other times and places. And it is a salutary mortification to discover that the answers we think we have to some present-day questions were suggested, perhaps, many centuries ago and have since been rejected as unsatisfactory.

I am not by any means suggesting that this situation is peculiar to our small society. The famous Spanish scholar, Ortega y Gasset, writes scathingly of the belief of the mass 'that it has the right to impose and to give force of law to notions born in the cafe.' It is one of the characteristics of our Mass Age and it is perhaps inevitable. But we must remember, those of us in this country, that whatever position we occupy in the social and intellectual structure of the West, we do not belong in the 'mass' of the society at home. We are, deservedly or otherwise, part of the elite. We must, therefore, be conscious of our responsibility.

I have been permitted – is it that I have permitted myself – to address you in the spirit of a leader calling his men to arms. That is how it may be interpreted, but with this qualifying plea: That everyone consider himself a leader in this struggle. Of course, the executive is expected to give leadership, and will give it, but for people in our situation the executive could hope to do little more than direct a composite leadership – which is what I am asking for – into a chosen channel.

The task, indeed, is not so much one for leaders and followers as for equally responsible men and women who have made up their minds to march together towards a common goal.

I stress this individuality because although we may collectively agree in our discussions and debates that a particular course of action is the best, it will be left to us individually to choose whether to follow that course. There are many who, whatever the argument, will pursue their ways. Much of our thinking in politics is special pleading – rather than seek after the truth, we look for facts and fancies to justify what we have already made up our minds to have. It is our values rather than our knowledge, our character rather than our intellect, which determine our course in politics. To organise for a purpose like ours it is more important that we want the same thing than that we argue to the same conclusions. May we have men and women who believe in our cause sufficient to bring us victory.

Source: *A Preface to Policy*, Nigeria Union, London 1953

Britain's largest colony
Ade Thomas

Nigeria is the largest remaining British colony. It covers an area of 375,000 square miles – larger than France and Italy put together – and has a population of over 31 million. It is mainly agricultural, supplying the world with cocoa, cotton, palm oil, and groundnuts. Its known mineral resources include tin, iron ore, uranium deposits, lead, zinc, coal and other resources.

The ever-increasing world demand for Nigeria's products and its growing share in world trade affect the class structure in Nigeria and undermine the former principle of the communal ownership of land. Growing numbers of landless peasants are being compelled to seek employment in the big towns, factories, railway yards, and in the mines.

Nigeria still remains a semi-feudal and colonial country. In some parts the feudal structure is being maintained by the imperialists to their own advantage. They see this as one way of maintaining their imperialist domination. The complex economic and social structure of Nigeria, created by imperialism, means far greater exploitation. Side by side with the dominant foreign exploitation is the brutal oppression of the feudal system. The peasant farmers still constitute the great majority of the population, but imperialism has also given rise to a growing national bourgeoisie, and the rise of the working class.

Growth of the National Movement
It was only in 1914 that the southern and northern territories of Nigeria were brought together into a single administrative unit. By 1922 the Nigerian people had begun to organise themselves into political parties. In that year the National Democratic Party was formed by Herbert Macauley.(sic)

Between 1923 and the outbreak of the second world war the imperialists exercised every wile to conceal the world-wide political awakening of the Nigerian people, and to prevent it from affecting the literate elements both in the coast towns and in the up-country administrative and trading centres. They were equally concerned to drive a wedge between these literate elements and the illiterate but militant masses. In this way, and through the absence of a central legislature for the country, they succeeded in carrying through their policy of 'divide and rule'.

Appendix

The years 1939-44 saw a new wave of national awakening in the country. Broad sections of the people, hitherto isolated from the national struggle, began to take an active part. Workers, young people, businessmen, ex-servicemen, market women, and secondary schoolchildren – all of them in varying degrees took their stand against imperialism. This created favourable conditions for the formation of a nation-wide united front in the struggle against imperialist domination.

The political impact of the second world war intensified the demand for self-government, while its economic impact increased the industrial ferment and the activity of the trade unions. In 1944 came the formation of the National Council of Nigeria and the Cameroons, the recognised expression of the rising national movement. At its inception it was a federation of all types of organisations in support of the declared aim of winning full political independence for Nigeria and the Cameroons.

The post-war history of Nigeria is one of bitter struggle, expressed in various forms, and directed against the imperialists. In 1945 the Nigerian workers brought the country to a standstill in a general strike which lasted 44 days, and forced the Government to grant increased wages. In 1949 the Enugu coal miners won world-wide support in the struggle against starvation wages. The shooting of 22 miners during the strike served only to expose the vicious nature of imperialist rule, and to raise the level of the anti-imperialist fight in Nigeria.

Already the imperialists had realised that the growing struggle and rising national movement was a menace to their rule. In 1947 they introduced the 'Richards Constitution' which divided Nigeria into three regions, north, east and west. Far from holding back the national movement, this constitution aroused great mass resentment, expressed in the nation-wide support for the N.C.N.C. delegation to London to oppose the constitution.

Within three years the British government had appointed a new Commission, under Macpherson, the British Governor, the result of which was the new Macpherson Constitution of 1951. This constitution perpetuated the division of Nigeria into three regions, created a new House of Chiefs in the west, and made provision for a complicated system of indirect elections.

On the eve of the 1951 elections new political parties were formed, but on a regional basis. Among these was the Northern People's Congress, expressing the interests of the feudal Emirs in the north; and the Northern Elements Progressive Union (associated with the

N.C.N.C.), whose policy was a challenge both to imperialism and the feudal elements in the north. In the west, the Action Group was formed, mainly in opposition to the N.C.N.C. As a result of the elections the N.P.C. got the majority in the Northern Assembly, the Action Group in the Western Assembly, and the N.C.N.C. in the Eastern Assembly-with an unstable combination of Ministers in the Central Assembly, dominated by the British Governor and the feudal Emirs.

The challenge in the Eastern Assembly in April 1953, to the reserve powers of the British Lieutenant-Governor was the first challenge to the Macpherson Constitution, spreading later to the Central Assembly with the resignation of Action Group Ministers. The Macpherson Constitution was faced with a crisis within less than two years of its existence. The N.C.N.C. and the Action Group formed an alliance in support of the demand for a revision of the Constitution and for self-government in 1956; and the British government was forced to convene a London Conference in August 1953 to consider revision of the Macpherson Constitution.

The sharp divisions at the London Conference among the representatives of the various Nigerian political parties enabled Oliver Lyttelton to take advantage of this lack of a united national front, in order to obscure the clear-cut demand for self-government for a united Nigeria and carry still further forward the system of regional division of the country.

Role of the Working Class
These experiences bring out clearly the urgent need for the working class in Nigeria to advance to the position of leading all anti-imperialist forces in the national front. Despite the early militant struggles of the working class, the imperialists have temporarily succeeded in weakening the working class and disrupting the trade union movement. But there are signs that the Nigerian workers will once more emerge and advance to the path of open mass struggle, and this alone can prevent the further worsening of their conditions and impart new vigour to the national liberation movement.

There is also a welcome sign of a growing interest in Marxism among the most active and younger elements in Nigeria. This is being expressed in the formation of various circles and groups claiming allegiance to Marxism. But serious divisions still exist among these organisations, as well as a tendency to isolation from the mass national struggle, and there is the most urgent need for them to find a common basis, a common programme, and united action.

There can be no real advance in Nigeria's fight for national liberation until all the genuine Marxist elements come together into a united party which can fulfil the role of Marxism and working-class leadership within the broadest national front, and so advance the struggle in Nigeria against imperialism and its reactionary puppets.

Let us, therefore, work with great zeal, vigour, and determination, for those aims which we have set ourselves at this conference, so that we can guarantee our peoples freedom, lasting peace, and socialism.

Source: *Report of the Second Conference of the Communist and Workers' Parties within the sphere of British Imperialism*, CPGB, London 1954

Abbreviations

AAC	Anglo-African Committee of the Missionary Council of the Church of England
ACWUK	Advisory Committee on the Welfare of Coloured Peoples in the United Kingdom
AG	Action Group
AHDC	Africa House Defence Committee
APU	African Progress Union
ASAD	Association of Students of African Descent
ASAPS	Anti-Slavery and Aborigines' Rights Protection Society
CBMS	Conference of British Missionary Societies
CO	Colonial Office
COPAI	Conference of Peoples of Europe-Asia-Africa Against Imperialism
CPGB	Communist Party of Great Britain
CPP	Convention Peoples' Party
CWAE	Committee for the Welfare of Africans in Europe
FCB	Fabian Colonial Bureau
GCARPS	Gold Coast Aborigines' Rights Protection Society
GCSA	Gold Coast Students' Association
IAFA	International African Friends of Abyssinia
IASB	International African Service Bureau
ILP	Independent Labour Party
ISR	International Student Relief
ITUC-NW	International Trade Union Committee of Negro Workers
IUS	International Union of Students
LAI	League Against Imperialism
LCP	League of Coloured Peoples
NCBWA	National Congress of British West Africa
NCCL	National Council of Civil Liberties

Abbreviations

NCNC	National Council of Nigeria and the Cameroons
NNDP	Nigerian National Democratic Party
NPU	Nigerian Progress Union
NTUC	Nigerian Trade Union Congress
NU	Nigeria Union
NUS	Nigerian Union of Students
NUSB	National Union of Students (Britain)
NWA	Negro Welfare Association
NYM	Nigerian Youth Movement
PAF	Pan-African Federation
PRO	Public Records Office, London
SCM	Student Christian Movement
SOL	Solanke Papers, University of Lagos, Nigeria
SOR	Sorensen Papers, House of Lords, London
SPAO	Society of Peoples of African Origin
TUC	Trade Union Congress (Britain)
UAC	United Africa Company
UGCC	United Gold Coast Convention
UNIA	Universal Negro Improvement Association
USAD	Union of Students of African Descent
WANS	West African National Secretariat
WASU	West African Students' Union
WAYL	West African Youth League
WFDY	World Federation of Democratic Youth
WFTU	World Federation of Trade Unions

Index

A Defence of the Ethiopian Movement 11
A Preface to Policy 173, 203-211
A Survey of Communism in Africa 160
Accra Riots 137-139
Action Group (AG) 144, 162-163, 172, 174
Ademola, Adenekan 152, 158, 162, 175, 182n
Ademola, Adetokunbo 41, 50n, 58
Adeniyi-Jones, C.C. 26, 30
Adenubi, A. 177
Aderemi, M.A. 155-156, 162, 173, 183n
Adjei, Ako 127, 138
Advisory Committee on the Welfare of Coloured Peoples in the United Kingdom (ACWUK) 113
Africa Bureau 174
Africa League 109, 159, 162, 175
African Economic Union 90
Africa Newsletter 141
Africa House Defence Committee (AHDC) 60-61, 64, 66
African Association 9
African Friendship Society 144
African International Trading Association 82
African News Agency 110
African Patriotic Students' Club 82
African Progress Union (APU) 4, 16-19, 22n, 26, 32-33, 43
African Progressive Association 125
African Provident Society 10
African Races Association 23
African Society 13-14, 16

African Students' Association (Edinburgh) 127
African Students' Association (US) 110
African Student in England, The 113
African Students' Union 15-16, 144
African Telegraph 17
African Times and Orient Review (ATOR) 13, 15-16
African Union 23
African Workers' and Students' Association 162
Africana 144
Afro-Asian Students' Association 175
Afro-Asian Students' Conference 175
Afro-West Indian Literary Society 10
Agbebi, Mojala 8
Aggrey House 57, 61, 64-66, 69, 75, 80-81, 92-94
Aggrey House Committee 58, 60
Aggrey, J.E. Kwegyir 26, 47n, 57
Ajibade, Okunade 53
Ajibola, J.O. 143
Akerele, Ekundayo 41
Akinloye, A.M. 152
Akpata, Bankole 127, 139, 142, 145, 148n, 161, 163, 165
Alake of Abeokuta 54, 74, 78
Alakija, Adeyemo 14, 21n
Alakija, O.A. 54
Ali, Dusé Mohammed 13-14
All-India Muslim League 144
Amponsah, A. 175
An African Survey 100

INDEX

Anglo-African Committee of the Missionary Society of the Church of England (AAC) [See also *Dean of Westminster's Committee* 113-114
Annan, J.S. 127
Annan, Nii Odoi 129, 139, 141-142, 145, 148n
Ansah, William 6
Anti-Slavery and Aborigines' Rights Protection Society (ASAPS) 13-14, 16, 101
Apithy, Sourous 131
Appiah, Joe 2, 127, 138-139, 145, 152, 158, 182n
Archer, John R. 17
Arikpo, Okoi 152, 171-172, 179
Asafu-Adjaye, E.O. 44, 50n
Asantehene, 73
Association of Students of African Descent (ASAD) 81, 95, 109-110, 122, 124, 127
Atlantic Charter 98, 105, 107
Atta, Nana Sir Ofori 40, 49n, 63, 65, 73,
Atta, William Ofori 80, 88n, 90, 138
Attlee, Clement 97-98, 133
Awolowo, Obafemi 111, 123-124, 127, 139, 144, 146n, 186
Awooner-Renner, Bankole 112, 119n, 129, 142, 148n
Azikiwe, Nnamdi, 79, 103-104, 111-112, 114, 123, 136, 144

Balogun, Kola 144, 150n, 172
Bamishe, O.A. 174
Banda, Hastings 127
Bankole, T.A. 124
Bankole-Bright, H.R. 10, 32-33, 139
Beoku-Betts, E.S. 16, 21n
Beoku-Betts, R.W. 105, 125, 127
Berry, Phillip 122
Bevan, Aneurin 155
Bevin, Ernest 107
Blackman, Peter 93
Blackman, The 47
Blaize, F.O.B. 102, 127, 132
Blay, R.S. 43, 50n

Blyden, Edward 12, 21n, 27, 35
Boadu, F.R. Kankam 127
Botsio, Kojo 129, 139, 142, 145, 148n, 155, 157, 171
Bourdillon, Sir Bernard 75, 81, 96
Bradley, Ben 84n
Bridgeman, Reginald 44-45, 60-62, 99, 125
British Africa Cultural Society 144
British Centre Against Imperialism 143
British Centre for Colonial Freedom 143
British Youth Conference on Democracy and War 78
Broadhurst, Robert 46, 78
Brockway, Fenner 143
Brotherhood of African Peoples 125
Brown, William Wells 8
Bruce, John Edward 11
Buckle, Desmond 80-81, 92-93, 127, 141, 162
Burns, Sir Alan 97, 101
Burns, Emile 143

Cadbury Brothers 52, 58, 73, 75, 95
Calabar Union 174
Cameron, Sir Donald 100
Campbell Bannerman, Sir H. 11
Caribbean Labour Congress 157
Carr, Henry 30
Cartwright, Albert 88
Ceylon Students' Association 126
Chen, Percy Acham 23
Churchill, Winston, 98
Church Missionary Society 8
Circle, The 129-130
Citizen, The 175
Clifford, Sir Hugh 24
Cocoa hold up 67, 73-74
Cole, Irene 109
Cole, Robert Wellesley 109, 112, 144
Colonial Centre (Cardiff) 122
Colonial Development and Welfare Act 100
Colonial and Dominion Students' Conference 160
Colonial and Young Dominions

217

Association 175
Colonial Office (CO) 3-4, 9-11, 14, 25-26, 29-32, 89-91, 95, 112-114, 121, 124, 151, 176, 178, 180; and student hostel 39-40, 52-53, 74-76, 153; and racism 41-43, 46, 54-55, 105-110, 159-160; Aggrey House 57-61, 64, 66, 72, 92-4; and student politics 80-81, 96-102, 104, 133-136, 138-142, 152, 161, 169-170; and Hans Crescent 154-157; Consultative Committee 157-158; and international student movement 164-165; and NU 173-174; Colonial Peoples' United Council 125
Colonial Problems 133
Colonial Students' Committee 81,
Colonies and Peace, The 126
Colonies: What Africa Thinks 90
Colour bar (see also *racism*) 12, 14, 16-17, 39, 52-54, 62, 90-92, 106, 121, 128, 140, 165
Coloured Alien Seamen Order 40, 55
Coloured Colonial Improvement Association 111
Coloured Film Artistes' Association 80
Colwyn Bay Training Institute 8
Comité de Défense de l'Indepeudence National de l'Ethiope 68
Comité de Défense de la Race Negre 55
Committee for the Welfare of Africans in Europe (CWAE) 18-19, 31, 52, 66, 74-75, 113
Common Wealth 111
Communist Party of Great Britain (CPGB) 4, 45, 60-61, 93, 130, 141-144, 161-163, 165, 170, 173-174, 181
Communism 139-143, 151-153, 160-164, 179-181
Conference of British Missionary Societies (CBMS) 130
Conference of Peoples of Europe-Asia-Africa Against Imperialism (COPAI) 143, 174
Congress of the African Peoples of the World 82
Constantine, Learie 108
Convention People's Party (CPP) 163, 171
Consultative Committee on the Welfare of Colonial Students in the UK 157-158, 161
Council of the Missionary Society of Great Britain and Ireland 112
Council on African Affairs 144
Cox, Idris 173
Creech Jones, Arthur 71-73, 91, 95, 100-102, 105, 112, 120, 131-136, 145, 151, 156
Crisis, The 82
Cummings, Ivor 64, 106, 133
Cunard, Nancy 78

Da Rocha, Moses 9-11
Dafe, I. 174
Dadzie, E.K 139, 174
Daily Comet 124
Daily Express 65
Daily Herald 160
Daily Worker 93, 168
Danquah, J.B. 33, 37, 44, 48n, 49n, 52, 63, 73, 138
Davidson, Basil 176
Davies, H.O. 2, 70, 86n, 111, 114, 122-123, 125-127, 132, 142-143, 146n, 170
Davis, Ben 175
de Graft Johnson, J.C. 109, 119n, 127, 149n
de Graft Johnson, J.W. 38
Dean of Westminster's Committee (See also *AAC*) 136-137, 145
Declaration to the Colonial Workers, Farmers and Intellectuals 128
Dinga, Madan Lal 13
Doherty, Ibidun 86n
Doherty, J.A. 40, 44
Doherty, J.H. 30
Du Bois, W.E. 11, 126-127, 187
Dutt, Rajani Palme 143, 145, 173

INDEX

Edinburgh African Association 81, 103, 109, 126
Edinburgh University 7, 9-10, 53
Egbe Omo Egba 174
Egbe Omo Ijebu 174
Egbe Omo Oduduwa 123, 144
Empire exhibition (Wembley) 24-25, 31, 44
Ethiopia 67-70
Ethiopia Unbound 12
Ethiopian Association 11
Ethiopian Defence Fund 69
Ethiopian Progressive Association (EPA) 11-12
Ethiopian Review, The 11
Ethiopianism 9, 11, 13
Evening News 24-25, 28
Evening Standard 93

Fabian Colonial Bureau (FCB) 4, 99, 101-102, 13-135, 141-142, 174-175
Fabunmi, Larry 174
Fadipe, Nathaniel A. 94-95, 115n
Fanimokun, A.M. 23
Folarin, Titi 86n
Ford, James 45
Fédération des Étudiants d'Afrique Noire en France (FEANF) 180
Federation of All Nigerian Women's Organisations 176
Federation of Student Societies 59
Fletcher, John 60, 93
Flight 107
Fourah Bay College, 103
Freetown Daily Mail 112

Gambia League 162
Gambia Students' Union (GSU) 175
Garba-Jahumpa, I.M. 127
Gardiner, Robert 101, 103, 113, 117n
Garvey, Amy Ashwood 28-29, 69, 77, 127
Garvey, Marcus 14, 28-29, 32
George, H.L. 175
Glasgow Students' Representative Council 53

Glasgow University 23
Gold Coast Aborigines' Rights Protection Society (GCARPS) 63, 129
Gold Coast and Ashanti Delegation 63
Gold Coast Leader 10
Gold Coast Farmers' Union 73
Gold Coast Revolution, The 171
Gold Coast Students' Association (GCSA) 32, 43, 57-58, 62, 64-65, 67, 69, 73-74, 77-78, 79-81, 90, 95, 109, 144
Gold Coast Students' Union (GCSU) 138, 144, 174
Gold Coast Union (GCU) 154-155, 158, 162, 169, 174, 178
Gold Coast Youth Conference 56, 73, 80
Grace, Canon H.M. 112-113, 130, 137
Guggisberg, Sir F. 26

Haden-Guest, Leslie 94, 105, 112
Hailey, Lord 100-101, 112
Hall, George, 96, 132-133
Hans Crescent Strike 154-157, 175
Hardie, Kier 10
Harris, John 14, 74-75
Hayford, J.E. Casely 9, 12, 20n, 27, 32, 36
Hayfron-Benjamin, A.M. 23
Henshaw, Richard 30
Hercules, F.E.M. 17
Hinden, Rita 99, 105, 131-135, 140
Hodgkin, Thomas 176
Horton, James Africanus B. 7, 12, 27, 35
How Russia Transformed Her Colonial Empire 133
Hughes, William 8

Ibare-Akinsan, O.K. 144, 150n
Ibeneme, V.O. 170
Ibo Union 122, 144
Ighodalo, Fola 176-177
Imoudu, M.A.O. 136

219

Independent Labour Party (ILP) 11, 44, 46, 143
Indian Home Rule Society 13
International African Friends of Abyssinia (IAFA) 67, 69, 77
International African Opinion 77
International African Service Bureau (IASB) 76-77, 127
International Coloured Mutual Aid Association 111
International Friendship League 111
International Student Relief (ISR) 164-165, 168
International Trade Union Committee of Negro Workers (ITUC-NW) 45, 50
International Union of Students (IUS) 141, 161, 164-168, 180
International Youth Council 111
Irish Republican Congress 78
Iyalla, Max 126, 149n

Jagan, Janet 157
James, C.L.R. 67, 77
Jardine, Sir Douglas 97
Jeffries, Sir Charles 140
Johnson, I.T.A. Wallace 77-80, 111, 127, 129
Johnson, Olive 106
Johnstone, Sir Harry 13
Jones, E.N. (Laminoh Sankoh) 91, 115n
Jones, Maurice 175
Jones-Quartey, K.A.B. 144-145, 150n

Keith, J.L. 91, 93, 104, 121, 136, 140, 152, 157-158
Kenyatta, Jomo (Johnstone) 45, 53, 65, 77, 126-127, 169-170
Kessie, Kobina 55, 58, 83n, 90, 97, 109, 170
Keys, The 68
Khama, Seretse 159
Kings College, Lagos 56
Koi, Alex Ansah 53, 57-8, 82n
Kpapkpa-Quartey, A.K. 53

Labour Leader 11
Labour Party 18, 44, 101-102, 105, 131-133, 135-136, 141-142
Lagos Standard 10, 14
Lahanmi, Oladipo 8, 16
Lamptey E.O. 138
Lamptey, Kwesi 131, 148n, 149n
Larbi, Koi 125, 129
Laski, Harold 132
League Against Imperialism (LAI) 4, 44-45, 55, 59-62, 64, 66, 67-69, 72-73, 76, 78
League for the Boycott of Aggressor Nations, 78
League of Africans 53
League of Africans and Peoples of African Descent 160
League of Coloured Peoples (LCP) 4, 53-54, 57-58, 64, 68-69, 72, 78, 80, 82n, 91-93, 106, 108, 127, 144, 157, 169
League of Nations 67-68, 71
Leverhulme Commission 94
Leverhulme, Lord 29
Lewis, Arthur 105
Leys, Norman 44, 60
Listowel, Earl 60, 91, 100, 106, 112-113
Little, Kenneth 105, 140
Lloyd, Lord 96-98
Lloyd George, David 41
Locke, Alain 36
London School of Economics (LSE) 55, 173-174
London University Graduates' Club 13
Lutterodt, Dr William 179

Macaulay, Herbert 27, 30
Macdonald, Malcolm 64, 97
Macdonald, Ramsey 11
Macmillan, Harold 103-104
Macpherson Constitution 172-173
Macpherson, Sir John 173-174
Maja, Akinola 114
Majekodunmi, Dr M.A. 106
Manchester Guardian 44, 71
Manchester Pan-African Congress

125-128, 130-131
Manifesto on Africa in the Post-War World 127
Marson, Una 106
Martin, Kingsley 60
Maxton, James 44
Maxwell, James Renner 9
Mbanefo, Louis 78-79
McMurray, John 60
Men of Two Worlds 108
Merriman Labor, A.B.C. 9, 14
Merton College, Oxford 9
Moody, Harold 53 57, 70
Moore, Tufuhin 62
Moscow New Times 130
Movement for Colonial Freedom (MCF) 175-176
Munster, Lord 157

National Congress of British West Africa (NCBWA) 10, 19, 27-28, 30, 32-33, 35-36, 43, 46, 111
National Council for Civil Liberties (NCCL) 59-60, 64, 66, 72-73, 95, 159
National Council of Nigeria and the Cameroons (NCNC) 102, 124, 144, 162, 174
National Union of Students, Britain (NUSB) 157, 166-167, 169, 178
Negro Anthology 78
Negro Association 125
Negro Citizen 111
Negro Welfare Association (NWA) 55, 59-60, 62, 72, 78, 80
Negro Welfare Centre 111, 125
Negro Worker 45, 62, 77
Negro World 46
New African 130-131
New India Political Group 59
New Leader 125
New Statesman and Nation 60, 62
New West Africa, The 176
Nicol, Davidson 144, 150n
Nigeria Union (NU) 143-145, 154-155, 157-158, 162, 169, 172-174, 176-178, 180
Nigerian Civil Service Union 101

Nigerian General Strike 124-125, 134
Nigerian National Democratic Party (NNDP) 27-28
Nigerian Progress Union (NPU) 27-30, 32, 43, 48
Nigerian Students' Union 174
Nigerian Trade Union Congress (NTUC) 124
Nigerian Union of Students (NUS) 109, 111,
Nigerian Union of Teachers 111
Nigerian Women's League (NWL) 177
Nigerian Women's Union (NWU) 176
Nigerian Youth Movement (NYM) 56, 111, 114, 123-124, 127
Nikoi, G. Ashie 127, 129, 132
Nkomo, Joshua 170
Nkrumah, Kwame 2, 125-131, 133, 137, 142, 153, 155, 157, 163, 171, 181
Northern Nigeria Association 174

Obahiagbon, E.E. 173
Obisanya, Olu 57
Odunsi, Ladipo 60
Ogunsheye, F. Ayo 144, 149n, 162-163, 175
Ojiako, T.O. 143
Ojo-Cole, Julius 36
Okafor, Amanke 142, 163
Omo, Uche 156, 173, 183n
Omoniyi, Bandele 9, 11-12
Open Letter to African Parents 31
Open Letter to the Prime Minister 127
Oxford University 9
Oyewole, M.A. 158, 169, 173-174

Padmore, George 77-78, 80, 88n, 124-125, 127, 130, 134, 136, 163, 171, 176, 187
Pan-African Conference (1900) 10-11
Pan-African congresses 22-23
Pan-African Federation (PAF) 4,

124-127, 134, 143
Pan-African Society 174
Pan-Africanism 2, 4, 9, 13, 79, 120, 130, 186
Pedler, F.J. 99, 104
Perham, Marjery 99
Portway College, Reading 8, 51
Pritt, D.N. 170
Profintern 45

Quaque, Philip 6
Queens' College, Taunton 8

Racism (see also *colour bar*) 9, 11-14, 16, 18-19, 39, 41, 54-55, 76, 90, 107-108, 127, 151, 158-160, 165, 186
Racial Relations Group 144
Ransome-Kuti, Funmi 176
Rassemblement Démocratique Africain (RDA) 180
Rathbone, Eleanor 71
Rathbone, H.P. 62
Residential Hotels and Caterers Association 54
Richards, Sir Arthur (Lord Milverton) 123, 135-136, 151-152
Richards Constitution 123, 136
Riley, Ben 101
Robeson, Paul 41, 63, 78
Roosevelt, F.D. 98
Rosiji, Ayo 142
Rothermere, Lord 71

Saklatvala, Shapurji 44-45
Saturday Review 25
Savage, Richard Akiwande 10, 27
Scottsboro Defence Committee 54, 62
Sekyi, Kobina 9, 14, 20n
Selassie, Haile 70
Shanu, E.A. 81
Sharp, Granville 7
Sierra Leone Student, The 175
Sierra Leone Students' Group 144
Sierra Leone Students' Union (SLSU) 109, 125
Sierra Leone Students' Union, UK (SLSU) 155, 157-158, 169, 175
Smith, Emma 51n
Society for International Studies 59
Society for the Cultural Advancement of Africa 109
Society of Friends 59
Society of Peoples of African Origin (SPAO) 16-17, 22n
Soetan, A.K. 25
Solanke, Ladipo 26, 103-105, 107-109, 110, 112, 122-123, 134-136, 152-153, 168; empire exhibition 24-25; Nigerian Progress Union 27-31; founder of WASU 32-34; West African nationalism 35-39;40, 42; and Marcus Garvey 45-47; missions to West Africa 52, 55-56;57-58, 114; Aggrey House 62-63, 65-67, 94-96; and cocoa hold up 73-74, 77-78; and AAC 136-137, 145; death of 151, 154;
Solanke, Olu 86n
Sorensen, Reginald 73, 91, 95, 99-102, 104-105, 108, 12, 114, 125, 131, 134-135, 152, 156-157, 181-182
Soviet Union (USSR) 79, 105, 127, 142, 169
Sowemimo, H.S. 164
Special Branch 53, 78
Spokesman, The 29
Stalin, Joseph 142
Stanley, Oliver 110
Student Christian Movement (SCM) 16, 18, 33, 52
Student hostel 13-15, 18-19, 39-40, 56
Student Labour Federation 144
Students' World Committee against Fascism and War 78
Subject Peoples' Conferences 126
Sunday Express 25
Swinton, Lord 100

Taylor, David 9
Taylor, John Eldred 17
Taylor, Samuel Coleridge 9
Ten Little Niggers 108

INDEX

Thomas, Ade 152, 162, 164, 184n
Thomas, J.H. 25
Thomas, Stella 82
Thomas, Stephen 82
Thompson, T.J. 9
Thomspson, T.J.D. 112
Times, The 44
Togoland Students' Union 175
Tokunboh, M.A. 124
Towards Nationhood in West Africa 38
Trinity College, Dublin 81
Truth About Aggrey House, The 59, 62, 94-98

Udoma, E. Udo 125, 147n
Union of Democratic Control (UDC) 174-175
Union of Students of African Descent (USAD) 23-28, 32-33, 42-43
United Africa Company (UAC) 66, 73, 75, 99, 99, 104, 135
United Ethiopian Students' Association 82
United Gold Coast Convention (UGCC) 137
United Missionary Board 18
United Nations (UN) 127, 130, 138
United West Africa at the Bar of the Family of Nations 37, 45
Universal Negro Improvement Association (UNIA) 46
Universal Races Congress 13
University College, London (UCL) 24, 27, 30

Vaughan, James 167
Victoria League 81, 109
Vischer, Hanns 29, 39, 42, 52, 57-61, 64-66, 75, 92-94, 97

Wachuku, J.A. 110, 127
Ward, Arnold 62
1Warri National Union 174
Warwick, Countess of 60
Washington, Booker T. 11, 29
Wasu 34-39, 41, 44, 55, 58, 65-66, 68-69, 77, 79, 82, 94, 104, 122, 131-132, 145, 168
Wasu News Service 160, 164-171, 179, 181
WASU hostel 57, 63, 74-76, 94, 100, 105, 112, 145, 151, 179, 182,
Watson Commission 138, 140
West Africa 24-26, 28, 41, 53, 56, 58, 70-71, 91, 93, 95, 101, 104, 124, 130, 144, 163, 178-179
West African and West Indian Christian Union 23
West African Christian Union 8, 16
West African Medical Service 10, 12
West African National Association (WANA) 53
West African National Secretariat (WANS) 121, 128-136, 139, 142-143, 145
West African Nationalism 34-39, 63, 79, 128
West African Parliamentary Committee 101-102, 114, 123-124, 145
West African Pilot 103, 124
West African Review 104, 111
West African Society 144
West African Soviet Union 142
West African Student, The 177, 181
West African Students' Club 103, 111, 138, 159
West African Students' Committee 175
West African Students' Union (WASU) 2, 10, 120-121, 158, 176, 186; founding 32-34, 43; and West African nationalism 35-39, 40, 111-112; and racism 41-43; 44, 106-108, 160; and Marcus Garvey 45-46; in West Africa 55-56; and Aggrey House 57-61, 64-67, 92-94; and Ethiopia 68-70; 71-72; and cocoa hold up 73-74; 77-79; and other organisations 80-82, 109-110, 113-114, 122-123, 144-145, 175-176; and Second World War 90-91; and anti-colonialism 95-102, 123-125, 131-136, 138-

139, 169-170; and Manchester Pan-African Congress 125-128; and WANS 129-131; and AAC 136-137; and communism 141-143, 151-154, 162-164, 180-181; and international student movement 166-168; attitude to decolonisation 171-172, 181-182;
West African Women's Association 144
West African Youth Festival Preparatory Committee 165
West African Youth League (WAYL) 78, 111, 125, 129
West African Youth and Student Organisation 162
West Indian Students' Association 53
West Indian Students' Union 155, 169
Wilkey, Babalola 77
Williams, Doris 51
Williams, Sylvester 9
Williams, Wadi 175
Women's Co-operative Guild 144
Wood, S.R. 63
World Congress against Anti-Semitism and Racism 78
World Federation of Democratic Youth (WFDY) 141, 164-165
World Trade Union Conference 124, 126
World Youth Conference 125-126
World Youth Council 125-126
Wyllie, William Curzon 13

Yergan, Max 44
Yoruba 27, 36
Yoruba Federal Union 144
Young Liberals' International Committee 143